Elisabeth O. Parsons

COLLECTION

SHENANDOAH
UNIVERSITY

ONE OF JACKSON'S
FOOT CAVALRY

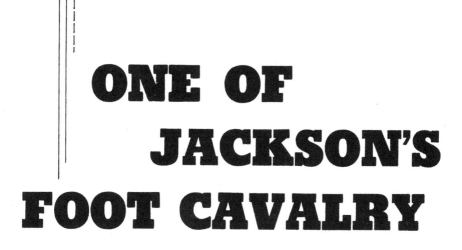

ONE OF
JACKSON'S
FOOT CAVALRY

By John H. Worsham
F Company, 21st Virginia Infantry

Edited By JAMES I. ROBERTSON, JR.
General Editor, Bell Irvin Wiley

Broadfoot Publishing Company
Monographs, Sources and Reprints in Southern History
Wilmington, North Carolina
1987

Library of Congress Catalog Card Number 64-24731

Copyright 1964 McCowat-Mercer Press, Inc.
Copyright 1987 Broadfoot Publishing Company
Route 4, Box 508C, Wilmington, North Carolina 28405

FOREWORD

One of the most absorbing and informative memoirs that came to my attention while I was writing the *Life of Johnny Reb* was that of John Worsham, a soldier of Stonewall Jackson's famous command. I wanted to add this excellent source to my personal library, but I soon found that it could not be obtained except at a premium price. Many years later I acquired a mutilated copy of *One of Jackson's Foot Cavalry* that had been discarded by a library and with this I had to be content.

In my unsuccessful efforts to locate a good copy of the book for a modest sum, I encountered many people who had been similarly disappointed. Among these was James I. Robertson, a Virginian who began his study of the Stonewall Brigade under my supervision at Emory, and Seale Johnson, bibliophile and publisher of Jackson, Tennessee. From this circumstance developed arrangements for Mr. Robertson to edit the Worsham memoir for republication by the McCowat-Mercer Press, headed by Mr. Johnson.

During his research for the new volume, the editor had the good fortune to locate in private possession thirty-five war-time letters of Worsham and these he used to a good advantage in preparing the introduction and documentation. He also made excellent use of unpublished service records in the National Archives and the intimate knowledge that he had acquired in his study of the Stonewall Brigade. His footnotes abundantly demonstrate the expertness of his scholarship; they also make interesting and informative reading for students of the Civil War.

Before Mr. Robertson's appointment as Executive Director of the Civil War Centennial Commission, he served for two years as editor of *Civil War History*. In preparing Worsham's account for republication, he utilized his editorial experience to make the narrative more readable, without altering the substance or diminishing the charm. He broke up long paragraphs, modernized punctuation and transferred tabular material to appendices. In footnotes he called attention to a number of factual errors. There can be no doubt that he succeeded admirably in his avowed desire "to convert an exceptionally good Confederate memoir into an even better one."

BELL IRVIN WILEY

Emory University

CONTENTS

Foreword VII

Introduction XIII

Preface XXXIII

1. The Commencement of Hostilities.................................... 1

2. The Western Virginia and Romney Campaigns.................. 13

3. Foot Cavalry in the Valley... 30

4. "High on the Scroll of Honor".. 54

5. Low Water Mark in Maryland.. 69

6. A Loss to the Confederacy.. 91

7. Camp Life 110

8. From the Wilderness to Cold Harbor............................. 126

9. "Hell Broke Loose Now!".. 146

10. F Company's Last Battles... 176

Appendix A
    Returning Home 189

Appendix B
    The Women of the South... 191

Appendix C
    Roster of F Company, 21st Virginia Infantry................ 194

Index 209

ILLUSTRATIONS

(Facing Page 6)

LAYING ON ARMS

UNIFORM 1861

UNIFORM 1862

UNIFORM 1863

UNIFORM 1864

SGT. JOHN H. WORSHAM

CAPT. R. MILTON CARY

CAPT. WILLIAM A. PEGRAM

CAPT. WILLIAM H. MORGAN

CAPT. REUBEN H. JORDAN

LT. COL. RICHARD H. CUNNINGHAM

BRIG. GEN. BRADLEY T. JOHNSON

BRIG. GEN. JOHN M. JONES

MAJ. GEN. EDWARD JOHNSON

JOHN AND MARY PILCHER WORSHAM

JACKSON AT WINCHESTER

INTRODUCTION

Ordinary men made the Civil War an extraordinary struggle. This is not to say that leaders like Lincoln, Lee, Grant, and Jackson were no more than normal men of common abilities; on the contrary, their greatness transcended their age. Yet in the sectional conflict of the 1860's the real heroes were in a sense those thousands of simple youths and men who left farms, schools, foundries, and shops to sustain by arms the American principles in which they each believed. "It was these these men and their kind," Bell Wiley, the authoritative spokesman for Civil War GI's, has stated, "whose strength was the bedrock of their respective causes and whose greatness made their war one of the most inspiring in the history of embattled humanity."[1]

John Worsham was such a man. Modest and unpretentious, raised in the middle-class atmosphere of Richmond, he fought for three years in the armies of Jackson, Lee, and Early. Only a crippling wound at Winchester in 1864 stopped his service to the Confederacy. "He was not only an intelligent observer of everything that went on," a Richmond newspaper commented, "but also a thoroughly reliable and courageous soldier—one of the wheel-horses of an organization that had some hard pulling to do."[2] As his memoirs vividly attest, Worsham did more than his share of "pulling."

His recollections, *One of Jackson's Foot Cavalry*, were first published by The Neale Company of New York in 1912. Initial reviews were highly laudatory. The Brooklyn *Citizen* of November 24, 1912, stated: "Worsham has made realistic the humorous, the dramatic, and the weirdly picturesque of the greatest game played by human pawns."[3] More recently, writers have termed his memoirs "invaluable" and "among the best" of Civil War narratives; "a well-written account with many plausible details;" "excellent in every way;" and "one of the really indispensables in a study of Lee's army."[4] Such commendation readily explains why the book has long been a choice collector's

---

[1] *Journal of Southern History*, XXII (1956), 35.

[2] Richmond *Evening Journal*, Dec. 9, 1912.

[3] For similar reviews, see the Birmingham *Herald*, Mar. 2, 1913; Pittsburgh *Post*, Dec. 21, 1912; Boston *Evening Transcript*, Jan. 1, 1913; Chicago *Evening Post*, Jan. 17, 1913; New Orleans *Times-Democrat*, Feb. 16, 1913; Chicago *Dial*, Feb. 16, 1913.

[4] D. S. Freeman, *Lee's Lieutenants* (New York, 1942-44), III, 565, 819; E. Merton Coulter, *Travels in the Confederate States* (Norman, Okla., 1948), p. 267; D. S. Freeman, *R. E. Lee* (New York, 1934-35), IV, 566; Clifford Dowdey, *Death of a Nation* (New York, 1958), p. 374.

xiv   INTRODUCTION

item and a source often consulted by historians treating of operations in the eastern theater.

Since the days of the Civil War mild controversy has existed as to who actually comprised "Jackson's foot cavalry." The men in the five Valley infantry regiments and artillery battery of the Stonewall Brigade always insisted that the designation was exclusively theirs. On the other hand, members of the twenty-eight regiments and one battalion in Jackson's Valley army likewise laid claim to the title; in their eyes their exploits under "Old Jack" were more than sufficient justification. Although Worsham was never a member of the Stonewall Brigade, his narrative nevertheless joins John O. Casler's *Four Years in the Stonewall Brigade*, Edward A. Moore's *The Story of a Cannoneer under Stonewall Jackson*, Henry Kyd Douglas's *I Rode with Stonewall*, and McHenry Howard's *Recollections of a Maryland Confederate Soldier* to form a superb quintet of personal recollections of the campaigns in the Valley. As a memoir of life and service in Lee's army, *One of Jackson's Foot Cavalry* has few equals.

Worsham himself was a descendant of Virginia's early settlers. In 1640 William Worsham and his brother acquired a large tract of land near Bermuda Hundred in what was then Henrico Shire. A son, Captain John Worsham, became prominent in Henrico affairs and numbered William Byrd among his close friends. Another forebear, William Worsham, was a member of the vestry that founded St. John's Episcopal Church, the Richmond site of Patrick Henry's cry for liberty or death. John Worsham's father, Richard, was born at the family's Bermuda Hundred estate in 1804. Nine years later, Richard's father died. The lad inherited considerable land and was then placed under the guardianship of his older sister's husband, Henry L. Carter of Strawberry Hill near Richmond. On May 29, 1833, Richard Worsham married Clarke Roxanna Goddin in Richmond. His wife came from a prominent Williamsburg family, and her father and grandfather had served with distinction in the War of 1812 and Revolutionary War, respectively.[5]

A merchant tailor by trade, Richard Worsham took his bride to a new home at the corner of Seventh and Broad (then H) Streets. From their union came two girls, Sarah Roxanna and Ann Eliza, and two boys, John Henry and Wellington Goddin. The third child, John Henry Worsham, was born July 8, 1839. Soon after his birth the family moved to a three-story brick home in the 500 block of North Seventh

---

[5] See Louis B. Wright and Marion Tinling (eds.), *The Secret Diary of William Byrd of Westover, 1709-1712* (Richmond, 1941), pp. 7, 22, 122, 410, 513; *Virginia Magazine of History and Biography*, XXXIII (1925), 178, 184-86.

Street. (The home still stands, one of the few in that locality that has not been razed for business and civic purposes.) John Worsham resided there until after the war, and other members of the family until the end of the century. The deaths of his father in 1847 and his sister, Sarah Worsham Parker, in 1854 marred the boy's childhood. Yet he received an above-average education at Richmond's Shockoe School for Boys, where he excelled in reading, arithmetic, and Latin, and then took employment as a clerk at Winston and Powers, Commission Merchants.

"The rumors afloat are pregnant with war," a young Richmonder soon to become Worsham's companion in arms wrote in April, 1861.[6] The bombardment of Fort Sumter made war a reality. Garbed in the new trappings of a nation's capital, Richmond became a hubbub of frenzied excitement and giddy optimism. Those "were gala days," one of the few serious-minded residents wrote. "The dire realities, the sickness, the mutilation, the sufferings, the miseries, were yet unknown. Only the glory which might accrue was shadowed forth. Absorbed in the contemplation of this, no thought was given to the darker events of the future. The shadows of coming events were not cast before, to chill the ardor of the young."[7]

John Worsham was caught up in this martial spirit even before Confederate batteries crumbled Sumter's uncompleted works. On April 1, 1861, this six-foot youth of twenty, with blue eyes, blond hair, and light complexion,[8] joined a Richmond militia unit known simply as F Company. In spite of its unimpressive title, this was an exceptional company. A Richmond matron observed that it contained "young men generally of wealth, education and refinement, enthusiastic, brave and generous. All . . . were well drilled in military exercises, and ready to use their skill in defense of the cause which had divided the North from the South, even to the death."[9] T. C. DeLeon remembered the company as containing "the brilliant advocate, the skillful surgeon, the man of letters, and the smooth-faced pet of the Mayday gatherings—all that made the pride, the boast and the love of Richmond."[10]

---

[6] Journal of J. Tucker Randolph, entry of Apr. 9, 1861, Randolph Papers, Confederate Museum.

[7] Sallie Brock Putnam, *Richmond during the War; Four Years of Personal Observations* (New York, 1867), p. 33.

[8] Pay and Clothing Voucher, 21st Va., June, 1861, War Records Group 109, National Archives. See also John H. Worsham manuscript, Randolph Papers.

[9] Putnam, *Richmond during the War*, p. 23.

[10] T. C. DeLeon, *Four Years in Rebel Capitals* (Mobile, 1890), p. 94. See also DeLeon's *Belles, Beaux and Brains of the 60's* (New York, 1907), pp. 60-61.

While F Company sported fancy uniforms and an extravagant patriotism, it also demonstrated both valor and ability. Of a total of 192 members, 31 were killed, 3 died of disease, 49 were wounded, and 19 were captured. These figures do not include 57 men who transferred to other commands. From that group ultimately came 3 colonels, 4 lieutenant colonels, and 10 majors.[11]

Following a day of alarm, April 21, 1861, (known in Richmond as "Pawnee Sunday"), the militia company moved to the Fredericksburg-Aquia Creek area for guard duty. A merry atmosphere characterized those first, peaceful days of the war. "We are having a very nice time of it," Worsham wrote his mother soon after their arrival at Fredericksburg. "If it was not for our confinement, [I] would think we were only on an excursion of some sort."[12] Three days later he stated to his sister: "You would hardly know me now, as I am about the color of a darky—and about as rough-looking. I have fattened 12½ [pounds] since I have been in camp."[13] Yet military life had its drawbacks. In one of his first letters home, Worsham told of pulling twenty-four-hour guard duty on Saturday. The next morning he fell asleep in church. To make matters worse, his head rolled back and struck a young lady seated behind him. "I never heard such a laugh as all of our company gave, which awaken[ed] me so thoroughly that I did not sleep any more that day."[14]

F Company shortly returned to Richmond; and at 10 A.M., June 28, 1861, it was mustered into Confederate service as Company F of the 21st Virginia Infantry.[15] Orders quickly came, assigning the regiment to duty in western Virginia. The Richmonders promptly loaded themselves down with food, luxuries, and excess equipment. Following tearful farewells at the R. F. & P. depot, the troops rode trains into the Valley of Virginia. Strenuous marches over mountainous terrain soon eliminated all baggage but the barest necessities, yet the men remained in good spirits. "We are having rather a gay time," Worsham wrote his sister late in July, "marching over mountains with roads as Rocky as can be, and so crooked that we sometimes go over the same place two or three times. . . . It would do you good just to see our

---

[11] These data supplemented Worsham's company roster in the original edition of his memoirs.

[12] Worsham to his mother, May 25, 1861, John H. Worsham Papers, in possession of the family. Unless otherwise stated, all letters quoted in the introduction are from this collection.

[13] Worsham to Annie Worsham Parker, May 28, 1861. Annie Worsham married her late sister's husband in 1860.

[14] Ibid., May 8, 1861.

[15] Randolph Journal, entry of June 28, 1861, Randolph Papers.

column crossing the streams. Some go over on rails, some on Rocks, and others right through the water—every man for himself."[16]

The gay and light-hearted attitude toward army life changed abruptly. In August, while the 21st Virginia was encamped in the mountains of western Virginia, measles, typhoid fever, and diarrhea struck with devastating effects. A long siege of bad weather accentuated the misery. Over one-third of the regiment was prostrated by illness. The men were still in various stages of recuperation when, on September 11, 1861, they had their first encounter with Federal troops. A skirmish of short duration occurred at Conrad's Store, but the first sight of a dead Yankee, Worsham wrote in his memoirs, "made a lasting impression." By October the regiment had regained its health. "The men soon improved so much and fattened too," Worsham wrote later, "that they became better looking than when they left home." The Confederate force soon moved back to the Staunton area, then marched down the Valley for a rendezvous at Winchester with the forces of General T. J. "Stonewall" Jackson. During this march Worsham experienced a burst of patriotic spirit, as evidenced in a letter to his mother. "I wish this war was over so that I could return home and be with you," he stated, "but as my Country wants ever[y] one she can get, my love for home and family must be sacrificed for her. I do not wish to return home until my time is out, and if the war is still going on then, [I] must again shoulder my gun and to my Country give assistance."[17]

A week after a bountiful Christmas feast—in which Worsham and a messmate devoured a whole mince meat pie,[18] the 21st Virginia embarked with Jackson's army on the ill-fated Romney campaign. The expedition, Worsham observed in later years, "tried men's souls—and bodies too."[19] The weather suddenly turned bitingly cold—"each day was colder than the day before," Worsham stated in his memoirs— and when the troops were not fighting Federals, they were battling the elements for survival. F Company suffered its first combat fatalities on this campaign. Worsham's narrative of the whole expedition is exceptionally vivid and detailed. After undergoing what Worsham called "the most terrible experience during the war," Jackson's army early in February returned to Winchester.

A month of rest followed, and Worsham took this opportunity to comment on Southern morale. On March 1, 1862, he wrote his mother:

16 Worsham to his sister, July 26, 1861.
17 Worsham to his mother, Dec. 13, 1861.
18 J. Tucker Randolph to his father, Dec. 30, 1861, Randolph Papers.
19 Worsham manuscript, Randolph Papers.

"I begin to think our people are beginning to wake up out of that long slumber and [to] see the importance of taking the field. [I] see signs around me every day. [I] saw a gentleman from R[ichmond] to day who says that they are showing themselves to be true Southerners, and are enlisting slowly. A few more disasters and the threatening of important places will make our men arouse to the full sense of our dangers, and then we can show our enemys that we can whip them at any time and place." On March 23, 1862, at Kernstown, Worsham and his comrades had the opportunity to make good that boast. They suffered instead a sharp defeat. In his memoirs Worsham gave a moving and full account of the battle. However, he was more informal in describing the action to his mother: ". . . and now comes the tug of war—they pouring in a tremendous fire, we returning it. And their we held our position for ¾ of an hour, being almost flanked on both sides, but we poured in such a galling fire that they would not advance. . . . I have heard of its raining pitchforks, but if it did not rain bullets on this occasion, I could not see or hear."[20] The Confederates, he grudgingly conceded in his recollections, "were whipped . . . only for want of ammunition."

Now began Jackson's famous Valley Campaign, and Worsham was as much amazed as he was pleased by the movements and victories of "Stonewall's Band." The 21st Virginia took little part in the May 8 battle of McDowell. Then Jackson accelerated his circuitous and secret marches. In mid-May Worsham voiced a mild complaint to the homefolk: "We need rest. We have been on the march now sixteen days in succession, marching from seven to twenty-five miles each day, starting early in the morning and not getting into camp until sundown. One more day without hearing the report of cannon. This makes about ten since the battle of Kernstown. This looks strange to one who knows nothing of Genl. Jackson. He never likes to be out of the hearing of guns, so he keeps us always near the enemy."[21]

Reading Worsham's account of this campaign gives one the sense of being a participant. The admiring soldier's comments about Jackson's exploits in the Valley are among the most oft-quoted passages in Confederate history. "We were retreating and advancing at the same time, a condition an army never undertook before," he stated. Jackson's "eagerness all through this campaign was surprising, and his escape from death was almost a miracle." The 21st Virginia struck the Federal army at Front Royal, captured a large number of wagons (many

---

20 Worsham to his mother, Mar. 25, 1862.
21 Fragment of a letter home, no date.

of which contained women's clothing, Worsham reported), and then routed the remnants of General N. P. Banks' army at Winchester on May 25. The next day, while resting in camp, Worsham penned a summary of the past week's activities. "Well, we have had some stiring times up in the Valley since my last [letter]," he wrote. Of the Front Royal-Middletown-Winchester battles, he observed: "This, Annie, I consider one of the most brilliant affairs of the war. We have driven a hated enemy from their positions, capturing a large number of Prisoners, all of their stores, wagons, baggage, and in fact every thing they had, not leaving them any clothing but what they had on." When the Confederates entered Winchester, he concluded, "even Genl. Jackson smiled, something I never saw him do before."[22]

The 21st Virginia guarded prisoners during the battles of Cross Keys and Port Republic, but Worsham saw and heard enough to give excellent accounts of both. His regiment rejoined Jackson's army at Charlottesville and marched to the Peninsula, where the men took part in the sanguinary Seven Days. At Gaines's Mill Worsham experienced "the heaviest musketry I heard during the war," and he termed the Federal position there "the strongest point I saw occupied by either army" throughout his war career. At Savage Station he came upon a dead soldier seated on a box and propped against a gate post as if taking a nap. On the night after Malvern Hill, Worsham shared his blanket with a wounded Confederate. The young Richmonder awakened the next morning to find his bed companion dead. Worsham was deeply impressed by the horror of this series of battles. "Mother, I'm realy sick," he wrote on July 5. "Dead, dying and wounded have been before my eye now for more than a week for ten miles along the road we came over. The dead and wo[u]nded are laid scattered over the ground in large numbers. Here a dead Yankey and one of our men lying beside him, their a wounded man and dead horse lying side by side. I laid down beside a wounded man a few nights ago and took a short nap. [I] have slept in the midst of dead & wounded, and now my heart sickens at the sights I have seen. Oh that this war was over!" However, in this same letter Worsham remarked that, where the enemy was concerned, Jackson "hangs on them like a blood hound; not a movement of theirs escapes him."

The men of F Company enjoyed short furloughs with loved ones in Richmond before tramping northward with Jackson on a new campaign that became their bloodiest. Eighteen men were in the company at the battle of Cedar Run on August 9, 1862; twelve were killed or

---

[22] Worsham to his sister, May 26, 1862.

wounded. Worsham was one of the few who emerged unharmed. His memoirs contain a detailed description of the severe hand-to-hand fighting in which he was involved and also give an insight into the reactions of his comrades. Less than three weeks later, still attached to Jackson, the 21st Virginia was one of those regiments that swooped down on General John Pope's supply depot at Manassas Junction. "It makes an old soldier's mouth water now," Worsham stated in his narrative, "to think of the good things captured there." Hungry gray-coats crammed stomachs, pockets, and knapsacks with a wide variety of food, burned what they could not carry, and then backed off to the Groveton area to await an aroused and irate Pope. The battles of Groveton and Second Manassas resulted. Worsham was a spectator at the former; yet in the vicious fighting of August 29-30 around the unfinished railroad cut, he was one of the valiant who threw rocks when no ammunition remained. At one point in the battle he narrowly escaped death when a cannon shell decapitated the man standing beside him.

The joy in Lee's army at the invasion of Maryland is evident both in Worsham's memoirs and in a letter he wrote home. On the day before Harpers Ferry fell to Jackson's troops, Worsham informed his sister: "Annie, it was one of the Grandest, most jubilant and exciting times [I] have ever seen. The [Potomac] River was about half a mile wide. Our troops went over in solid column, with bands playing, bugles blowing, and men singing. I would like so much for you to have seen those barefooted, rag[g]ed and half starved 'Rebels' waist deep in water but in the highest spirits [they] could possibly be."[23] Such exultation vanished along the banks of Antietam Creek. Posted in the West Wood, the 21st Virginia received the first series of assaults on that bloody Wednesday, September 17, 1862. Fighting in that area lasted throughout the morning and was as savage as any in the Civil War. F Company shrank to three men, and for a time thereafter its members were known as "the guerillas of the 21st Virginia."

In the two months of inactivity following Sharpsburg, homesickness engulfed Worsham as it did a goodly number of his comrades. On November 5, 1862, from the regiment's camp near Berryville, he wrote his sister: "I should go perfectly wild with delight to spend a day with a party of young Girls who are somewhat wild. [We] expect the presence of some young ladies in camp to day, but [we] have just received marching orders, so all that is knocked in the head." Those marching orders were preliminaries for the battle of Fredericksburg,

---

[23] Worsham to his sister, Sept. 14, 1862.

fought December 13, 1862. As a reserve element of Jackson's line, Worsham's regiment took little part in the fighting. However, after the battle Worsham witnessed "one of the most uncommon and interesting things which it has ever been the fortune of this old Division to see." Both sides had established the customary picket lines. The Federal infantrymen then agreed to honor an "unofficial" flag of truce; and to prove their good intentions, their whole line threw down its arms.

Then, stated Worsham, "our men did the same and both parties walked forward and began holding a lively conversation." Federal and Confederate soldiers swapped tobacco, sugar, newspapers—even such equipment as haversacks and canteens. "In fact the battle field was for a while the scene of a trading match on a grand scale." The truce soon ended. "Now the field is clear, except [for] the forms of men peeping from behind trees and bushes, and back of these is their line of battle extending as far as the eye could reach. Curious things happen on the battle field but this beats all we have had any experience with."[24]

The handful of veterans remaining in F Company were on recruiting duty in Richmond during the battle of Chancellorsville, and Jackson's death was a particularly hard blow for them. In his memoirs Worsham devoted several eulogistic paragraphs to "Old Jack" and his value to the Confederacy. Augmented by a large contingent of volunteers and conscripts, F Company acted as a provost guard in the Harpers Ferry area throughout the Gettysburg campaign. As such, the unit took part in the little-known but bloody battle of Williamsport, Maryland, July 6, 1863. This, Worsham recorded in his memoirs, was "the best fight of F Company during the war;" and referring to the new men in his company, he boasted to his mother that "the Orangotangs have sustained the reputation of old 'F'."[25] Worsham's reminiscences again provide a comprehensive and interesting insight into battle.

Two weeks later, from Martinsburg, West Virginia, the newly promoted Sergeant Worsham reassured his family that all was well. "Every thing is quiet here now. . . . Every thing is dull, but it always is after an active campaign. Every one tries to see what kind of rumor he can start, so when our bodys are still we have our minds puzzled and harrassed by things from the reliable man."[26] Speculation and false reports apparently intensified in the ensuing weeks. Early in September, with the army then encamped near Montpelier, Worsham wrote dis-

---

24 Worsham to his mother, Dec. 21, 1862.
25 *Ibid.*, July 8, 1863.
26 *Ibid.*, July 20, 1863.

gustingly: "If all the camp rumors are true, I expect to start on a trip around the moon soon."[27] The regiment instead moved in November to the Mine Run area and took an active role in that campaign. Worsham's memoirs are especially valuable here, for they reveal not so much the details of the battle itself as they do individual acts and oddities. For example, he recounted the humorous episode of Confederates breaking from their battle line to give chase to a frightened rabbit. During the actual fighting, an officer attempting to rally his men volunteered to lie down on the brow of a hill and permit the men to use him as a breastwork. The troops accepted the offer.

During the five-month lull in the fall and winter of 1863-1864, Worsham spent a short furlough with his family. His narrative for these months, treating exclusively of camp life, rivals in interest and value Carlton McCarthy's *Detailed Minutiae of Soldier Life in the Army of Northern Virginia*. War weariness took hold of Worsham on at least one occasion during this period. Writing to his mother from Mt. Pisgah Church on February 28, 1864, he simultaneously bemoaned his plight and pledged his fidelity to the Southern cause. "I wish more and more every day for this war to end. The suffering it causes and the hardships to the poor as well as the soldier is very galing to my feelings. You may think [by] my saying this [that] my patriotism is weakening, but not so. I reinlisted sometime ago for the war and I expect to do my portion of the fighting as long as any Yankee vandals are arranged in battle against us." As evidence of his devotion to cleanliness and duty, Worsham took a bath in Madison Run in the dead of winter —after chopping a hole through ice he adjudged "about seven inches thick."

For pure battle narrative, Worsham's description of the fighting from the Wilderness to Cold Harbor ranks with the best. At the Wilderness he related in detail both the big maneuvers and the desperate hand-to-hand fighting in which his 21st Virginia was involved. In this same engagement he witnessed an incident novel to modern warfare. Two opposing soldiers, isolated by the action, got into a fistfight between the main battle lines. The fierceness with which they fought caused both sides in that sector to cease firing and to raise a cheer for the antagonists. Once the fistfight had been decided, the battle broke out anew.

A few days later, to counter Grant's flanking movement, the Confederates moved to the Spotsylvania area. From newly dug earthworks Worsham wrote his mother of some of the Wilderness action. "We

---

[27] *Ibid.*, Sept. 5, 1863.

drove the enemy, and my regiment captured and killed as many Yanks
as we had men. Our loss was very small. My Co. had 5 of the recruits
wounded and two are missing, supposed to be in the hands of the
enemy. . . . The enemy dead are laying as thick in our present front
as I ever saw."[28]

The day after this letter was written, Worsham's brigade and
division ceased to exist as organized units. At Spotsylvania they occupied the "Bloody Angle." Here two Federal corps launched an assault
the like of which, according to Worsham, "was not witnessed during
the war." He stated further: "I expect that it was the heaviest attack
ever made at a single point by any army in the world." He and a handful of men in the 21st Virginia barely escaped capture, and his experiences were recorded in moving passages both in his memoirs and in a
letter home. "We have had one of the hardest fought battles I have
ever been in," he informed his mother. "The enemy made the attack
at light. They came forward without any line of skirmishers preceding
them, as is always the custom. The whole mass with a yell and double
quick threw themselves on our Division and captured two regts. in my
Brigade that were in the front." When he and the remnants of his
regiment reached the Confederate reserve line, Worsham added, "I
never had such a feeling of safety and gratification." He reported being
struck twice by spent balls, "but [they] did no damage."[29]

Remnants of four shattered brigades, including survivors in the
21st Virginia Regiment, were combined into one brigade as the defen-
sive campaign against Grant continued. "Although we did not know it
at the time," Worsham wrote in his recollections, "Grant's 'hammering' had commenced and was telling." He took little part in the
slaughter of the Federals at Cold Harbor, and his unit was among
those detached shortly afterward for service in the Valley with General
Jubal A. Early. This little band of Confederates chased General David
Hunter's army into the mountains of West Virginia, after which the
Southerners swept down the Valley on an invasion of their own.
Worsham's division, under General John B. Gordon, proved a key
factor in Early's victory of July 9 at Monocacy, described by Worsham
as "one of the most complete victories I have ever seen."[30]

Jubilant Confederates moved optimistically on Washington; yet
Early fell back to the Valley without making an assault on the city's
improvised defenses. Scores of writers subsequently censured Early for
his strategy—or lack of it; but Worsham expressed a viewpoint more

[28] *Ibid.*, May 11, 1864.
[29] *Ibid.*, May 19, 1864.
[30] *Ibid.*, July 15, 1864.

favorable to his general. He felt that excessive straggling by Confederates made it impossible for Early to attack, and he was convinced that the campaign and General Early had both been successful. In a letter to his mother Worsham commented: "I must say that we have met with continual success and captured more stores than ever before. Gen. Early has gained the confidence of us all. . . . I am about twice as large since taking a look at Washington City."[31]

On July 24, 1864, Early's army defeated a Federal force at Second Kernstown in what Worsham was sure was the "most easily won battle of the war." In this action a portion of his brigade charged the enemy in disobedience of orders and left a major "stamping with rage." Fortunately for the "insubordinates," they routed the Federals. Early's army then encamped at the head of the Valley, where the men "engaged in our old occupation of tearing up the Baltimore and Ohio Rail Road."[32] Cut off from the main action around Petersburg, the Richmonders knew nothing of the state of affairs at home. "Write me all the news," Worsham begged his mother. "We know nothing of what is going on in the Confederacy. . . . No papers reach us, nothing but rumors."[33]

On September 12, 1864, Sergeant Worsham received appointment as acting adjutant of the 21st Virginia. Exactly a week later occurred the second major battle of Winchester. Here Worsham's military career ended. At the height of an engagement "as hotly contested as any in the war," a bullet shattered his left knee. Worsham painfully endured a bumpy wagon ride to Woodstock where, twenty-four hours after being wounded, he received his first medical attention.[34] He made his way home to Richmond and spent the last seven months of hostilities in bed. In early April, 1865, Worsham heard and witnessed part of the chaos accompanying the fall and occupation of Richmond. His memoirs indicate unrestrained admiration for the Federal troops who displayed benevolence to the city's residents.

Late that year, through the assistance of Joseph Mayo, a close and influential friend, Worsham became tollkeeper for Mayo's Bridge that spanned the James River at the foot of Fourteenth Street. The wounded soldier's health and means soon improved sufficiently to enable him to

---

[31] *Ibid.* For a different view of this campaign, see John N. Opie, *A Rebel Cavalryman with Lee, Stuart and Jackson* (Chicago, 1899), pp. 245-46.

[32] Worsham to his sister, July 27, 1864.

[33] Worsham to his mother, Aug. 8, 1864.

[34] According to the family, the army surgeon instructed Worsham to apply cold compresses to the wound. On his arrival at Richmond, however, Worsham used hot applications, which possibly prevented gangrene. He purposefully kept his injured joint but slightly bent so as to avoid permanent stiffness in either extreme. As a result, he thereafter enjoyed a quick step with only a slight limp.

establish partnership in a small Richmond tobacco firm. On February
15, 1871, he married Mary Bell Pilcher, daughter of John A. and
Elizabeth Parsons Pilcher of "Bleak Hill" in Richmond. Worsham
then moved to Scottsville and entered the milling business. Shortly
afterward he and a Luther Pitts began operating a line of freight
barge on the James River and Kanawha Canal. The boating firm ceased
operations when the Richmond and Allegheny (now a part of the
Chesapeake and Ohio) Railroad purchased exclusive rights to the
canal.

In 1882 the Worsham family returned to Richmond and thereafter
resided at 1001 Main Street. Worsham joined the auditing
section of the Virginia State Insurance Company, located at Fifth
and Main Streets. When that business dissolved, he became the
bookkeeper for the Richmond Press, Incorporated, a Governor
Street printing firm of which his son Gibson was co-owner and president. The elder Worsham held this position until his death. He
was actve in Confederate historical affairs; and on May 29, 1890,
he was one of forty-one surviving members of F Company who took
part in ceremonies for the unveiling of the Lee Statue in Richmond.[35]

Worsham remained vigorous long after most men of his age had
retired or died. He was extremely proud of his family, which included
four children: Bell (Mrs. E. Edward Bates, Jr.), Jessie (who died in
infancy), George Gibson, and Natalie (Mrs. William Wirt Henry),
as well as his six grandchildren. After the death of his wife in 1914,
the gray-bearded septuagenarian went to live with his son at 3601
Brook Road. (Two grandchildren live there still.) He rose very early,
prepared his own breakfast and usually was on his way downtown
before the rest of the family, including Alberta, the maid, awoke.
When not caring for his rose bushes and garden, Worsham could
usually be found in a rocker on the front porch of his home. There he
would watch with interest the old and the new in the city he had
helped to defend. Those who remember him vividly state that his deep
blue eyes with their ever-present twinkle were his most distinct
physical characteristic. According to descendants, he was a man who
spoke rarely but with authority.

An accidental fall led to pneumonia and on September 19, 1920
—the fifty-sixth anniversary of his wounding at Winchester—John
Worsham died at the age of eighty-one. The Reverend William Hedley
of Ginter Park Baptist Church conducted funeral services at the home,

---

[35] See *Southern Historical Society Papers*, XVII (1889), 285, 289. Hereafter cited
as *SHSP*.

after which Worsham was interred in the family plot at Hollywood Cemetery, near many of his comrades-in-arms.

Sergeant Worsham began work on *One of Jackson's Foot Cavalry* in the early 1890's. He refreshed his memory by consulting a wartime notebook that contained short, daily entries of his movements and the principal events of which he was a part. He also relied on thirty-five letters written from the field to his mother and sister. Excerpts from these unpublished letters have been incorporated into this introduction. Worsham read avidly in his postwar years, and he faithfully jotted down notes on the 21st Virginia from such works as the *Official Records* and the *Southern Historical Society Papers*. Printed reminiscences written by fellow veterans soon after the war provided him with additional material. For the company roster at the end of his memoirs, Worsham used a list of his own, available personal records, and E. H. Chamberlayne's pamphlet, *Record of Richmond City and Henrico County Troops, Confederate States Army* (Richmond, 1879).

To enrich this material, Worsham conducted a constructive correspondence with former members of his regiment. He would customarily write one or two persons and give his version of a specific battle or event; then he would ask for their comments. From their replies he made whatever revisions in his account he considered feasible or necessary. Apparently Worsham did not write his memoirs in chronological order, for his recollections of Cedar Run, Second Manassas, and the 1862 campaign for Front Royal and Winchester appeared in the *Southern Historical Society Papers* in that order.[36]

Worsham spent the better part of twenty years writing his memoirs. He submitted the finished manuscript, written in long hand on legal-size paper, to the publisher in the summer of 1912.

One of Jackson's Foot Cavalry has many virtues and few vices. It is an excellent collection of those small and personal incidents in war that tend to be washed away by the tidal wave of war itself. Worsham was as adept in describing battlefield terrain as he was in portraying the various escapades of the men in the ranks. The spontaneous humor which made him such an engaging associate is apparent throughout his book. He referred to the Valley of Virginia on one occasion as "that great place for wheat, flour, hogs and democrats;" he often broke a battle narrative to recount a witty act by some individual on the field; and he was ever quick to point out (most of the time facetiously) instances of timorousness or cowardice.

---

[36] See *ibid.*, XXVII (1899), 144-51; XXXII (1904), 77-88; XXXVIII (1910), 327-34.

At the same time, Worsham did not gloss over his own short-comings and irregularities. He recorded with apparent satisfaction that, during the 1862 Maryland campaign, he bought a barrel of flour for six cents a pound and then sold a portion of it to his comrades at more than four hundred percent profit. Moreover, he twice described robbing dead Yankees. (Only John O. Casler of the Stonewall Brigade ever confessed as frankly to a similar act in printed Confederate recollections.) However, as Worsham's memoirs reflect, he harbored no animosity for the enemy after the war ended. While his wartime letters contained references to Federals as "vandals," his memoirs often mention the gallantry of bluecoats against whom he fought. Any hatred that Worsham might have borne for the enemy in later years seems to have been concentrated on three men: Generals Nathaniel P. Banks, John Pope, and Philip H. Sheridan.

Worsham possessed a keen sense of observation and a retentive memory. During the Valley Campaign, he recalled, two members of the 21st Virginia owned pet roosters. Everytime the regiment passed a farmyard, the soldiers loosed their cocks—and enjoyed fresh fowl for supper that night. He related the erratic flights of Federal cannonballs in two battles. He recounted in detail all aspects of camp life. His book tells of marches, picket duty, punishments, sick call, deaths, mail service, winter quarters, food, clothing, fraternization, provost duty, battles, equipment wounds and foraging. His narrative, in short, is a comprehensive story of the common Confederate soldier.

Comments about the rank and file are interspersed with descriptions of Jackson, Lee, Early, Gordon, and other Confederate generals. Because Worsham had a penchant for moving rapidly from one subject to another, his memoirs rarely drag and are never dull. Although the recollections were written four decades after the Civil War, they contain very few inaccuracies. Worsham occasionally confused dates; for example he stated that Jefferson Davis was on the field at Gaines's Mill when actually the President was with Lee the day before at Mechanicsville. He was also guilty of misspelling names, but this practice was so prevalent among soldiers of the 1860's as not to be startling. The original narrative contained long and complicated sentences; nevertheless, inexorably present at all times is the vision of a soldier: on the one hand gallant and devoted to duty, on the other hand observant and able to record what he saw and did. This combination makes the Worsham memoirs a classic in Confederate military history.

Among Worsham's personal papers is a publisher's blurb on *One of Jackson's Foot Cavalry*. A portion of it merits repeating:

"If Dickens had followed Stonewall Jackson, he would have written just such a book as this. Worsham's sense of humor, his pathos, his fancy, his descriptive power, made him just the man to write this splendid account of the great campaign in which he took part. Like Dickens, too, he knew how to appraise greatness; consequently his pictures of the noted leaders that he followed are finely drawn. . . .

"But Worsham's story does not concern itself primarily with officers and strategy and battles. It is the war experience of a private soldier, told with spirit, and a persuasive humor that is delightful. The narrative is intimate and charming. One sees in detail the daily life of the man in the ranks; what he was doing when he wasn't fighting, wasn't marching, wasn't sleeping; precisely what he was doing when he *was* fighting and marching and sleeping—or desiring to! With all the high romance cut out, the gold braid and the red tape abbreviated, and the truth given pleasant precedence, this is Worsham's story, and it is thoroughly good.

"No. The War of the States was not uninterrupted 'hell,' nor was it uniformly 'glorious.' But it was not the less superb. Worsham's book rivets this fact in the mind, once and for all."

The original version of Worsham's memoirs, published in 1912, was indifferently edited. In this reprint, therefore, I have performed those editorial tasks normal to and expected in modern publishing. Worsham's thirty-eight short chapters have been combined into ten chapters of average length and two appendices. Cumbersome sentences have been shortened and, in the interest of clarity, some minor revisions of phraseology have been made. Obvious misspellings have been corrected; yet dangling prepositions and similar grammatical irregularities have been retained to preserve the flavor of Worsham's writing.

In two instances I converted Worsham's use of the third person into the first person when it was obvious that he was describing his own activities. To help the reader keep his bearings I have occasionally inserted the name of a battle which Worsham failed to identify. The engagement of June 27, 1862, at Savage Station is a case in point. I have deleted a few completely irrelevant sections and indicated the excisions in footnotes. I have also omitted some fragmentary statistics on the human cost of the war, a list of battles in which F Company participated (all of which are duly mentioned in the narrative), the number of miles the company marched daily from April, 1861, through mid-November, 1864 (a total of 4,266 miles), and a list of the fifty-one counties through which it passed.

In making these revisions, I have striven at all times to preserve Worsham's true meaning and interpretation of events. All changes were motivated by one desire: to convert an exceptionally good Confederate memoir into an even better one.

Many persons have aided in the preparation of this new edition. Foremost among them are Miss Bell Worsham, Mrs. Sarah Worsham Landrum, and John G. Worsham, all of Richmond, Va. These surviving grandchildren of Sergeant Worsham generously placed at my disposal his meticulously preserved papers and wartime memorabilia. Their keen interest, voluntary suggestions, and patient answers to many queries helped me immeasurably in my editorial labors. John R. Peacock of High Point, North Carolina, kindly loaned me a copy of the scarce first edition when I initially began work on the memoirs. My first knowledge of the value of Worsham's recollections came several years ago from a fellow student of the Stonewall Brigade, the late Hugh McAllister of Covington, Virginia. Now among my most prized possessions is "Mr. Hugh's" copy of *One of Jackson's Foot Cavalry*, bequeathed to me by his son. Ray D. Smith of Chicago, ever willing to help, again provided many research leads through his massive index to the *Confederate Veteran*. Mrs. Ann L. Merriman of the Richmond *News-Leader*, Miss India Thomas and Miss Eleanor Brockenborough of the Confederate Museum, Lewis N. Barton of Winchester, Virginia, E. Porter Hopkins of the Maryland Historical Society, and Hirst D. Milhollen and E. E. Billings of the Library of Congress each assisted substantially in solving many of those minute riddles that inevitably plague an editor. Lastly, I am particularly indebted to Bell I. Wiley, the general editor of this series. My graduate director and former colleague at Emory University, he has continued over the years to give me wise counsel and warm encouragement in all my scholarly endeavors. To him this edition is gratefully dedicated.

JAMES I. ROBERTSON, JR.

Washington, D. C.

ONE OF JACKSON'S
FOOT CAVALRY

PREFACE

In writing my experiences and what I saw during the war as one of Jackson's "foot cavalry," it is not my intention to make a comparison of commands, but simply to state what was seen and experienced by me. When other commands are mentioned, it is done to give their position, so that the reader may better understand the situation; and when I have a word of praise for them, it is because they came under my eye. It is needless to make comparisons between different commands of the Army of Northern Virginia. The world never saw such courage, devotion, and patriotism as was displayed by the men of that army, and every man in it who did his duty was a hero.

J. H. W.

Richmond, Va.
August, 1912

Chapter I

THE COMMENCEMENT OF HOSTILITIES

Soon after the secession of South Carolina, December 20, 1860, a military spirit prevailed all over Virginia. All the old volunteer companies were filled at once, and new ones were organized. When the State seceded, a large portion of the men had already joined some of the military organizations. I joined an old volunteer company known as "F Company" of Richmond. It was one of the crack companies of that day; in its ranks were some of the best men of the city. It numbered about eighty men, but new members were added so rapidly that it soon numbered about one hundred and fifty.[1]

This company had a fine cadet gray uniform. It consisted first of a frock coat which had a row of Virginia fire-gilt buttons on its front. Around the cuff of the sleeve was a band of gold braid and two small fire-gilt buttons. On the collar the same gold braid was so arranged that it looked very much like the mark of rank for a first lieutenant which was afterwards adopted by the Confederacy. The pants had a black stripe about one and a quarter inches wide along the outer seams. The cap was made of the same cadet gray cloth, trimmed with black braid and two small fire-gilt buttons. On its front was the letter F. The non-commissioned officers had their mark of rank worked on the sleeves of their coats with black braid.

The differences between the uniforms of the officers and the privates were in these particulars: the officers' coats were a little longer; the coat sleeves were highly ornamented with gold braid (something like that of the Confederate uniform); the officers had gold braid down the outer seams of their pants; and their caps were trimmed with gold braid. Each sergeant carried a sword attached to his belt in addition to his gun. When on duty every man was required to wear white gloves. He carried in his knapsack a jacket made of cadet gray cloth. We had black cloth overcoats—the skirt reaching a little below the knees, the capes a little below the elbow—and the buttons were Virginia-gilt.

---

[1] The original muster roll of F Company contained the names of 107 men. By May, 1861, the company numbered 134 men. Letters Received, Va. Forces, War Records Group 109, National Archives.

Our knapsacks were a specialty. They were imported from Paris, made of hairy calfskin wrapped around a frame box, and red and white in color. Inside they were divided into partitions; outside were openings into some of these partitions so that one could handle articles inside without opening the whole knapsack. There were straps on the outside for blanket, overcoat, oilcloth, and shoes. Other straps and some hooks were handy for attaching any article we wished to carry. We also imported our canteens.

For a week or two before Virginia seceded, the companies in Richmond were drilling nearly all the time: a squad of green men at one hour, another squad at the next, and so on throughout the entire day. At night a company drill was held. Each man was required to report at company headquarters once during the day. The tolling of the fire bells was the signal to meet at the companies' armories and be prepared to go wherever ordered.

I was quietly walking home from church after the morning service on Sunday, April 21, 1861, when the bells commenced to toll. I broke into a run at once, going home as fast as I could. I put on my uniform, etc., and was soon at our armory. Here it was rumored that the gunboat *Pawnee* was coming up the James River with the intention of either capturing or bombarding the city. As soon as all the men reported, the company was formed and marched to Wilton on the James River, about ten miles below the city. Passing Rocketts, the port of Richmond, we found the citizens assembled there by thousands: old men, boys, women, girls, women with babies in their arms—in fact, nearly the whole population. The fields and wharves in Rocketts were literally alive with human beings, commingled with horses and vehicles (as some had ridden down in buggies and carriages). Some people had shotguns, some had rifles, some pistols, some swords, some canes, and some had made large piles of stones on the wharves to use against the enemy. They were all determined that the ship should never get to the wharf. It makes me laugh now, after my experience of war, to think what the citizens were then doing!

We arrived at Wilton about sunset and were joined by the Richmond Howitzers.[2] A picket from F Company was established along the river. The Howitzers' guns were placed in position. Orders were given to fire on the *Pawnee* as soon as she came within shooting

---

[2] Another elite unit from Richmond, the Howitzers were initially fancy-dressed and belligerently proud of their little naval six-pounders. In the ranks of the three companies was an unusually high proportion of educated men. Notable among them were such writers and artists as John Esten Cooke, Robert Stiles, Nicholas Couch, and William L. Sheppard. See Frederick S. Daniel, *Richmond Howitzers during the War* (Richmond, 1891).

distance. Those men of F Company not on duty were ordered to stack arms and remain near them during the night. We had nothing to eat and did not know when or where we would get anything. However, one of our officers had remained behind and, about eight or nine o'clock that night, he came up with a wagon loaded with cooked ham, bread, etc. We had a jolly time over our supper, the first of the war. After eating the men gathered about in squads and talked; finally we lay down on the grassy ground and went to sleep without either blanket or oilcloth. The night passed without incident; the expected *Pawnee* did not come.[3]

The next day we returned to Richmond on two barges that were sent down the river for us. We won a great deal of glory in this campaign, as everyone thought we had done wonders. In marching from Rocketts up Main Street to our quarters, which were between Eighth and Ninth Streets, we had an ovation nearly all the way. Thus closed the "Pawnee War."

By now Virginia was thoroughly aroused. Soldiers were coming into Richmond from all directions, the streets were filled with marching men, and the sound of the drum was heard every hour of the day and night. It is said that four weeks after Virginia seceded, 80,000 organized soldiers had offered their services in defense of the cause!

On the morning of Wednesday, April 24, 1861, several telegrams were received in Richmond announcing that the enemy were landing at Aquia Creek, the terminus of the Richmond, Fredericksburg & Potomac Railroad. Our company and the Richmond Light Infantry Blues[4] were ordered at once to that place. We marched to the R. F. & P. depot, then at the corner of Broad and Eighth Streets, and embarked on cars for the seat of war at Aquia Creek. On reaching Fredericksburg we were informed that the Yankees had made a demonstration at Aquia Creek but had not landed. We received orders to stop at Fredericksburg. F Company debarked, marched to the courthouse, and camped for the night. A load of straw that was sent to us was spread on the floor and benches and made a very good bed. Citizens invited us into

---

[3] Of the first scare caused by the *Pawnee,* Mrs. Putnam wrote: "The different companies of infantry were all mustered . . . [and] were drawn out into the street; almost every man carried a gun of some description, and boys, who had learned to shoot, appeared with light fowling pieces. The ridiculous was singularly blended with the solemn and impressive." *Richmond during the War,* pp. 24-25. See also DeLeon, *Four Years in Rebel Capitals,* pp. 103-04. Supper for the camping soldiers that night consisted of "half done Bacon & crackers, but it was devoured with great relish." Randolph Journal, entry of Apr. 21, 1861.

[4] The proud Blues had its antecedents in pre-Revolutionary War days. Commanded by Capt. O. Jennings Wise, son of the ex-governor, it shortly became Co. A of the 46th Va.

their homes for supper. We went to bed that night in regular military order—had a camp guard, lights out by taps,[5] etc. During the day some of the boys had purchased whistles, tin horns, and other noisy things. As soon as the lights were put out, the fun commenced. One blew a horn; another in a distant part of the building answered on a whistle. This went on for a few minutes. When the officers commanded silence, no attention was paid to them. When the officers ordered the sergeant to "arrest those men," the sergeant would strike a light and go to where he thought the noise originated. But each man looked so innocent that he could not tell who it was. By this time, another would blow. Soon four sergeants were running here and there, trying to catch the delinquents. This kept up until the perpetrators became tired. Not one was detected.

In the morning citizens supplied us with breakfast. We remained in the town, living in this manner, for several days. Then we marched to the Fair Grounds, where we found that the Blues had preceded us. Here we went regularly into camp, which was called Camp Mercer.[6] Our company was assigned to the sheds of the horse department. The floors were covered with straw, and three men were assigned to a stall.

Camp duty, with its guard mounting, policing, drills, etc., began at once, and dress parade was held every fair evening. Most of the young ladies of the town came out to witness the drill, and they seemed to enjoy it as much as we did their presence. The men formed messes, each consisting of about ten men and each employing a Negro man as cook. We got on nicely, as we thought. The regular rations were issued to us; but in order to become accustomed by degrees to eating them, we sent the cook or some member of the mess into town to get such articles as the market afforded.

While in Camp Mercer we were joined by a company of infantry, one of cavalry, and the Purcell Battery of artillery from Richmond. W. R. J. Pegram of F Company ("Specks," as he was called) helped Captain Lindsay Walker drill this battery and was soon made a lieutenant. This is the same W. R. J. Pegram who was soon known in the

---

[5] Prior to 1862, the call for "Taps" was a drab, little-known melody found for the most part only in such military manuals as Silas Casey's *Tactics*. Gen. Daniel Butterfield of the Federal army composed the "Taps" that we know today shortly after the conclusion of the Seven Days campaign. See Oliver W. Norton, *Army Letters, 1861-1865* (Chicago, 1903), pp. 327-28.

[6] The Fredericksburg fairgrounds were converted into a permanent camp of instruction and named Camp Mercer in honor of a local son, Hugh Mercer, of Revolutionary War fame. At the outset camp drainage was inadequate, and at least one heavy rain drove the companies quartered there into the shelter of the city's buildings. Fredericksburg *News*, May 3 and 7, 1861.

Army of Northern Virginia as the fighting captain, major, lieutenant colonel, and colonel, and who was killed at Five Forks in April, 1865. I saw the first man of the war punished for disobedience of orders while we were in this camp. He was a member of Walker's battery and was strapped on one of the cannon wheels in such a manner as to keep him from moving. We were treated most hospitably by the citizens of Fredericksburg. Some of us visited the city each day. We were always welcomed and sometimes invited to meals. We left with sad hearts. This was the most comfortable camp we had during the war, but at that time we thought it was execrable.

We stayed at Fredericksburg about three weeks, and were then ordered to Aquia Creek. At Game Point, about three-quarters of a mile from Aquia Creek, we camped in a house situated on a high hill to the left of the Richmond, Fredericksburg & Potomac Railroad. The Richmond Light Infantry Blues also went to Aquia Creek and camped about one and a half miles from us lower down the river.

As the cook of my mess would not leave Fredericksburg, we determined at Game Point to cook for ourselves. I will never forget the first meal. We made a fire under the shade of a tree, made up our bread of meal (the government commenced to give it to us thus early), sliced our fat meat, and commenced to cook. In about two minutes both meat and bread were burned black on one side! We took them off the fire, cooled them, tried again, and succeeded very well in burning the other side. We finally cooked everything we had and sat down on the ground to eat. The bread had no salt in it (no one had thought of that), and the meat was so salty we could not eat it. We were disgusted; but the next day we had better success, and in a few days we got along all right.

In addition to a camp guard we had two picket or lookout posts. The duty of each was to watch the river for the enemy. One night while I was on guard at our quarters, General Daniel Ruggles, the commanding officer of this department, paid us a visit.[7] As soon as I saw him I presented arms and turned out the guard, thinking to do him all the honor we could. I was horrified when a non-commissioned officer slipped up to me and told me such honor was not done after dark.

The following letter was written while we were in this camp and explains itself:

---

[7] A native of Massachusetts, heavily built and heavily bearded Daniel Ruggles (1810-1897) joined the Confederacy largely because of his marriage to a Virginia girl. He commanded state forces until Aug., 1861, when he was transferred to the western theater. The end of the war found him a commissary general of prisoners.

"George W. Peterkin, Esq.:

Dear Sir—We, the undersigned comrades in arms with yourself, have been struck with the propriety of evening prayer, and desire, if agreeable to you, that you, from this time, and so long as we remain together, conduct that service."

Signed by fifty-three members of Company F.

This gallant young soldier and truly good man, George Peterkin, conducted the service each night. By his Christian example he won the respect and affection of every member of the company. When he left us in 1862 to take a staff appointment, it was like breaking up a household.[8]

On May 29, 1861, we had our first experience of war. One of the enemy's gunboats stopped in front of Aquia Creek, fired a few shots and left. On June 7, three gunboats made their appearance and commenced to bombard the earthworks near the wharf. The enemy threw six-, eight-, and ten-inch shots at Captain Walker, who put some of his small three-inch rifled cannon into the works and replied. The firing lasted several hours. The enemy withdrew about two or three miles down the river, stayed all night, and renewed the attack the next morning with five gunboats. They kept the fire up until about 5 p.m., when they withdrew. During the firing the Richmond Light Infantry Blues and F Company were stationed behind some hills in the rear of the works, and nearly all the shots of the enemy passed over us. The family living inside the earthworks had a chicken coop knocked to pieces. The old cock confined in it came out of the ruins, mounted the debris, flapped his wings, and crowed. That was the only casualty on our side. Captain Walker's shots struck the vessels several times; as they were wooden boats, he must have damaged them some. We afterwards heard that one of them was the notable *Pawnee*.[9]

We had several alarms at night, when the entire command would turn out and march to the river to the place designated. On one of

---

[8] Another soldier in F Company stated that Peterkin "would be an angel if they existed in uniform." C. G. Chamberlayne (ed.), *Ham Chamberlayne—Virginian* (Richmond, 1932), p. 39. Hereafter cited as *Ham Chamberlayne*. Peterkin later became Bishop of West Virginia. See *Confederate Veteran*, XXV (1917), 419; *Magazine of History and Biography by the Randolph County Historical Society*, XII (1961), 97-99. Hereafter cited as *Randolph County Historical Society*.

[9] On May 29, according to Ruggles's report, two small Federal steamers attacked the Aquia Creek Railroad battery at sunset and fired fourteen shells. A more concentrated bombardment on May 31 likewise failed. No action occurred for the next few days, but the *Pawnee* was ever visible, "lying off at the point." U. S. War Dept. (comp.), *War of the Rebellion: A Compilation of the Official Records of the Union and Confederate Armies* (Washington, 1880-1901), Ser. I, II, 55-57. Hereafter cited as *OR;* unless otherwise stated, all references will be to Ser. I. For a vivid description of the May 29 action, see Tucker Randolph to his father, May 30, 1861, Randolph Papers.

LYING ON ARMS

"At night we lay down on our arms. The next morning, expecting a renewal of the battle, we were up bright and early."
From a drawing by William L. Sheppard.

1861

"This company had a fine cadet gray uniform. . . . When on duty every man was required to wear white gloves."

1862

"He carried a knapsack, oilcloth, blanket, extra shoes, haversack, tin cup, canteen, and a tin can for cooking." (From Worsham's original caption.) Worsham himself posed for this picture shortly after the war.

1863

"Our army at this time was in a sad plight as to clothing. Hundreds had no shoes, and thousands were as ragged as they could be."

1864

"He carried an oil cloth, in which was wrapped a cotton fly tent;
haversack in which was towel, soap, and needle case; canteen, tin
cup and tin can for cooking." (Worsham's original caption)

One of Jackson's Foot Calvary, Made 1912

SGT. JOHN H. WORSHAM

From a photograph taken presumably around June, 1865.

CAPT. R. MILTON CARY

"He was the organizer of F Company, a fine soldier, strict disciplinarian, and splendid drill master."

CAPT.
WILLIAM A. PEGRAM

"Young, unassuming, but a true soldier, he was noted for his gallantry on many a battlefield."

CAPT. WILLIAM H. MORGAN

"He was a splendid soldier, and the best informed man on military matters that I knew during the war."

CAPT. REUBEN J. JORDAN

"Capt. Jordan, by his bravery and coolness, had with only seven men stopped the advance of the enemy."

LT. COL. RICHARD H. CUNNINGHAM, JR.

"As gallant a man as the cause ever lost, he was conspicuous on every battlefield for brave deeds."

Confederate Museum

BRIG. GEN. BRADLEY T. JOHNSON

"His personal interest in the men went right to their hearts, and they showed their appreciation by obeying every order with cheerfulness and alacrity."

BRIG. GEN.
JOHN M. JONES

"A strict disciplinarian . . . he was
the only officer who made the men
take care of themselves as far as they
could."

MAJ. GEN.
EDWARD JOHNSON

"In the presence of many spectators
General Johnson, in patriotic and
thrilling words, presented to our regiment its first battle flag."

JOHN AND MARY PILCHER WORSHAM

From a photograph taken presumably in the 1880's.

JACKSON AT WINCHESTER

"On entering Winchester, even Gen. Jackson smiled, something I never saw him do before." From a painting by William Washington.

Cook Collection. Valentine Museum

these occasions we marched in rain which poured down in torrents. The darkness was illumined by most vivid flashes of lightning, and great peals of thunder intensified the storm. We stayed out all night, putting a picket along the river—two men on a post. We crossed Aquia Creek twice during alarms, one time staying all night on the point.

We were joined by the 1st Arkansas Infantry, Walker's Tennessee Legion, and several Virginia companies. The hills around Aquia were fortified by earthworks, and large naval guns were placed in them. Our company turned out one night and pulled one of those large guns up one of the steepest hills to its position, after a failure on the part of a large team of horses and oxen! It was demonstrated very forcibly that men are the best and quickest force for handling large and heavy guns like those.

We drilled every good day and took our first lessons in skirmish drill, as well as the bayonet exercise, or Zouave drill.[10] Before we left, we became very well drilled in each. Notwithstanding the duties, we enjoyed ourselves very much by fishing on the wharf, bathing in the river, and taking rambles through the woods. On one of the hills in the neighborhood was a fine and extensive view of the Potomac.

On June 14 F Company was ordered to Richmond to join a regiment that was being formed there. The men were told it was to be a crack regiment. Our own and a Maryland company, commanded by Captain J. Lyle Clarke[11] and then in Camp Lee, were to be the nucleus, with the other companies to be of the same standing. No time was designated for the formation of the regiment; when formed it would be an independent one. With these inducements the men readily consented to the arrangements. The order therefore came to go to Richmond.[12]

---

[10] In those rare instances when bayonet drill was conducted, men had to stand at a distance from one another at least equal to the combined length of their arms, musket, and bayonet. One Federal soldier likened a squad of men performing such a drill to "a line of human beings made up about equally of the frog, the sand-hill crane, the sentinel crab, and the grasshopper; all of them rapidly jumping, thrusting, swinging, striking every way, and all gone stark mad." Francis A. Lord, *They Fought for the Union* (Harrisburg, Pa., 1960), p. 27.

[11] Twenty-seven-year-old Lyle Clarke commanded a company composed of members of some of Baltimore's most aristocratic families. The company disbanded in May, 1862; Clarke later became a major in the 30th Va. Battalion of Sharpshooters. See *Confederate Veteran*, IV (1896), 386.

[12] Since the company at this time had not been mustered into Confederate service, the men were reluctant to relinquish their pleasant duty. Ruggles reported to Lee that the men wished to become part of a regiment being formed at Fredericksburg, and that their return to Richmond "would give the greatest dissatisfaction." As Worsham stated, the troops soon changed their minds. *OR*, II, 874, 944.

While we were at Fredericksburg and Aquia Creek, some changes took place in officers and non-commissioned officers. First Lieutenant James R. Crenshaw and Corporal Edward T. Robinson did not accompany us, and soon after we got to Fredericksburg Captain R. Milton Cary was made a colonel. These vacancies and others were filled as follows:

Captain, Richard H. Cunningham, Jr.
1st Lieutenant, Edward Mayo
2nd Lieutenant, Phillip A. Wellford
Junior 2nd Lieutenant, Henry T. Miller
1st Sergeant, John A. Pizzini
2nd Sergeant, Edward G. Rawlings
3rd Sergeant, John Tyler
4th Sergeant, Thomas Ellet
1st Corporal Jesse Child (who succeeded M. Louis Randolph)
2nd Corporal, J. Tucker Randolph (who succeeded Jesse Child)
3rd Corporal, Shirley King (who succeeded J. Tucker Randolph)
4th Corporal, George R. Pace (who succeeded Shirley King)

F Company gave up Captain Cary with much reluctance.[13] He was the organizer of F Company, a fine soldier, strict disciplinarian, and splendid drillmaster. They tell this on him to show his promptness: At the time of the John Brown raid, Governor Henry Wise one night sent for him, told him he wanted his company to go to Harper's Ferry at once, and asked him, "How many men can you carry, and how soon can you meet me at Richmond, Fredericksburg & Potomac Railroad depot?"

Captain Cary replied, "Sixty men in sixty minutes."

The old governor, much pleased with the answer, told him to report within two hours.

When F Company left Richmond for Fredericksburg, each man carried as equipment a gun, knapsack, canteen, tin cup, and haversack. Most of them wore linen gaiters and havelocks, the latter being a head covering for protection from the sun. Many wore around their waists, next to the skin, a flannel belt or worsted string to prevent bowel complaint.[14] In our knapsacks we carried a fatigue jacket, several pairs of

[13] A native of Hampton, Va., Milton Cary was a successful Richmond attorney who had served in a militia company at Harpers Ferry during John Brown's 1859 raid. After the Civil War he became a successful cotton and tobacco broker in England. In May, 1861, he was placed in command of a battalion. The subsequent addition of companies to his unit led to the formation of the 30th Va. and Cary's promotion to colonel.

[14] Civil War soldiers often tried to combat intestinal disorders by "the general adoption of the habit of wearing flannel body bandages or stomach belts." Bell I. Wiley, *The Life of Billy Yank* (Indianapolis, 1952), p. 137. For other primitive treatments of

white gloves, several pairs of drawers, several white shirts, undershirts, linen collars, neckties, white vest, socks, etc.—filling our knapsack to overflowing. Strapped on the outside were one or two blankets, an oilcloth, and extra shoes. Most of the knapsacks weighed between thirty and forty pounds, but some were so full that they weighed fifty pounds!

The best article carried by the soldiers was a "needle case" containing needles of various sizes, thread, buttons, etc. It soon became the most valuable of our possessions. When we went into camp we would see the men occupied in sewing or patching their clothing, and towards the last of the war it was in almost constant use. Notwithstanding this, it was hard to keep the ragged clothing from showing a portion of the skin of its wearer.

I suppose every man in the Confederate army carried a Bible, given with blessing by a mother or sweetheart. This Bible was read as a book never was before. I read mine through the first year. They were a blessing to many—and life savers too, as I heard of and saw many lives saved by bullets striking the Bible carried in the breast pocket.

On our arrival at Camp Lee[15] we were given tents, which we put up in regular military style near the center of the grounds, and commenced a regular camp life: drilling, guard mounting each morning, policing, inspections, and evening dress parade. The last-named was witnessed daily by quite a number of our lady friends from Richmond.

We were mustered into service for one year on June 28, 1861 (to date from April 21), on the Capitol Square by Inspector General J. B. Baldwin. Each boy under twenty-one, and there were many, brought a written permit from parent or guardian. This was approved by the Governor of Virginia before he was mustered in.[16]

While in Camp Lee, some of the company visited the city daily. Some had passes; others "ran the blockade" on their uniform. As before stated, our uniforms gave the impression of a first lieutenant; and when we wanted to go to the city and could not get a pass, we would march boldly by a sentinel on duty at one of the many openings around the grounds, give him the salute, and he would present arms as we

these maladies, see Bell I. Wiley, *The Life of Johnny Reb* (Indianapolis, 1943), pp. 257-58.

[15] Named in honor of "Lighthorse" Harry Lee, the camp was located on the western outskirts of Richmond in what was known as Monroe Park, or the Hermitage Fair Grounds. For the camp's later history, see *SHSP*, XXVI (1898), 241-45.

[16] At this point in his original narrative, Worsham gave a partial muster of F Company, plus some official correspondence relative to the mustering of the unit. The more important of that data has been incorporated into the roster at the end of the text.

passed out. So many of the company went to the city in this way that orders were finally issued that everyone leaving the grounds should go out of the gate. As some officer was always stationed there, we were afraid to try it too often.

I cannot help telling of a good thing I heard from an officer. One night I was particularly anxious to go to the city, but no one was allowed to go out at night unless he had the countersign. This was only given to those on duty, and in consequence none of us could go out at night. As night approached, I walked to the guard quarters at the gate and took a seat among some of my company who were on duty, hoping something would turn up and let me into the secret. I was there some time, but no one would talk about it. As it was getting dark, I had about made up my mind to leave and try to dodge the sentinel by walking out, hoping he would think me one of the guards. The captain of the guard now made his appearance, called by name the non-commissioned officer who was on duty, and said, "The countersign tonight is 'Richmond,' and the password, 'Chickahominy'." I was so overjoyed that I came near letting the officer know that I was not one of the guard. As soon as he walked away I quietly left, went to our quarters, told many of the company, and they left for the city. About half of the company did the same.

On Monday, July 1, our company was called on suddenly about sunset to "fall in," and we marched at a double quick through rain and mud to the Penitentiary. Here we found the weaving department on fire and much excitement. Our company was put on guard duty. After several hours the fire was put out and quiet restored. We were again ordered to "fall in" and were marched to the corner of Fifth and Franklin Streets in the city, where we were dismissed and allowed to go to our homes for the remainder of the night. We were given orders to assemble at the same point the next morning at 10 o'clock, when we marched back to Camp Lee.

Quite a stir was created in camp one day by the announcement that a flag would be presented to Company B. This was a very handsome silk flag. Made by the ladies of Baltimore, it "ran the blockade" into Richmond and was presented to the company by President Jefferson Davis. He made one of his brilliant speeches in the presence of the regiment and a large number of visitors from Richmond, most of them ladies. The occasion passed off with great enthusiasm.

About two weeks after reaching Camp Lee, the 21st Regiment of Virginia Infantry was formed and included the Maryland company, two or three others, and F Company. The following officers were appointed:

Colonel William Gilham of the Virginia Military Institute
Lieutenant Colonel John M. Patton, Jr., of Richmond
Major Scott Shipp of the Virginia Military Institute
Adjutant William H. Morgan of the Virginia Military Institute
Surgeon Robert T. Coleman of Richmond
Assistant Surgeon R. Lewis of Richmond
Commissary H. E. C. Baskerville of Richmond
Sergeant Major Virginius Dabney of Richmond
Commissary Sergeant Timothy H. Kellogg of Richmond

In a few days orders were sent to these officers to complete the regiment at once from such companies as were then in camp and to be ready to move as soon as possible, as troops were very much needed in the field. This order was complied with, and the regiment was completed. The following is a list of the companies, their origins and captains:[17]

A — "Red House Volunteers," Charlotte County, John B. Moseley

B — "Baltimore Company B Maryland Guards," Baltimore, J. Lyle Clarke

C — "Oliver Grays," Buckingham County, James Oliver

D — "Cumberland Grays," Cumberland County, Francis D. Irving

E— "Buckingham Leaches," Buckingham County, James P. Leach

F — "F Company of Richmond," Richmond, Richard H. Cunningham, Jr.

G — "Brunswick Grays," Brunswick County, Thomas B. Robinson

H — "Chalk Level Grays," Pittsylvania County, Sherwood T. Mustain

I — "Turkey Cock Grays," Pittsylvania County, William A. Witcher

K — "Meherrin Grays," Mecklenberg County, William R. Berkeley

The regiment numbered about 850, rank and file. We were soon ready, and reported to the authorities. Our company now equipped itself with everything that could be gotten to make us comfortable. As we had been in the field several weeks and knew the necessities, and as we had marched, slept without protection, done picket duty,

---

[17] In his memoirs Worsham listed nine of the ten companies, in alphabetical order and with several errors in the names of the company commanders. This revised list was compiled from muster rolls in War Records. Group 109, National Archives.

and been in one engagement, we thought ourselves veterans. As such, we were going to take along with us everything the authorities would allow. Each man purchased a nice chest. As our own was a fair specimen, I will try to describe it and its contents. The chest was made of oak, and was about three feet long, eighteen inches wide and eighteen inches deep. In it were several trays. It was strapped securely with iron. At each end were iron handles, and its top was secured by substantial iron hinges and a strong lock. We had in it a dozen knives and forks, two or three butcher knives, a dozen teacups and saucers, a dozen plates, several dishes and bowls, a sugar dish and cream pitcher, salt and pepper boxes, a tin box containing a dozen assorted boxes of spices, a dozen glasses, a sifter, rolling pin, coffee tin, etc. Besides these, we carried outside a frying pan, coffee pot, camp kettle, teapot, bread oven (that afterwards played such a prominent part in the army as the "spider"), two water buckets, ax, etc. In addition to the usual arms of an infantryman, each man carried a long bowie knife and a pistol in his belt.

On July 17, 1861, the regiment got orders to take the cars at the Central Depot for Staunton.[18] Promptly on the next morning we marched out of Camp Lee into Broad Street, where we wheeled into platoons, F Company in front, and marched to the depot. Our friends turned out by thousands, and the march was made amidst the inspiring cheers of the multitude that bade us goodbye. The day was terribly hot, and many of the men, overcome by the heat, fell out of ranks during the march.

---

[18] Many men in the 21st Va. had hoped that they might be ordered to the York-town area. Se DeLeon, *Four Years in Rebel Capitals,* p. 108.

Chapter II

THE WESTERN VIRGINIA AND ROMNEY CAMPAIGNS

We left Richmond about 11 a.m. on July 18 and reached Staunton in slow time about 7 o'clock on the next morning. We marched to the Fair Grounds and camped in a wood on a large hill overlooking the depot and city. During the day we made additional purchases of articles that we thought would be of use and comfort to us, and we hired teams to carry our company baggage. The next morning we left Staunton, marching toward Buffalo Gap. The regiment had a train of forty-five wagons, most of which were four-horse mountain wagons. Our company had five, having hired four of that number to carry our baggage, knapsacks, chests, etc., and the one furnished by the government carrying our tents and cooking utensils. When we reached Buffalo Gap flour was issued to us as rations. We were promised beef as soon as some of the regiment killed some cattle that were nearby in a pen. Several of the F Company boys volunteered to do the killing if others would do the dressing, etc. The force was soon made up. The F boys quietly loaded their guns and shot the required number of beeves. The others dressed them, and in a short time we had our regular supper. This was the commencement of our rations of beef and flour—a ration that was issued to us many years. While the beef was being dressed, camp was laid off, tents were pitched, and fires were made. Some of the men took a delightful bath. Others climbed the steep mountain and viewed the surrounding country. Guard was placed around the camp and, as bedtime approached, we went quietly to rest after our first regular march as a regiment.

The next morning we continued our march, and during the day we heard the firing of artillery so plainly in our front that our officers sent someone ahead to find out what it meant. After waiting some time one of them rode forward; when he returned after several hours' absence, he could give no account of it. He said that as far as he went it seemed just ahead, and no one he saw could give any information in regards to it. We went into camp at Ryan's. While we were eating supper, we received a dispatch by courier saying a great battle had been fought and won by the Confederates at Manassas. We must have been 100 miles in an air line from Manassas. The firing was as distinct that day as any I heard afterwards that was five to six miles off.

The company's first misfortune overtook us at Ryan's: the government took one of our company wagons, and the driver of another refused to go any farther. Some of the mess chests were abandoned, and some of the men had to carry their knapsacks. The next day we reached McDowell in a drizzling rain and met the men of General Robert Garnett's command, who had been defeated a few days before at Carrick's Ford.[1] They were a forlorn looking set, and told awful tales of having nothing to eat except berries and roasting ears! None of us believed what they said, but it was not many months before we were made to realize that it was the truth. We now lost another of our company wagons, and more mess chests were left behind. The next day we marched to Monterey. We were living high, buying as many nearly grown chickens as we wanted for six pence (8 1/3 cents) each, butter and eggs at corresponding prices per pound and dozen, and a meal—when we could stop for one—for nine pence (12½ cents).

Continuing our march, we reached Napp's Creek Valley on July 25. We forded that creek seventeen times during the day's march, the road crossing from one side to the other every few hundred yards. General William Loring,[2] the officer in command of this expedition, passed us today while we were on the march. His attention being called to the 21st Regiment, he remarked that they were a fine look-ing body of men, but not soldiers. "Until they are able to sleep in winter amidst the snow and ice without tents, they are not soldiers!" This was repeated to our company. The men were very indignant and put Loring down at once as an officer who knew nothing. Each man in the company wanted to call him to account for the insinuation, and they would have told him they never expected to sleep in snow or be surrounded by ice. Alas for our judgment! It was not many months before we were of the same opinion as General Loring, and we then knew that we had at this time learned nothing about the duties of sol-diers in the field. On the evening of the 26th we reached Huntersville, the seat of Pocahontas County.

We stayed there several days, concentrating a force large enough to cope with the enemy in our front. We were joined by several regi-

---

1 For reports of the July 13, 1861, action at Carrick's Ford, see *OR*, II, 204, 206-08, 220-23, 285-88. Another Confederate verified the shoddy appearance of Garnett's men as they joined Lee's army. See *SHSP*, XXVII (1899), 47-48.
2 William Wing Loring (1818-1886) was a brusque and belligerent North Caro-linian who had lost an arm in the Mexican War. His notable clash with Jackson after the Romney campaign led to his transfer to the West, where Loring proved a reliable but unspectacular commander.

ments of infantry, several companies of cavalry, and several batteries of artillery. During our stay there a great many of the men became sick with measles and typhoid fever. When we left on the evening of August 3, at least one-third of the 21st Virginia Regiment was sick in the hospitals.[3] The courthouse and only church had been converted into hospitals; some of the private houses were full of the sick; and tents had to be erected for others. Our company's baggage was reduced so much that we only had one wagon when we left. The march continued until we reached Valley Mountain on August 6, where our regiment pitched tents on the side of this mountain and we went into camp.

General Robert E. Lee, having been assigned to the command of this department, joined us here and pitched his headquarters tent about one or two hundred yards from our company. He soon won the affection of all by his politeness and notice of the soldiers.[4] He very often had something to say to the men; and it soon became known that when some of the people in the neighborhood sent him something good to eat, the articles were sent to some sick soldier as soon as the messenger got out of sight. This affection increased as the years rolled on, and I suppose no body of men under his command had more love and respect for our great leader than these men who first served under him!

Here is an incident showing General Lee's kindness of heart. He was well aware of the arduous duties we had to do at that time. On a rainy night a private of Company E of our regiment was on guard duty. Soon after getting to his post he took a seat on a log, thinking he could protect himself and his gun from the rain better in this position. While in this position he was approached by the corporal of the guard, who accused the man of being asleep on his post. This the man denied, stating that, the ground being so soft from rain, he did not hear the corporal approach. The corporal arrested him, took him to the guard house, and turned him over to the officer of the guard. At that time it was considered a capital offense for a man to be caught asleep on post; the offense was punishable by death.

In the morning the captain of the guard consulted with the officers of the regiment as to what should be done. All of them thought the

[3] George Peterkin of F Company wrote after the war that 600 of 900 men in the 21st Va. were prostrated by sickness during the month of August. The regimental surgeon, R. T. Coleman, called the area around Huntersville "the Valley of the Shadow of Death," and Ham Chamberlayne informed his mother that "camp disease weakened us mightily for a time." Worsham to his sister, July 26, 1861; *Randolph County Historical Society*, XII (1961), 98; *Ham Chamberlayne*, p. 38.

[4] "General Lee was at that time the very personification of dignity and grace," Peterkin recollected, "and I can never forget the impression he made upon us all." *Randolph County Historical Society*, XII (1961), 98.

private ought to be shot. Things began to look blue for the man when, as by inspiration, the captain said, "Well, General Lee is here, and he knows, and I'll carry you to him."

As they approached General Lee's tent, they saw that he was alone and writing at a table. On getting to the tent the general bade them good-morning and invited them in. When they entered, the general said, "What can I do for you, Captain."

The captain stated the case and added that, as the officers of the regiment did not know what to do, he had come to consult him. General Lee at once replied: "Captain, you know the arduous duties these men have to do daily. Suppose the man who was found on his post asleep had been you, or me. What do you think should be done to him?"

The captain replied that he had not thought of it in that way.

Then General Lee turned to the man and said, "My man, go back to your quarters, and never let it be said you were found asleep on your post."

The sick became so numerous here, and the regiments were so diminished, that at one time I suppose there were not more than one-fourth of the men available for duty. I know that in my own regiment we had to picket at the front; and when one picket was relieved and the men returned to camp in the evening, most of them were re-detailed immediately and ordered to get ready with rations, etc., for duty again in the morning.[5] We worked a great deal on the roads. While at work one day under the direction of a corporal, we were observed by General Loring on his rounds. He dismounted, gave some directions to the corporal as to the work, and then took a seat on a log near him. The corporal joined him, seated himself near the general, and made some remarks about the work. He then said to General Loring: "General, we officers have a good time up here, don't we?"

General Loring looked at him and then asked his rank.

"Corporal," he replied.

The General, who was a profane man, let some "cuss words" loose at him and told him to take a spade. It is said the corporal made the dirt fly as long as General Loring was in sight.

General Lee ordered a forward movement on September 9. Each man was given thirty rounds of ammunition, which a short time there-

---

[5] Ham Chamberlayne, either belittling the misery or attempting to boost the morale of his family in Richmond, was more optimistic of conditions in mid-August. "F's health generally is surprising," he wrote home reassuringly. "The band box Co. of parlour soldiers has done better than any other Co. in the Regt.; having in proportion to its numbers more men fit for duty." *Ham Chamberlayne*, pp. 25-26.

after was increased to forty rounds. This number was always carried by each man to the end of the war, unless on some special occasion we were required to carry eighty.

We met the enemy at Conrad's Mill on the 11th; some skirmishing and artillery firing took place. As we advanced up the road, we passed our first dead Yankee. He made a lasting impression, for he lay on the side of the road, his face upturned and a fresh pool of blood at his side, showing that his life had just passed away.[6]

The enemy retired during the night. The next day a picket from the 21st Virginia Regiment was sent to the front and remained there until the 15th. We then fell back to Valley Mountain, reaching there on September 17.

The failure here was owing more to mud than anything else. In all my experience of the war I never saw as much mud. It seemed to rain every day. It got to be a saying in our company that you must not halloo loud; for if you should, we would immediately have a hard shower. When some of the men on their return from picket had to shoot off their guns to get the load out, it brought on a regular flood. Granville Gray always said it rained thirty-*two* days in August. I was told by wagoners that it was hard for them to haul from Milboro (sixty miles away) any more than it took to feed their teams back and forth. I saw dead mules lying in the road with nothing but their ears showing above the mud.[7]

We remained at Valley Mountain until September 24, when General Lee left us and joined General John B. Floyd on Sewell's Mountain. He took all the troops with him but our regiment, the Irish Battalion,[8] a battery of artillery, and a company of cavalry. These troops were left in command of Colonel William Gilham of the 21st Virginia Regiment.[9] Gilham fell back to Middle Mountain—about two

---

[6] The Federals at Conrad's Store belonged to Co. F of the 15th Ind. The dead man that the Virginians saw was either Pvt. Alexander Kent or Pvt. George Bealer, since these were the only Federals killed in the skirmish. *OR*, V, 188.

[7] Worsham's exaggeration is perhaps not too extreme. George Peterkin wrote later that "it was indeed a fearful summer. We camped on Valley Mountain forty-three days, and it rained thirty-seven days out of the number." *Randolph County Historical Society*, XII (1961), 97.

[8] Composed of five companies, the Irish Battalion was organized in May, 1861, and mustered into service June 30, 1861. Maj. John D. Munford was its first commander, but Maj. John Seddon led it at this time. For the wartime letters of one of its members, see Catherine Thom Bartlett (ed.), *"My Dear Brother": A Confederate Chronicle* (Richmond, 1952), pp. 51-57.

[9] "Old Gil" Gilham, a native of Indiana, champion of military ideals, and author of a popular army manual of instruction, had commanded the VMI Corps of Cadets at the hanging of John Brown. He was a quite scholar with high-pitched voice and ready wit, but he was known too for a hot temper. See Jennings C. Wise, *The Military History of the Virginia Military Institute from 1839 to 1865* (Lynchburg, Va., 1915), pp. 55-56, 90-96, 114-15.

miles from Valley Mountain, a position that could be more easily defended. We marched to the place of our encampment on Middle Mountain, stacked arms, and returned to Valley Mountain for our camp equipage. Having no wagon, we had to carry everything needed on our backs, and we had to make several trips to do it. What was left at Valley Mountain was gathered together and burned. What a fall for F Company! We had left Staunton with five wagons loaded with company baggage. We were now moving the camp of our regiment without a single wagon.

We left Middle Mountain on September 28 after a heavy rain. All the creeks had become small rivers; as we forded them, the water came up to our waists. We had now one two-horse and one three-horse wagon to move everything belonging to the command. We began to think, as General Loring did, that we were men but not soldiers. After a short march on each day we reached Elk Mountain about dark on October 1. A detail from F Company, composed of a lieutenant, a non-commissioned officer, and six men, was sent back eight miles on the road to picket. We reached our destination about midnight. Two sentinels were posted at once, one in the road and the other in a path that led over the mountain. Headquarters of the camp was at a spring on the road near a house, but on the opposite side of the road.

The next morning, not long after daybreak, the inmates of the house—a woman and her children—commenced to stir and soon made their appearance. About sunrise the woman came to the yard fence and commenced to abuse us in the most violent language I ever heard from a woman. It was some time before we could tell why she was abusing us. She had quite a large number of beehives, and the troops marching by her house the day before had not molested any of them. Yet when she arose in the morning and realized that one of her beehives was gone, and that a squad of men was at her spring, it was quite natural that she should think we took it. Our lieutenant, Edward Mayo, tried to impress on her that we did not. But she knew better, as she had gone to bed with everything all right; and when she awoke, we were there and the hive was gone. This was convincing proof to her.

We were ordered not to go on her side of the road nor have any talk with the inmates of the house, as Lieutenant Mayo wanted to show her that we were gentlemen at any rate. We had no rations, as we had moved in the night before we could get any. It is true that some of the men had a little sugar and coffee, and some a little raw meat and a few biscuits. After the old lady had cooled off (as we supposed), our lieutenant went over to the house and tried to borrow or rent a coffee pot. But the old lady said she would see him and us in a hot place sooner. On his return we built a small fire, boiled the meat, and divided the bread amongst ourselves.

Now, to add to our misery, the woman commenced to bring out her milk and carry it to the hog pen, where she poured gallon after gallon to the hogs. We did not say a word to any of the household during the day. A little before nightfall our lieutenant went over again to see what he could do. With the offer of a little coffee, an article he found the old lady was very fond of and had been without for some time, he got the use of a teakettle to make some coffee in, and she baked us an oven of cornbread. He carried the articles back, then returned to the porch and had quite a long chat. On returning, he told us she had promised to let us have the kettle and some more bread in the morning. We got them the next morning, with the promise of a dinner for the party. About dinner time we were relieved and ordered to report back to camp. We waited for our dinner, and the old lady certainly did try herself. She gave us as nice a dinner as we ever had; it included dessert, which made amends for the way in which she first treated us. She also apologized; we left truly friends and all kissed the baby.

On October 9 we left Elk Mountain for Edray, marching amidst the most beautiful scenery I ever saw, the trees having taken on their brilliant colors of fall. We remained in Edray and had a picket on Elk Mountain until the 14th, when we moved to Greenbrier River. Soon after leaving our camp and getting into the road, we passed two men who were sitting on the ground and facing a fence rail. Their hands and feet had been put through the rails and tied on the opposite side of the fence in such a position that they could not move. A little further on, we passed two who were lying on top of the fence, their hands and feet tied to some of the rails underneath so as to keep them from moving. These men, guilty of disobeying some order, were being punished in that manner.

We went regularly into camp on the banks of the beautiful Greenbrier, on a piece of low ground that was almost level and afforded plenty of room for camp and drill. It was a magnificent camp. The weather was fine, and the time of year such as to make it bracing. The men soon improved so much, and fattened too, that they became better looking than when they left home. We had a picket on the other side of Edray, about twelve miles from camp. About fifteen men and an officer went and stayed three days at a time. It was my fortune to go there with the first detail. I went again afterwards, and I thought it the most delightful duty of the war.

While we were in this camp, we were informed that in a few days there would be an election for President and Vice-President of the Confederate States of America. This had been talked about with much interest for some time—but without the usual excitement of an election, as there was only one ticket in the field. All the South looked to Mr. Jefferson Davis as their leader, and no other person was even thought of. As it would be the first election held in camp, much interest was taken by the soldiers. They discussed who was entitled to vote and where the voting place would be located. On a cloudy morning in November, it was announced that the eventful day had arrived and that the precinct was open. Some of the regiment had been appointed election judges. The voting precinct was in a tent in our camp. Across the entrance of the tent a pole had been placed to mark the line between the voters and the judges. It had been decided that all enlisted soldiers of good standing, regardless of age, could vote. The following ticket was eagerly voted:

VIRGINIA ELECTORAL TICKET
Election of November 6th, 1861
For President
Jefferson Davis of Mississippi
For Vice-President
Alexander H. Stephens of Georgia
ELECTORS
For the State at Large
John R. Edmunds, Halifax
A. T. Caperton, Monroe
For the Districts
1st—Joseph Christian, Middlesex County
2nd—Cincinnatus W. Newton, Norfolk
3rd—R. T. Daniel, Richmond
4th—W. F. Thompson, Dinwiddie County
5th—Wood Bouldin, Charlotte County
6th—W. L. Goggin, Bedford County
7th—B. F. Randolph, Albemarle County
8th—James W. Walker, Madison County
9th—Asa Rogers, Loudoun County
10th—Samuel C. Williams, Shenandoah County
11th—Samuel M. D. Reid, Rockbridge County
12th—H. A. Edmundson, Roanoke
13th—J. W. Sheffey, Smyth County
14th—H. J. Fisher, Mason County
15th—Joseph Johnson, Harrison County
16th—E. H. Fitzhugh, Ohio

The election passed off with much enthusiasm. At the close of the day, when it was announced the entire regiment had voted for Jefferson Davis and Alexander H. Stephens, there were loud and repeated cheers for them and the Confederacy.[10]

One morning while we were in this camp, the guard near the river reported a deer swimming the stream and making for the middle of our camp. In a minute all was in commotion. The deer came over, ran down the middle street of our encampment, and took to the hills in the rear. Many men, I amongst them, took their guns and went in pursuit. Hoping to head the deer off and get a shot, I ran in an oblique direction to the top of the hill. I did not see the deer, as it had been turned the other way by some of the men. As the exertion made me breathe rapidly, I took my time back to camp. One of the guard quietly approached, told me I was arrested, and marched me to the guard house, which was the shade of a tree on the river side. During my absence, an order had been issued to the guard to arrest every man found with a gun in his hand. My comrades, being near enough to hear the order, dropped their guns, quietly walked into camp, and afterwards went back for them. I was the only man arrested. Before we left, another deer ran through our camp. We made excursions in the neighborhood, sometimes fording the river, or sometimes mounting a log and riding over on that. We often got a ducking by the logs turning.

On November 11 we left Greenbrier River. We reached Warm Springs on the night of the 13th, having marched twenty-two miles that day, the last five (on Peter Sublett's dead level) all the way uphill! The hotel was open at that time, and the officers of F Company treated the company to supper. I cannot tell you of that supper. I only know none was ever enjoyed more. After supper we took a bath in the warm pool. We though the water hot, but we enjoyed it. The next morning the men of F Company took breakfast at the hotel; then we marched to Bath Alum Springs, pitched tents, and went regularly into camp. We had a good snow here. Our camp was on the edge of a piece of land that had been recently cleared of its wood—the wood being cut into logs about eight feet long and piled ready for burning. Every day we toted enough of these logs to our tents to make a great fire that would last about twenty-four hours. At night we gathered around these fires and had a big time telling tales, singing, etc. I think the company enjoyed this camp very much.

---

[10] Worsham's ardor for the political ticket must have waned in later years, for he spelled the Vice President's name "Stevens."

While here a comrade, J. E. Mayo, and I took our muskets and went out of camp to see if we could get a deer. We cut our bullets into slugs and loaded with them. We had not gone more than 300 yards when two deer sprang up; but we thought they were too far for our slugs. A little farther on we came to a branch that seemed to run around a hill. It was agreed that Mayo should go over the hill and that I would follow the branch. When he got in sight of the branch, Mayo should halloo. I waited for the signal; hearing it, I started up the bottom, went a short distance, and jumped a doe. I called out to Mayo to look out, and soon heard a shot which killed the deer. We carried it at once to camp and had a big time over our deer.

We remained at Bath Alum Springs until November 30, when we marched to Milboro. We stayed there until December 4, then took the cars for Staunton. We left Milboro late in the evening on flat cars and did not reach the camping place on the side of the railroad near Staunton until late in the night. That was a fearful ride at that season of the year. It was cold, and our riding on a flat car made it more so. The water tank at Panther Gap was literally one mass of ice. Some of the men got a small quantity of wood and built fires in the spiders and ovens; this afforded a little warmth for a few. It was only a few minutes after leaving the cars before we had trees cut down and rousing fires going. Did it ever occur to the reader how quickly soldiers could make fires? It made no difference whether it was raining, snowing, or blowing a great gale. In five minutes after getting into camp, a regiment would have fifty fires burning. Wet wood and green wood made no difference.

We were encamped about one and a half miles north of Staunton. In the Valley of Virginia, that great place for wheat, flour, hogs and democrats, the last-named could always be heard from in counting the votes after an election.

While we were in this camp, we elected officers to fill the vacancy occasioned by the resignation of First Lieutenant Edward Mayo.[11] P. A. Wellford was made first lieutenant, W. Granville Gray, Jr., second lieutenant.

We remained at Staunton until December 10, when we took up our march to join General Thomas J. Jackson at Winchester.[12] We

---

[11] Mayo's personal service file in the National Archives contains no explanation for his resignation.

[12] "The Regt generally is disgruntled at going to the Winchester line," Ham Chamberlayne wrote home, "but to me there seems no reason for such feeling. A foot knows where its shoe pinches but these men forget that other men perhaps all other men have pinching shoes & doubtless every Regt thinks it has the worst luck." *Ham Chamberlayne*, p. 52.

marched along quietly each day until, on the 20th, we reached Mt. Jackson. During the war it was the custom to march with the right of the regiment in front one day and the left the next day. On the 20th the left was marching in front. That threw our company in the rear, as we were on the right. During the day the left led off several times in quick time, which gave our company hard marching. That night our company decided that we would get even the next day. If the officers did not interfere, we would give it to them. Soon after getting on the road the next morning, our captain told Sergeant Edward Rawlings, who was leading the company, to step out. Now Sergeant Rawlings was just the man to do it, as he was a powerful man physically and had great endurance.[13] He stepped out at quick time and kept that pace during the march. Six and a half hours after leaving Mt. Jackson, we went into camp at Strasburg—having marched twenty three and a half miles. It was said by some of the boys who timed us that at one time we marched three miles in thirty-three minutes. This was the quickest march we made during the war.

We had a snow storm while at Strasburg. We marched to Winchester on December 25, passing through the town the next day and going into camp on the Romney road. In marching through Winchester, as we filed to the left at one of the cross streets, we saw standing in the crowd on the sidewalk a man with full dark whiskers and hair, dressed in uniform, and wearing a long dark blue overcoat with a large cape. His coat reached to his boots, which were worn outside of his pants in regular military style. On his boots were bright spurs. His head was covered by a faded gray cap, pulled down so far over his face that between cap and whiskers was very little to see. Yet as we passed we caught a glimpse of a pair of dark flashing eyes from underneath the brim of his cap. That man was Stonewall Jackson, and this was our first sight of him.

In our march on the third day after leaving Staunton, we met a woman and five children riding on the same horse. The woman had large bags fastened together after the fashion of saddlebags on the horse behind the saddle. A child's head was looking out on each side of the horse. Two children were on the horse behind her, and she held a baby in her arms. When she came into our midst and realized that the war was actually going on, she broke down and commenced to cry. One of our officers rode up to her, hat in hand; and with the politeness of a Virginian, he said some pleasant word to her. This, and the respect shown her by the passing men, soon restored her. She said her

---

[13] Thirty-six when the war began, Rawlings was the oldest man in F Company.

husband was in the army; and she, fearing to stay at their home by herself in the lower valley, was going to her mother's higher up, where she hoped to be out of reach of the enemy, in case the lower valley should be abandoned by our army. She would have to travel about fifty miles. The children seemed to be in splendid spirits and to enjoy our passing. Although this was a sight none of us ever saw before, everyone treated her with the respect due the first lady of the land. Here is war, real war. Such scenes as families leaving home with nothing but what they could carry on their person was witnessed many times by the writer.

In going down the Valley, we had a feast all the way. The people had just finished killing hogs, and every house had sausage, spare ribs, chine, liver, etc. to give us. We passed Lacy's Spring, or Big Spring, situated on the side of the Valley Pike, for the first time. The volume of water from this spring is large enough to run a large mill, and it looked more like a small river than a spring branch.

At that time everything in the Valley had a thrifty look. The horses and cattle were fat and sleek; the large barns were overflowing with the gathered crops; the houses, small in comparison with the barns, looked comfortable; and the fences—post, rail, or stone—were in splendid order. In fact, everything looked well and showed a thriving population. It was truly a land of milk and honey.

While in camp at Winchester, the Irish Battalion and the 21st, 42nd, and 48th Virginia Regiments were formed into a brigade to be known as the Second Brigade of Jackson's Division. Colonel Gilham, who was the ranking officer among the units, took command. The marching we had now done made all of us discard everything but necessaries, and we began to think that, on leaving Richmond, Ritchie Green did a very smart thing by carrying nothing in his knapsack but one paper collar and a plug of tobacco!

We elected a lieutenant here to fill the vacancy occasioned by the resignation of Second Lieutenant Henry T. Miller.[14] W. Granville Gray, Jr., was made senior second lieutenant, and James B. Payne, Jr., junior second lieutenant.

Having decided on a winter campaign, General Jackson marched his army from the neighborhood of Winchester on January 1, 1862. It was a beautiful day with the sun shining brightly and the atmosphere bracing. The Second Brigade camped near Pughtown that night. The 21st Virginia was in a large wood, where we gathered the fresh fallen

---

[14] Miller's resignation resulted from his appointment in November, 1861, as Adjutant of the 26th Va. In March, 1864, he became captain of the 25th Va. Bttn. and surrendered with the unit at Appomattox.

leaves into large piles, placed our oilcloths on them, and then laid down. Covered with our blankets, we enjoyed the bed as much as any we ever slept on.

We marched the next morning at early dawn and camped that night at Unger's Crossroads. The next day, January 3, we met the enemy about five miles from Bath in Morgan County. The 21st Virginia was marching near the rear of the column. General Jackson sent an order for F Company to report to the front, and we marched by our troops who had halted in the road. When we reached the front, we halted and were ordered to load. This was done under fire, as the enemy were a short distance in front, on a hill behind a fence. As soon as we had loaded, we were deployed as skirmishers and ordered forward through a wood. Halting on its edge behind a fence, we became heavily engaged with the enemy and kept up a fire until it was too dark to see. Firing ceased; returning to our regiment, we went into camp. This was the company's first real fight, and the men behaved splendidly. William Exall was killed, and Lieutenant Payne seriously wounded.[15]

It snowed during the night, and the weather became very cold. The enemy were now at Bath in force.

In the morning General Jackson advanced on their position in three columns, the Second Brigade moving along the road with F Company as advance guard. We moved slowly in order to let a column on our left get into position on the mountain ridge. We came in sight of the enemy, who were in line of battle on that ridge, about one and a half miles from Bath. Our column marched along the road and got almost on the flank of their line before they moved. It was too far for musket firing, but men on each side engaged in much abuse of one another. As soon as our skirmish line on the ridge came within shooting distance, firing commenced and the enemy began to retreat. General Jackson now arrived at the front and, with a few couriers following him, took the lead on horseback. As he passed our company he ordered us to double quick, and we soon ran. This was a grand sight: the Second Brigade marching by the flank and running down the road, the Yankees in sight on the ridge to our left and running too, with our column on the ridge following them as fast as they could run!

In this way our column entered and passed through Bath, then doubled back on the road that wound up the ridge. When we reached

---

15 Worsham's company was one of four dispatched by Loring to attack part of Co. D, 39th Ill., under Capt. Samuel S. Linton. The Federals lost 3 wounded, 8 captured, and 1 missing. Exall was shot in the leg above the knee, and died apparently of hemorrhage. Payne took a musket ball through the neck; both his arms were temporarily paralyzed as a result. Randolph Journal, entry of Jan. 3, 1862; OR ,V, 400-02, 1066, 1070; SHSP, XXIII (1895), 125.

the top of the ridge, we could see the Yankees disappearing at the far end of a field, going toward the Potomac River. We followed; but the road ran through a defile and we could not go as fast as the enemy because we had to look out for their rear guard, who occasionally came in sight and fired. The enemy went over the river during the night. We captured some stores and a few prisoners.

Today I saw Colonel Turner Ashby for the first time.[16] He impressed me as being a dashing man. With a company of cavalry he passed us and took a road to our left. One of our columns, following on another road, had a spirited combat with the enemy. On the next day, January 5, General Jackson moved his force toward Hancock, a village on the the Maryland side of the Potomac. He sent for F Company to come to the front and lead the column across the river. Coming from him, this was a high honor. We marched out of camp singing, and kept it up until we arrived at the front. We were singing the "Pirate's Glee," every man having joined in with a zest. We had taken up the inspiring words, "We'll nail the black flag to the mast," when we came suddenly on General Jackson. He pulled off his cap, and his eyes twinkled with evident delight as we passed.

We halted at a certain point for several hours. The Yankees threw a shell at us occasionally from a battery in Hancock. The ground was covered with snow, it was cold, and we were not allowed to make fires. As night approached we marched back and camped with our regiment. It snowed and hailed all night,[17] and was intensely cold. The next morning the ground was covered with several inches of snow and ice. Owing to the ice in the Potomac River, General Jackson gave up the advance on this road. On the 8th we returned to Unger's Crossroads. The march was a terrible one. The road had become one sheet of ice from frequent marching over it, and the men would march in the side ditches and in the woods where it was practicable. Guns were constantly being fired by men falling, and many accidents were occasioned thereby. In some instances the horses had to be taken from the cannon and wagons, which were then pulled by men with chains and ropes. At many hills the pioneers had to cut small trenches across the road in order that the men might have a footing. It was late in the night when we stopped to camp. Although the men underwent great exertion in this march, the cold was so intense that their suffering was

---

[16] The thirty-three-year-old Ashby, void of any formal military training, soon rose to command of Jackson's cavalry. He received promotion to brigadier general only two weeks before his death in June, 1862.

[17] Throughout his discussion of this campaign Worsham referred to snowing and hailing. He obviously meant that it was snowing and sleeting. Subsequent references to winter precipitation have been corrected.

great. Several times I saw General Jackson marching along the road on foot with the men.

Colonel Gilham[18] and Major Scott Shipp[19] of the 21st Virginia received an order to report to the Virginia Military Institute for duty, and they left on January 9. The men had become very much attached to both and were sorry to give them up. As a token of its respect, F Company purchased a fine horse and presented it, along with a bridle containing one of our company insignias, to Colonel Gilham.

The next day we had sleet again. The Second Brigade marched only about four miles, with the men helping cannon and wagons as they did the day before. The next day my regiment marched about 500 yards, and the head of the brigade marched about four miles. Owing to the terrible weather, our line was scattered over ten miles of road. My mess was so near the camping place of the preceding night that we went back to it, put the chunks together, and in a short time were comfortable and asleep for the night. We rejoined the company in the morning in time for roll call. The only way we could get along at all was to have heavy details of men help, and at times pull, each wagon and cannon. Each day was colder than the day before, and cannon, wagons, and men crossed most of the streams on the ice.

On January 14 it snowed and sleeted again. For several miles along the road we passed a growth of flat cedar and arbor vitæ. We continued our march until we reached the neighborhood of Romney on January 17. There the head of the column had quite a spirited combat with the enemy and captured their camp and some stores. The Second Brigade went into camp in a wood near the town and picketed the road we had marched over. Here the sun came out and shone on us for the first time in nineteen days.

Our mess lost its "spider" on this march, and I thought one might be purchased in the neighborhood to replace it. One day I took a stroll into the country to get one, and I went to several houses without success. Finally I came to a very comfortable looking house and found an old lady who was very talkative. She made many inquiries: where we were from, how long we were going to stay, etc. She seemed particularly pleased on learning I was from Richmond, and we had a long

---

[18] Following this campaign, Jackson preferred charges of "neglect of duty" against his former VMI colleague for alleged slowness in the Jan. 4 movement on Bath. The charges were later dropped. At Gilham's departure, F Company presented him with a horse which they purchased for $250. *OR,* V, 391; Randolph Journal, entry of Jan. 10, 1862.

[19] Shipp was "a large man, with close-trimmed black hair and beard, a solemn bearing, and a deep voice." To one associate, he seemed fifteen years older than he actually was. He commanded the battalion of VMI cadets in their famous 1864 charge at New Market. John A. Wise, *The End of an Era* (Boston, 1927), pp. 246-47.

chat about the city. I finally told her what I wanted. She called a servant girl, held a consultation, and finally decided that she would let me have a certain oven that was too large for her family. It was brought from one of the outhouses and, after much discussion, a bargain was made. She wished to know if it suited me. It was an unusually large oven and had a broken lid. It did not suit me; but as it was the only one I had been able to get, I told her that it did. As to the price, she did not know what to say. She finally said, "That is a good oven. I bought it in Winchester sixteen years ago, and gave two dollars and fifty cents for it. It's a good oven, even if the lid is cracked. It's done me good service. Well, as you want it, under the circumstances you may have it for two dollars and seventy-five cents."

That took all the wind out of me. I am sure you could have knocked me down with a feather, but I paid her the money and the service that oven rendered us proved it was a bargain.

A night or two later the ground became covered with snow. We cleaned off the snow so as to have the ground to lie on; but the thawing of the ground underneath us made it muddy, and our oilcloths would be badly soiled when we got up in the morning. We then tried the snow, and found it made a better bed and was equally as warm. After that, on going into camp we never removed the snow. Some nights we would spread our tents on the snow, put our oilcloths on that, and a blanket on top. The party would then lie down; a comrade would cover them up with the remaining blankets and then throw the sides of the tent over that. This left nothing but the head out. The comrade would then crawl from the bottom into his place. In this way I managed to sleep very comfortably several nights on this expedition.

On January 24 the 21st Virginia marched into the town of Romney and took up its quarters in the houses that had been deserted. F Company had the bank building. We lived well there. My mess employed an old darky, about two squares off, to cook our rations. She added to them any good thing she could get. There was a hotel that had buckwheat cakes in splendid style, plus fine butter and syrup for breakfast, and it only charged twenty-five cents for meals. It took only three days for us to eat it out.

Leaving General Loring in command at Romney, General Jackson took part of his force and went to Winchester. We stayed until the evening of February 3, when Romney was given up and General Loring's force was marched toward Winchester.[20] We marched late

20 Worsham prudently glossed over the details surrounding the recall of Loring's command from Romney. The men under Loring were highly dissatisfied at being left in so remote an outpost. Accordingly, on Jan. 25, 1862, eleven regimental colonels

in the night, and it snowed again. Our wagons had gone ahead. When I arrived at their camping place, I sat down on a bucket at one of the wagoner's fires to warm, fell asleep, and stayed on my bucket until morning! On February 6 we reached Winchester and went into camp—after being away a little over a month and undergoing the most terrible experience during the war. Many men were frozen to death; others were frozen so badly that they never recovered. The rheumatism contracted by many was never gotten rid of. Many of the men were incapacitated for service, and large numbers, having burned their shoes while trying to warm their feet at the fires, were barefooted.

Do any of my readers recollect Randall Evans at Winchester?[21] He is the old colored man who could get up such famous dinners. After a long time in camp, or on a march with the usual army fare, to go to Randall Evans and get a meal such as he could serve would make one forget all about bread and beef—both without salt! I never saw a soldier leave *his* place who was not perfectly satisfied with the army and everything else, and it was brought about by being full of food, as Randall did not keep anything to drink. What Tom Griffin was to Richmond, so was Randall Evans to Winchester. After the Romney campaign, we came very near eating Randall out.

(Cunningham was the tenth of eleven to sign) sent a petition to Loring, urging that he ask the War Dept. for their recall. Loring bypassed channels and sent the petition to Richmond; his command was consequently ordered by Sec. J. P. Benjamin to retire from Romney. Jackson issued the order—and simultaneously tendered his resignation to Richmond. In the end, Loring was transferred from the Valley and Jackson withdrew his resignation.

[21] Evans operated a restaurant on N. Loudoun St. near its intersection with Piccadilly St.

Chapter III

FOOT CAVALRY IN THE VALLEY

General Jackson sent several regiments of his army to General Joseph E. Johnston at Manassas.[1] We remained in our camp on the Romney Road until February 27,[2] when my brigade marched through Winchester and camped on the Berryville road. We stayed there until March 7, at which time we marched through Winchester and camped on the Staunton [Valley] pike until March 11. Then everything was packed, and we were ready for a general move. These movements were occasioned by the enemy having crossed the Potomac, and it was reported that they would advance on Winchester. We marched through Winchester again, this time to the Martinsburg road, as we had heard that the enemy were advancing on this road and were not too far off. They were commanded by General Nathaniel P. Banks, afterwards known as "Jackson's Commissary" because he supplied our army so bountifully. General Jackson made disposition to meet them. A line of battle was formed across the pike, a battery placed on Fort Hill, and the 21st Virginia ordered to support it. We took our position along with the battery and lay down to await the enemy. We heard occasional guns in our front. When night came the enemy had not made their appearance.

Considering the enemy too strong for him, General Jackson withdrew during the night, marched through Winchester a short distance, and rested until morning. Then we continued our march slowly up the Valley until, on March 18, we reached Mt. Jackson. The Second Brigade went into camp about one mile below Mt. Jackson; the balance of the army marched to Rude's Hill, about two miles above the village,

---

[1] Owing to the strained relations between Jackson and Loring, President Davis dissolved the Army of the Northwest. Loring went to southwestern Virginia (with a major general's commission); segments of his command joined Confederate forces at Fredericksburg and at Knoxville, Tenn.; and the 1st, 7th, and 14th Tenn. transferred to Johnston's army.

[2] Worsham neglected to mention the hardships of winter camp at this time. His messmate, Tucker Randolph, on the other hand, wrote bitterly: "The command is nearly used up." He told of seeing two soldiers die in the road from pneumonia, and he reported many of F Company suffering "from Rheumatic affections." He concluded: "Genl. Jackson has a great load on his shoulders to answer for in *this* Campaign." Randolph to his father, Feb. 9, 1862, Randolph Papers. See also *Ham Chamberlayne*, p. 70.

and camped. We sent a picket down the Valley pike and, on the 20th, marched to Rude's Hill and joined the balance of our little army. The enemy had followed us slowly, but they stopped at Mt. Jackson and retired down the Valley.[3]

General Jackson was a great man for saving everything captured from the enemy. His way was to save everything already on hand and never destroy anything there was a chance to save. It was a saying in the command that he would carry off a wheelbarrow load rather than let it fall into the hands of the enemy. While we were camped around Winchester, he was diligently at work getting everything out of reach of the enemy, in case he should be compelled to leave. Even the locomotives and cars captured at Martinsburg were sent to the rear. Because the Valley pike was such an excellent road, he could do this. At Jackson's orders parties of men cut down trees along the pike and used the timber in bracing the bridges so as to enable them to endure greater weight. When everything was ready, large teams of horses and mules were hitched to the locomotives and cars at Martinsburg. They were hauled to Strasburg, a distance of about fifty miles, and put on the Manassas Gap Railroad for the use of the Confederacy. In this way many locomotives and cars were saved. During this movement I saw at one time five cars on their way to Strasburg.

While General Jackson's army was at Rude's Hill, the enemy retired from our front to obtain, as we supposed, a better camping place.[4] On the evening of March 21, we received orders to cook three days' rations and to be ready to move at early dawn the next morning. When the line was formed in the morning and we marched onto the road, instead of turning up the Valley pike, as we supposed our course would be, we took a quick march in the direction of the enemy and soon passed through Mt. Jackson.

The day was raw and blustering. We marched twenty-seven miles, stopped near Fisher's Hill and bivouacked for the night. Early the next morning we marched, and kept it up for about sixteen miles until we reached Barton's Mill about noon. Our brigade stopped to rest until most of the troops came up. We had heard cannon firing in our front and knew our advance under Ashby had overtaken the enemy. It was

---

[3] Readers unfamiliar with the geography and popular terminology of the Valley should remember that one goes "down" when he travels northward toward Harpers Ferry and "up" when moving southward toward Lexington.

[4] The withdrawal from Strasburg of Gen. James Shields' division was an obvious indication to Jackson that Federal troops in the Valley were heading east to the assistance of McClellan on the Peninsula. This was the very movement that Jackson had been ordered to prevent. He therefore started down the Valley to thwart Shields' transfer, and the battle of Kernstown resulted.

a surprise to the men that we had come so far without encountering them. But it was known to General Jackson that they had fallen back to the neighborhood of Winchester and were sending some of their number away to join their army at Manassas. Our march was to find out what they were doing. It was ascertained that they had made a stand at Kernstown.

The 21st Virginia was now ordered forward. After going down the pike a short distance, it turned to the left and marched across an open field toward the hills that were covered with woods. When we were about halfway across the field, we came in sight of the Yankee line of battle near Kernstown, with a battery posted on a hill a little in their rear. The battery opened on us at once. We were ordered to double quick; we soon began to run and reached the hills without an accident. F Company was thrown forward as skirmishers, the rest of the regiment following in line of battle a short distance to the rear. The company was soon ordered to join them, and we marched by the flank. A gun or two of the Rockbridge Artillery now joined us. While we marched under a hill, the battery went to the right on top of the ridge. In their movement these guns were occasionally exposed to the view of the enemy's battery. The Yankees fired at them, the shells passing over our regiment. One shell struck one of the drivers of the guns, tearing his leg to pieces, and going through a horse. Both fell. The shell descended and passed through our ranks; it struck a stump not far off and spun around like a top. Before it stopped spinning, one of the company ran and jumped on it, taking it up and carrying it along as a trophy. This is the first man in the war I saw struck by a shell, and it was witnessed by a majority of the regiment.[5]

General Jackson now made his appearance and had a talk with with our commander, Lieutenant Colonel John M. Patton.[6] We were thrown forward into line of battle again and marched a short distance to the top of a hill, in full sight of the enemy's line of battle. At this point they were advancing, too. I saw five flags. We opened fire at once and they scattered. In a few minutes I saw only two flags, and

---

[5] This same shell chopped off the foot of an artilleryman walking beside his gun. Both wounded soldiers died that night. Randolph Journal, entry of Mar. 24, 1862; Edward A. Moore, *The Story of a Cannoneer under Stonewall Jackson* (New York, 1907), pp. 30-31. Hereafter cited as Moore, *Cannoneer*.

[6] Patton was a frail man whose weight, during the Valley Campaign, dropped from 164 to 128 pounds. Ill health finally forced his resignation from the army in July, 1862. One soldier thought him "a pigeon headed fellow, tho' Lieut Col—, with a mind as narrow as any King's that ever tormented mankind." Patton's personal service file, War Records Group 109, National Archives; Patton to John Worsham, Oct. 19, 1893, Worsham Papers; Percy H. Gilmer to William Gilham, Oct. 22, 1861, Patton Family Papers, Virginia Historical Society; *Ham Chamberlayne*, p. 60.

soon after only one, which was marched in a field on our right and planted on a pile of rocks. Its regiment gathered about it. Our regiment and the guns of the Rockbridge Artillery had been fighting this force. Our line was lengthened by the arrival of the Third Brigade on our left. A part of our regiment moved to a fence on the right and, facing the enemy, in the field, fired at them. Some of F Company were kneeling down, firing from behind the fence; some were standing straight up. Soon all were standing, and taking deadly aim as they fired. As the excitement increased, many men in F Company mounted the fence and sat on it, loading and firing until every cartridge was shot away.

A regiment was sent to the support of the Yankees; yet they never got any nearer than the party around the flag, and they soon became intermingled with them.[7] All our ammunition being gone, we gradually retired, passing through the 5th Virginia, that had formed in our rear. Our artillery had taken position and were firing on the enemy; but when we retreated, they were compelled to do so. In going through a gap in a stone wall, one of their guns became entangled and disabled, and it was left. In going to the rear one of our company encountered General Jackson, who inquired where he was going. The soldier answered that he had shot all his ammunition away and did not know where to get more. Old Stonewall rose in his stirrups, gave the command: "Then go back and give them the bayonet!" and rode off to the front.

The remainder of the little army had been heavily engaged. Although confronted by large odds, it held its own and retired only after shooting all its ammunition away. It seems to me that the 21st Virginia would have held its line indefinitely if it had been supplied with ammunition. It was a regular standup fight with us and, as stated, the men along the fence left its protection and fought as I never saw any fighting during the war. After this, they were glad to take advantage of anything.

We were whipped after desperate fighting, and I think only for want of ammunition. Night found our little army in retreat toward the Valley pike, where the stragglers were gathered up and the men lay down on the ground for a few hours' rest. The next morning we took up a slow and sullen march up the Valley, with the enemy following. Arriving at Middletown, I learned that Tucker Randolph, one of my messmates, was in one of the houses. Wounded, he had been sent to

---

[7] Opposing Worsham's brigade were the 14th Ind., 8th Ohio, 67th Ohio, and 84th Pa., all under Col. Nathan Kimball. In the battle these regiments lost 45 killed, 200 wounded, and 1 missing. See *OR*, XII, pt. 1, 346, 360-71.

the rear the evening before. I soon found him and, seeing the condition of my dear old comrade, I made up my mind to stay and nurse him if I could obtain my captain's permission. Dear old fellow! How he thanked me when I said it. I had long ago made up my mind never to be taken prisoner, but I could not leave my messmate. All our wagons and ambulances had long passed. Our lieutenant had promised to send an ambulance back; the surgeon had also promised.

I finally became so uneasy that I went to all the town folks to see if I could get a vehicle of some kind to take him away; but I could get nothing. All the infantry had now gone; even the stragglers had left the village. Our rear guard, the cannon of the horse artillery, were near and had ceased their firing. I could hear the exchange of carbine shots. I went to the door and looked up the street for my long looked-for ambulance, but nothing was in sight. I looked down the street and saw the horse artillery entering the village. I now made up my mind to ask the officer in command to take my friend on one of the caissons. I went into the street to meet him when, taking another look up the street, I saw an ambulance coming on a run. We put Randolph into it in a hurry, pitched in his knapsack, etc., and off we went. We passed out of the village in time to get away, but the Yanks gave us a parting shot from a cannon as we left. The shot passed over without damage. The ambulance horses received some heavy whacks from the whip of the driver, and we were soon out of danger.

I went along with my comrade and, before nightfall, had collected about half a dozen of the wounded of my company. I took care of them until we arrived at Staunton, where I put them on the cars en route to their homes. I then returned to my company.

This was the first regular battle of the regiment, and it was said we displayed great gallantry.[8] F Company had six wounded: Tucker Randolph, Ned Taylor, Charles Taylor, Henry Picot, Charles Skinker, and Joe Nunnally.

This attack of General Jackson on the enemy was a very daring one. It was also the means of helping our army at Manassas, as the troops the enemy were sending away were recalled. The enemy were far superior to us in numbers.[9] Although Jackson was whipped, Con-

---

[8] In his official report Jackson stated of the 21st and 27th Va.: "Well did these two regiments do their duty, driving back the enemy twice in quick succession." OR, XII, pt. 1, 381. The 21st Va. at Kernstown lost 7 killed, 44 wounded, and 9 missing. Ibid., 384.

[9] Shields' force numbered 8,000 men; that of Jackson was 2,742. Ibid., 335, 383.

gress thought it did the cause so much good that it at once passed a resolution of thanks to Jackson and his army.[10]

On March 24 our brigade moved to the vicinity of Strasburg, where we halted about midday and camped. The enemy were in hot pursuit. We could hear firing in the rear all day, and during the march, from some high points, we could see the enemy. We had built fires in our camp, drawn rations, and were busy cooking when a shell, followed by another, came screaming over our heads. In a few minutes the woods were full of shells from the enemy, who had driven our rear guard far enough to command our woods from one of the neighboring hills. We loaded our cooking utensils and baggage on the wagons, and they went off in a run. We soon followed in a slow march and continued it until we reached the neighborhood of Woodstock, where we quietly went into camp out of hearing of the enemy. The next day we went into camp near Mt. Jackson. On the 26th the Second Brigade was sent back to near Woodstock to meet the enemy, with whom we skirmished until March 28, when we marched to Mt. Jackson.

On April 3 we returned to near Edinburg to meet the enemy again. We were to cooperate with Colonel Ashby in any movement he made. F Company was ordered forward as skirmishers through a wood and halted on its edge. A large open field was in our front, Edinburg was in full view, and the Yankee skirmish line was on the opposite side of the creek. We engaged them at once. Colonel Ashby came along, riding his white horse. He had the dwarf courier with him. He told us not to fire unless the enemy attempted to cross the creek and, if they should make the attempt, to give it to them. Accompanied by the little courier, Colonel Ashby rode out in front to a small hillock to see what was going on. The enemy immediately shot at them. As they reached the hillock, the courier's horse fell dead. We could hear Colonel Ashby tell him to take off his saddle, bridle, and accouterments and to carry them to the rear, which the courier did as quickly as possible. Colonel Ashby sat on his horse as quietly as if he had been in camp until the courier reached the woods. Then he quietly turned his horse and walked him off toward us, passing through our line on his way to the rear.[11] Soon afterwards, he gave orders for our brigade to go back to camp, as he would have nothing for us to do that day.

---

[10] The resolution was passed early in April. U. S. War Dept. (comp.), *Journal of the Congress of the Confederate States of America* (Washington, 1904-05), II, 127-28; V, 183, 187, 201.

[11] The "dwarf" was a short youngster whom the troops called "Dixie," and regarded as a protégé of Ashby. A fuller account of this incident is in Lenoir Chambers, *Stonewall Jackson* (New York, 1959), I, 478.

On April 5 we marched to Rude's Hill and went into camp. The next morning I was ordered to report with arms to the brigade quartermaster. On arriving at his quarters I saw two large wagons, four mules hitched to each, and learned that a detail of six men had been assigned to accompany the wagons on a trip to get corn. As soon as all the men reported, a quartermaster sergeant, who went with us, ordered three men to get in each wagon. The wagons started at once and turned down the Valley pike. Reaching Rude's Hill we passed some artillerymen who had a cannon trained on the bridge over the Shenandoah River. At the foot of the hill we passed the cavalry outpost of about thirty or forty men who were dismounted and awaiting events, their horses strung along and fastened to the fence on each side of the road. When they learned our destination, all of them bade us goodbye, saying they would never see us again as the Yankees would certainly capture us. Going about a half a mile farther, we passed the cavalry vidette on the outpost. He said goodbye too, and pointed out to us the Yankee vidette, a little above the bridge and on the other side of the river in his front. We went about a fourth of a mile farther, pulled down two panels of fence on the left of the road, entered a large corn field, and loaded those wagons more quickly than any were ever loaded before. When we had them about half full, a Yankee cavalryman rode to his vidette in plain view of us, had a short talk, and then rode off at full speed. That made us pull corn faster. The wagons were driven back to the road and headed for camp. A countryman who was with us said that was "the slickest job he ever saw." When we reached our vidette, he gave us a hearty welcome and the outpost cavalry gave us a big cheer.

On the 7th we marched below Mt. Jackson and camped in our old place. On the 10th all of Jackson's force marched up the Valley and stopped near New Market. On the 13th our brigade marched to the gap of Massanutten Mountain that leads into Luray Valley. It had been rumored that the enemy were making a demonstration from that direction. On the 17th all the force marched up the Valley to Big Spring, staying there all night. The next day we marched up the Valley, left the Valley pike near Harrisonburg in the direction of Swift Run Gap, crossed the Shenandoah River, and went into camp the next day. We were now safe from pursuit. With our backs to the Blue Ridge Mountains, our little force could easily keep off thrice as many as had been in pursuit of us.

This was the boldest retreat I ever saw. General Jackson was defeated at Kernstown on March 23 by an overwhelming force. The next day he retired up the Valley more slowly than I ever saw him march; and when we went into camp at night, we tarried as long as possible. If the enemy did not hunt for us, General Jackson would hunt for them. The regiments had orders to drill just as if no enemy was within 100 miles of us. It can be seen that our movements were slow, since it took us from March 24 to April 18 to march about 100 miles. Yet we marched about half that distance in two days when we advanced to Kernstown.

We rested at this camp and made ourselves as comfortable as we could in the shelter of brush, oilcloths, etc. On the day that we reached here, General Jackson ordered all the wagons containing tents and extra baggage to the rear—so far to the rear that we never saw them again! This was a hard blow to us, since we had gotten in the habit of smuggling many articles into our tents to avoid carrying them. When our tents left, they had in them dress coats, underclothing, etc. "Old Jack" flanked us that time.[12]

We had a snow storm while we were in this camp; but as it did not turn cold, we got along very well.[13] In this place we also first felt the strict hand of Jackson. During the snow storm our regiment and several others burned some of the fence railing. Seeing this act, General Jackson gave orders for each regiment to maul rails and put the fence up again. If we repeated the burning, he said, every man would be punished.

The reorganization of the army took place while we were in this camp. This was a great misfortune to us. Many good officers were thrown out, and men who were popular were elected in their stead. In many instances men were elected who were utterly unfit for their positions. The 21st Virginia elected John M. Patton as colonel, Richard H. Cunningham, Jr., as lieutenant colonel, and John B. Moseley as major. F Company elected the following: Adjutant William H. Morgan, captain; W. Granville Gray, first lieutenant; and George W. Peterkin and E. G. Rawlings, Jr., second lieutenants.

In one of the regiments of our army, two men each had a game cock. On a march the cocks perched on the shoulders of their owners and seemed as well contented as if on their roost. Their crowing and the flapping of their wings always brought forth a lusty cheer from

---

[12] Jackson ordered half the wagon trains to Staunton because he was preparing to launch a campaign of rapid marches and quick maneuvers—the type of campaign which could not be burdened by wagons.

[13] The snowstorm to which Worsham referred occurred on April 24. Describing the countryside, one writer stated: "The scene is curious, bright green fields, peach and plum trees in full blossom covered with snow." David H. Strother, *A Virginia Yankee in the Civil War*, edited by Cecil D. Eby, Jr. (Chapel Hill, 1961), p. 31.

the men. The roosters, like everything else in the Confederate army, had their use. Whenever we marched past a farmyard where there were a lot of fowls, one of these men would break from ranks. His game cock would fly to the rooster at the head of the fowls, and a battle would take place at once. The owner of the game cock would pick up both roosters and quickly rejoin his command. That night he would have stewed rooster for supper.

I must not forget to tell about our umbrella man. In Company H of our regiment was 1st Sergeant John H. Kelley, who was an old country gentleman. When he left home for the army, he carried an umbrella which he kept until he left us at this camp. During a march on a hot day, one would see the old sergeant marching along at the head of his company with his umbrella hoisted. The boys would call out to him: "Come out of that umbrella!" The sergeant took it kindly, and would generally reply that he knew they wanted it. Whenever he hoisted it during a rain, he always had numerous applications for a part of it. When the umbrella was not in use, the sergeant carried it strapped to his knapsack.

We stayed in this camp until April 23, when we moved our camp to a cove with a large opening within the outer mountain. On the 30th we marched from this camp toward Harrisonburg. We crossed the Shenandoah River, marched a mile or two, turned back on a road to the right, and marched up the river to Port Republic. The road on which we marched was an ordinary country road, yet it had been raining and snowing so much that the road had become very soft. When the artillery and wagons came along they sank up to their axles, and there was no way to get them out unless the men put their shoulders to the wheels. This general Jackson had foreseen, as details of men were sent along with the wagons. As evidence of General Jackson's anxiety and solicitude, I saw him personally getting rocks and putting them in the holes of this road. We reached Port Republic on May 2 after one of the most severe marches we had undergone.

We were now retreating and advancing at the same time, a condition an army never undertook before. We were retreating from Banks; but in leaving Port Republic on May 3, we commenced the great Valley Campaign—the most brilliant campaign of modern times, and I do not know that it was ever surpassed.

We marched across the Blue Ridge Mountains to the Central Railroad near Meachum's Depot; there we took the cars to Staunton, where we arrived on May 4. On the next day we were joined by the 10th

Virginia Infantry,[14] which was assigned to the Third Brigade, and by the cadets from the Virginia Military Institute.[15] On May 6 we left Staunton, marched toward Buffalo Gap, and about midday joined General Edward Johnson's force that had fallen back about six miles from Staunton. He had been in great danger before we arrived. A force in his front was pressing him, and Banks' army was threatening to march to his rear. With Jackson's coming, all was changed.

Near Buffalo Gap we went into camp for the night. The next morning, with Johnson's force in front, the advance was continued. We encountered some of the enemy near Ryan's and captured some stores, tents, a sutler's outfit, etc. Lying just outside the sutler's store door was about a bucketful of "sutler's coin," used by him in his traffic with the soldiers and having on it his name, regiment, and the value of the coin. The head of the column skirmished some with the enemy. We crossed the Shenandoah Mountain and passed through the fortifications used by General Johnson while he was there. In descending this mountain, we could see a long line of the enemy in position on the opposite mountain. However, they withdrew without firing, and we halted for the night.

On May 8 we marched in about the same order. General Jackson's command was in front, the Second Brigade next, then the Third Brigade, with the Stonewall Brigade in the rear. The V.M.I. cadets marched, I think, in front of the Stonewall Brigade. In the afternoon the Second Brigade was ascending Bull Pasture Mountain. We marched a few yards and halted, then a few more yards and another halt—a type of march that fatigued men more than one in which they take an even step and march for a length of time. We marched in this way for a long time, and evening soon approached. It was rumored that we could not cross the mountain that night, that we would return to the valley (or bottom of the mountain) and camp for the night, and that the remainder of Jackson's division would join us there. The men had begun to think that there was some truth in the report.

---

14 One of the few Valley regiments not a part of the Stonewall Brigade, the 10th Va. was commanded by Col. S. B. Gibbons and, after his death at McDowell, by Col. E. T. H. Warren. "The regiment acted nobly," one Confederate later wrote, "and had a high reputation during the whole war." John O. Casler, *Four Years in the Stonewall Brigade* (Girard, Kan., 1906), p. 72. Hereafter cited as Casler, *Stonewall Brigade*.

15 The cadets, under their commandant, Gen. Francis H. Smith, voluntarily joined Jackson's army to do their share in defending the Valley. Their principal activities, however, consisted of guarding prisoners, collecting discarded equipment, and burying the dead. "The natty appearance" of the 200 cadets, a staff officer stated, "afforded a striking contrast to the seedy and delapidated veterans, but before they returned from McDowell much of the gloss was gone." *OR*, XII, pt. 1, 471, 473; Moore, *Cannoneer*, p. 47; Henry Kyd Douglas, *I Rode with Stonewall* (Chapel Hill, 1940), p. 48. Hereafter cited as Douglas, *Stonewall*.

Soon the idea was discarded, for the 21st Virginia was rushed forward. On reaching the top of the mountain, we could hear firing; going a little farther, we could hear that it was heavy. We hurried along the road until we reached and occupied the position of the 31st Virginia, which rejoined Johnson's command heavily engaged on our left. We formed in line of battle across the pike. General Jackson now arrived and gave orders in person to Lieutenant Colonel Cunningham, who was in command of the 21st Virginia. Jackson told him to protect his men as much as possible and to hold the position at all hazards. He ended by saying, in that sharp way of his, "Tell your men they must hold the road!"[16]

This was the only road by which Jackson could get his forces out if he should meet with disaster. If the road was taken, the enemy would be directly in his rear. This was therefore the key to Jackson's position; and if it were lost, all was lost. The men of the 21st Virginia now took their positions behind trees and big rocks. As we took our places it was with the determination that no enemy should drive us away. We were not called on for a test of our courage. Only a few skirmishers appeared in our front, as the enemy attacked from our left next to the village of McDowell.[17] It is said that General Jackson had no idea of fighting this battle. He and General Johnson had ridden to the front and examined the situation of the enemy. As Jackson had obtained information that the enemy could be attacked in their rear, he had intended to send a force to that point as soon as it became dark and to make an attack the next morning. Some of his staff had actually gone to our rear to show our troops where to camp.

General Robert H. Milroy, who was in command of the enemy, received some reinforcements about noon. Not knowing of Jackson's presence, he had thought best to make an attack at once on General Johnson. This was the cause of the battle.

The enemy made a gallant and spirited attack, but were promptly met and, after some hard fighting, were driven back with loss. We lost a number of men and some valuable officers. General Johnson was shot through the foot in the thickest of the fight.[18] We had no artillery on

---

[16] Cunningham's own report, while void of specific quotations, is nevertheless mild in comparison with Worsham's recollections of what Jackson said. *OR*, XII, pt. 1, 476-77.

[17] One man in the 21st Va. was wounded at McDowell. *Ibid.*, 476.

[18] Fighting in Johnson's sector reached very close quarters and Federals, seeing the old warrior deploying his troops, shouted: "There's old Johnson—let's flank him!" The crusty leader thereupon waved his hickory walking stick over his head and roared back: "Yes, damn you, flank me if you can!" However, Johnson was so disabled by the wound in his ankle that he did not return to duty until after Jackson's death, at which time he was given command of Jackson's old division. Casler, *Stonewall Brigade*, p. 74; Douglas, *Stonewall*, p. 49.

our side, as we could not get a position on the mountain side; and not more than two-thirds of Jackson's force was up in time to take part in the battle. The enemy used artillery from the other side of McDowell. When we passed through the town the next day, we could see the holes they made in the ground in order to elevate their guns so as to shoot at us on the mountain side.

During the night the enemy retreated. They burned some of their stores, however some fell into our hands. They threw a large quantity of ammunition into the creek from a bridge on the road. We followed in hot pursuit as far as Franklin in Pendleton County, where we overtook them on the afternoon of May 11. There the enemy took position in a narrow valley that ran between the mountain hills. These hills were covered with woods, and the enemy had set fire to the woods on both sides of the valley in their front. As soon as we came in sight, their artillery commenced firing at us. We could not locate the guns because of the smoke. General Jackson sent a small force to the enemy's rear to obstruct the road at the mountain gaps. This force was driven off before it accomplished the work. We remained in front of the enemy, trying to find their position with skirmishers, but the fire and smoke from the burning woods prevented this.

Having other and more important plans, General Jackson abandoned this place about 10 o'clock on the morning of May 13 and retraced his march back through McDowell. We marched about eleven miles, then turned east on a road leading to Harrisonburg. We stopped on the 15th at Lebanon Springs and remained there on the 16th to observe the day of national humiliation and prayer ordered by the President of the Confederacy. On May 17 we resumed our march and, on Sunday the 18th, stopped near Mossy Creek, where most of the command had religious worship. At early dawn on the 19th we resumed the march. Passing through Bridgewater we crossed the Shenandoah on a bridge of wagons placed in a row across the river, with planks laid from one wagon to the other. This thus made a very good footbridge. On May 20 we passed through Harrisonburg and were joined by Brigadier General Richard Taylor's Louisiana brigade of Richard S. Ewell's division. This brigade made an unusually good appearance, as the men were more regularly uniformed than any we had seen.

When General Jackson moved from Swift Run Gap, General Ewell with his division and two regiments of cavalry occupied a position in Culpeper County on the Rappahannock River. Ewell moved his command to Swift Run Gap and occupied the position just vacated by Jackson. This was to prevent Banks from making an attack on Jackson's rear while Jackson was advancing on Milroy. After Jackson had disposed of Milroy, he turned back to the Valley. The junction with Taylor showed that he had reached that great country. We then went into camp on the Valley pike.

On May 21 General Jackson marched down the pike. When we reached New Market we took the road leading to the Luray valley and, on the 22nd near Luray, formed a junction with the balance of General Ewell's command which had marched down the Luray valley from Swift Run Gap. Jackson now had the largest army he had ever had.[19] He had brought General Edward Johnson's force of six regiments and some artillery with him from the Shenandoah mountain, and had Ewell's command as well as his own.

On May 23 Jackson's army left its bivouac near Luray and took the road to Front Royal. The head of the column arrived at Front Royal about 3 or 4 o'clock in the afternoon. General Jackson, as usual, made an immediate attack on the enemy with the few men who were up. His eagerness all through this campaign was surprising, and his escape from death was almost a miracle. The enemy were found drawn up in line of battle in a strong position on the opposite side of the Shenandoah River. Jackson personally formed a line of skirmishers, gave them the command to move forward, and pushed them and some advance cavalry toward the Federals. The Yanks, finding things getting so hot, set fire to two bridges. Our cavalry and skirmishers immediately charged them and saved the damaged bridges. Our men crossed over and were right in the midst of the enemy, Jackson along with them. The enemy made a bold stand and fought well, but they could not withstand Jackson's mode of warfare and retreated to a farm orchard and buildings. Here they made a gallant stand. Yet our two regiments of cavalry from Ewell's command came up, formed under Jackson's eye, and charged the protected enemy. The cavalry swept everything before them, and soon the entire enemy force was killed and captured. In the charge at the bridge, the gallant Captain George F. Sheetz,[20] Ashby's right hand, was killed. A large amount of stores and several hundred beef-cattle were captured. The Second Brigade did not come up until night, having marched twenty-seven miles.

---

[19] Jackson's force then numbered about 16,000 men and 48 cannon. Being brought to bear on him were approximately 63,000 Federals under Banks, Fremont, and Shields.

[20] When the war began, George Sheetz had left his grocery store in the Unionist stronghold of New Creek Station, raised a cavalry company, and joined Ashby's command. He was "the most promising cavalry officer on the continent," one writer stated, but that promise, observed another, "had no time to ripen." Frank Cunningham, *Knight of the Confederacy: Gen. Turner Ashby* (San Antonio, 1960), pp. 101, 187-88; Douglas, *Stonewall*, p. 52.

On the next morning, as our brigade passed the prisoners that had been captured the evening before, one of them hallooed out: "How are you, Tom?"

Tom replied: "What are you doing in such bad company, Bob?"

However, Tom left ranks, went inside the prison lines, and had a hearty shake of the hand and a few minutes' conversation with Bob. On returning, he informed us that Bob was his brother. Literally is brother against brother.

At this point also, Company B of Maryland, which was mustered into service for one year and which had served out its term of enlistment, left us for home. After that date the 21st Virginia had only nine companies.

We kept up our march toward Winchester until we reached Cedarville. Jackson's division and Taylor's brigade took the road on the left; the remainder of the army, under Ewell's command, continued on the direct road to Winchester. Jackson's command, after leaving the road at Cedarville, marched to Middletown.[21] When we came in sight of the Valley pike, it was filled as far as we could see from one end to the other with Yankees on their way to Winchester. We had surprised them on the march. We attacked at once and cut their marching column in two. One part continued on toward Winchester, and the other turned back toward Strasburg. This latter part of their command the Second Brigade was ordered to pursue. We followed them until they crossed the bridge over Cedar Creek. Then we were recalled and joined in the general pursuit. In marching through Middletown we found long lines of knapsacks behind the stone walls on the pike, as if whole regiments and brigades had unslung them in order to make a stand and, as soon as we attacked them, had left in such a hurry as to leave them behind.

Near Newtown we came on a long wagon train of the enemy's that was standing on the side of the road. The enemy had set fire to some of them. As we passed, one thing struck the writer as singular about the contents of those wagons. In every one that had articles in

---

[21] In later years Col. J. M. Patton told of the hard march of his regiment during this period. The heat and dust were almost unbearable, he stated. Referring specifically to F Company, he wrote: "As the men limped along with weary limbs and feet throbbing with pain, on what seemed to them an aimless march, I heard them denouncing Jackson in unmeasured terms for 'marching them to death to no good end.' It was my duty no doubt to have rebuked these manifestations of insubordination, but, feeling that their sufferings in some measure condoned their offence, I took no notice of the breach of discipline." *SHSP*, VIII (1880), 141.

sight, I could see portions of women's clothing.[22] In one wagon was a bonnet, in another a shawl, a dress in the next, and in some was all of a woman's outfit. I never saw the Yankee soldiers wearing this kind of uniform, and why they carried it was beyond my knowledge. Some of our men suggested that it had been confiscated from citizens of the Valley.

Marching a little farther we halted, as the enemy had some artillery on the opposite hill shelling our road. Our advance ran out some guns; these, with our advanced skirmishers, soon had them retreating again. It was now dark. We soon came to another long train of captured wagons and a pontoon-bridge train. The men looked at these with much interest, as they were the first we had seen. Marching a little farther we saw a string of fire along a stone wall and the crack of muskets told us it was from the Yankee rear guard. They stopped at nearly every cross wall and gave us a volley. General Jackson, who was always in front in an advance, came near being shot by Yankees from behind one of these walls.[23]

We captured over 100 wagons during the night and kept up the pursuit without intermission until about dawn, when we halted and were allowed to rest an hour or two in our places along the road. Soon after daybreak on May 25 we were on the move again. When we reached the mill about two miles from Winchester, we saw that the enemy had made a stand on the hill behind it. We soon met one of our men; he was hatless and wounded, having been shot in the head, and the blood streamed down his face so freely that the poor fellow could hardly see. The Second Brigade took the left road here, marched a short distance, filed to the right, and formed a line of battle under the foothills and on the left of the Stonewall Brigade. Our 21st Virginia was supporting the Rockbridge Artillery.[24]

We could see Ewell's command on the Front Royal road far away to our right. They were engaged, and we located Ewell's line by the smoke from his artillery and musketry. We could also plainly see the

---

[22] Abandoned Federal wagons—some overturned, some burning, and others simply standing on the pike—formed an unbroken train that stretched six miles down the Valley. Jackson was irate that many of the foot cavalry "were forgetful of their high trust" and "deserted their colors" in order to pillage the loaded wagons. *OR*, XII, pt. 1, 703; *SHSP*, XLIII (1920), 221n.

[23] Douglas verified this incident in his *Stonewall*, pp. 55-56.

[24] The Rockbridge Artillery was one of the most celebrated batteries in Confederate service. Formed in Lexington in 1861, and initially commanded by the town's Episcopal rector, William N. Pendleton, the unit entered the army with 28 college students, 25 theological students, and 7 men who held master of arts degrees. In the course of the war, 45 of its members received officers' commissions. See James I. Robertson, Jr., *The Stonewall Brigade* (Baton Rouge, 1963), 11, 17.

Yankee shells bursting over his lines, and see his shells bursting over the Yankees!

The enemy in our front were behind a stone wall that ran entirely across an open field. A little way behind them were two batteries of artillery. A piece of the Rockbridge Battery was run out on a knoll on our left, where they were met by grape and Minie balls. Every man at the piece was killed or wounded.[25] Undaunted, the battery ran forward another piece—but were careful not to expose it as in the case of the other gun. The men were soon picked off by the infantry behind the wall, and they were forced to abandon both pieces. However, as the guns were in our line, they were safe; and if the enemy wanted them, they must fight for them. About this time General Jackson made his appearance and rode to one of the hillocks in our front. Our brigade commander, Colonel John A. Campbell, accompanied him on horseback, while Colonel Patton of the 21st Virginia and Colonel Andrew J. Grigsby[26] of the Stonewall Brigade followed on foot. They were met by a hail of grape and musket balls. Campbell was wounded; Grigsby had a hole shot through his sleeve and said some ugly words to the Yankees for doing it. General Jackson sat there, the enemy continuing to fire grape and musketry at him.

It was right here that Jackson issued his celebrated order to the commander of the Stonewall Brigade: "I expect the enemy to occupy the hill in your front with artillery. Keep your brigade in hand and a vigilant watch, and if such an attempt is made, it must not be done, sir! Clamp them on the spot!"[27]

After satisfying himself as to the location of the enemy, General Jackson quietly turned his horse and rode back in a walk. Arriving at the road in our rear he called for Taylor's brigade, led them in person to their position, and gave General Taylor his orders.

General Taylor acknowledged the orders, then added: "You had better go to the rear. If you go along the front in this way, some damned Yankee will shoot you!"

---

[25] The battery took 89 men into the battle and lost 2 killed, 15 wounded, and 9 horses slain or disabled. The two cannon disabled in the action were Parrotts. See *OR,* XII, pt. 1, 761-62; Robert L. Dabney, *Life and Campaigns of Lieut.-Gen. Thomas J. Jackson* (New York, 1866), p. 377. Hereafter cited as Dabney, *Jackson.* The best account of the battery's role in this battle is in Richard Taylor, *Destruction and Reconstruction* (New York, 1879), pp. 56-59.

[26] Andrew Jackson Grigsby (1819-1895) at this time commanded the 27th Va. His fearlessness, hatred of Yankees, and profanity were well-known throughout the Valley army.

[27] Jackson issued this order to the Dunkard commander of the 33rd Va., Col. John Neff. See *OR,* XII, pt. 1, 755; Dabney, *Jackson,* p. 378.

General Jackson rode back to him at once and said, "General, I am afraid you are a wicked fellow, but I know you will do your duty."

Taylor formed his brigade in the road about two or three hundred yards to our left. We were on his flank and could see nearly the whole of his advance. His march was in an open field, up a steep foothill or high bank, and then on a gentle rise to the top. Near the top stood the same stone wall that was in our front, with the enemy's line of battle extending beyond Taylor's left. As soon as General Jackson saw that Taylor had commenced the advance, he rode back to the hillock in our front to watch the effect of Taylor's attack.

The enemy poured grape and musketry into Taylor's line as soon as it came in sight. General Taylor rode in front of his brigade, drawn sword in hand, occasionally turning his horse and at other times merely turning in his saddle to see that his line was up. They marched up the hill in perfect order, not firing a shot! about halfway to the Yankees Taylor, in a loud and commanding voice that I am sure the Yankees heard, gave the order: "Charge!" up to and over the stone wall they went! This charge of Taylor's was the grandest I saw during the war.[28] There was all the pomp and circumstance of war about it that was always lacking in our charges. Yet it was no more effective than ours which were inspired by the old Rebel Yell, in which most of the men raced to be foremost.

As Taylor's men went over the stone wall, General Jackson gave the command in that sharp and crisp way of his: "After the enemy, men!" Our whole line moved forward on a run. The enemy broke and ran in all directions. The Rockbridge artillerymen rushed to their two abandoned pieces and gave them a parting salute.

Near Winchester our artillery, which had been firing from every elevation over the heads of our infantry at the fleeing enemy, halted its advance. A scene was witnessed that had no parallel in history that I know of. The men of several batteries unhitched the lead horses from cannon and caissons, threw the traces over the horses' backs, and charged the enemy through the town! They captured and brought back many prisoners. As our regiment passed through Winchester, the citizens were so glad to see us that men, women and children ran into the streets to welcome us. They wrang our hands with both of theirs, some

---

[28] "I have rarely seen a more beautiful charge," wrote Lt. Douglas of Jackson's staff. Jackson himself officially reported that "steadily, and in fine order," Taylor's men mounted the hill, "and there fronting the enemy, where he stood in greatest strength, the whole line magnificently swept down the declivity and across the field, driving back the Federal troops and bearing down all opposition before it." In Taylor's Louisiana brigade were the 6th, 7th, 8th, and 9th Regiments, plus Wheat's battalion of infantry. Douglas, *Stonewall*, p. 58; *OR*, XII, pt. 1, 705.

embraced the men, and all cried for joy. The bullets from the enemy were flying through the streets, but this made no difference to these people! It seemed that joy had overcome fear. Such a scene I never witnessed.[29]

After following the enemy about five miles below Winchester, the Second Brigade was ordered to halt and go into camp while other troops followed the fleeing enemy. Some of the men followed the enemy into Maryland, but were stopped by Jackson when he received notice of the effort of other forces of the enemy to get into his rear.

The enemy on this occasion were commanded by General Banks, from whom General Jackson captured vast stores: several hundred beef cattle, several hundred wagons and teams, 11,000 new muskets in boxes that had never been opened, a large amount of ammunition, and over 3,000 prisoners. Although Jackson lost a very small number of men, he had led us for three weeks as hard as men could march. In an order issued to his troops the next day, he thanked us for our conduct and referred us to the result of the campaign as justification for our marching so hard. Every man was satisfied with his apology. To accomplish so much with so little loss, we would march six months! The reception at Winchester was worth a whole lifetime of service.

On May 28 the 21st Virginia was ordered to Winchester to take charge of the prisoners. This job was little relished by the men, since we had only about 250 men to guard about 3,000 prisoners![30]

The enemy had a large force in the valley of the South Fork of the Potomac under General John C. Fremont, and another on the Rappahannock River under General Irvin McDowell. As soon as it was known that Jackson had routed Banks, the authorities in Washington gave these two commanders orders to march at once to Strasburg, which was twenty to thirty miles up the Valley in Jackson's rear. There they were to form a junction, and the united force of between 30-35,000 men would fall on Jackson, whip him, and capture his army. McDowell ordered General James Shields and his division to the Valley. Shields

---

[29] A Maryland soldier substantiated Worsham's account with the observation: "The joy of the citizens of Winchester at once more having the protection of Confederate troops knew no bounds, and as we filed through the streets in pursuit of the enemy, provisions and delicacies in abundance were lavished upon us, while more than one of our young fellows came in for an earnest embrace from the matron of some well-grown household." W. W. Goldsborough, *The Maryland Line in the Confederate States Army* (Baltimore, 1869), p. 69. Col. Cunningham's report of the 21st Va. at Winchester is in *OR*, XII, pt. 1, 764-65.

[30] The 21st Va. numbered 270 men at Kernstown. On May 3 Jackson placed its strength at 600, which is far too high. In any event, the regiment was in charge of 2,300 Federal prisoners. *Ibid.*, 403, 708; pt. 3, 879.

moved promptly and rapidly, and actually burst into the Luray valley at Front Royal before Jackson was advised of his movement! Learning that Fremont was moving on a road that led to Strasburg, Jackson divined their purpose, recalled his advance, and ordered the other troops to concentrate at Strasburg. At that time the Stonewall Brigade was the advance of Jackson's army. It was in the neighborhood of Harper's Ferry, and the 2nd Virginia of that brigade had crossed the Shenandoah and gone to Loudoun Heights. On May 31 the brigade received the order to march to the other side of Winchester before they stopped. The brigade marched over thirty-five miles, and the 2nd Virginia marched over forty to accomplish it.

On May 31 also, Jackson sent all his captured stores and his wagon train up the Valley pike. Our regiment with the prisoners followed in the afternoon. We marched to Cedar Creek and stopped for the night. Our guard line was around a large barn, in order to allow the prisoners to have the benefit of shelter from the rain. Some amusing scenes were witnessed the next morning. The barn had a large quantity of hay in it. We went to the door and ordered all prisoners out; we then called for those who were concealed to come out or they would be punished when found. None came, so some of our men were ordered to go in and see if they could find any prisoners. Two or three were pulled out of the hay—amidst shouts from their comrades as well as our men. Then we fixed bayonets and told them we were going to thrust the bayonets into the hay in the entire building. One or two came out. Presently the bayonets began to be used. A few strokes and a man is struck; but, fortunately for him, not hard enough to hurt him. He and several others then came out. We then formed our line and commenced the march.

At Strasburg we could see Ewell's division in line of battle on the right of the road. It was awaiting the advance of Fremont, whose skirmishers had made their appearance and were then engaged with Ewell's skirmishers. Our prisoners became very much excited about this, and they declared loudly that Jackson had met his match now, would be badly whipped, and that it would be only a few hours before they would be retaken. After all the wagons and prisoners had passed, Jackson waited for the Stonewall Brigade to arrive. As soon as it had passed, Ewell withdrew his division and followed the column up the Valley. Fremont made a big show at one time in Ewell's front. Yet hearing nothing from Shields, who for some reason had not made his appearance, Fremont withdrew his men back into the mountain fastness while his skirmishers followed Ewell a short distance.

The plan to bag Jackson at Strasburg had failed. "Old Jack" was too quick for them. Besides, he had some plans of his own.

The next day, June 2, Fremont followed us in hot pursuit, and so closely that our guard and the prisoners could plainly see his advance from the tops of some of the hills on our march.

Reaching the Shenandoah at Mt. Jackson, General Jackson gave General Ashby orders to burn the bridge across the stream after our army had passed. General Ashby left this task to an officer and some men, but they were driven off by the enemy before it was accomplished. Learning this, Ashby took a few men with him, went back and drove off the Yanks, then set fire to the bridge and retired. But as he rode off, Ashby's famous white horse was shot! This beautiful and great horse, known by the enemy as well as it was known in our own army, was thought by the Yanks to be enchanted. I have heard prisoners repeatedly say that they have often taken deadly aim at that horse and its rider, sometimes rested their guns on a fence or wall, and the ball had no effect on either! He was a grand horse. After being shot, he carried General Ashby about a mile from the bridge before he fell dead. This was the first intimation Ashby had of his horse being wounded.[31]

Shields marched up the Luray valley with the intention of getting into Jackson's rear at New Market, but "Old Jack" defeated that by burning the White House bridge over the Shenandoah. Shields continued his march up the valley, expecting to force a fight with Jackson as soon as he and Fremont could unite somewhere in the neighborhood of Port Republic. Again Jackson frustrated their plans by turning on Fremont at Cross Keys on June 8 and easily whipping him.

Yet in the combat of June 6, we lost the great Ashby! He was killed while leading some infantry who had been sent to the front to aid him. At this time he was the most gallant and conspicuous cavalry officer we had. General Jackson thought a great deal of him and said that he was a born soldier who also seemed to have the faculty of knowing *what* the enemy was doing and when they were doing it. The army and the Confederacy could ill afford to lose him, and I think his loss was never repaired. In this short time his name was known all over the Confederacy, and amongst the enemy just as well. He was a tower of strength to us, and he was more feared by the enemy than any man

---

[31] Douglas alleged that this was the same horse Jackson had used at First Manassas. Douglas, *Stonewall,* pp. 79-80. See also *SHSP,* XXIX (1901), 136.

on our side at that time. His remains were carried to the University of Virginia and buried there.[32]

After defeating Fremont at Cross Keys on June 8, Jackson sent most of his troops that night to Port Republic. Left in Fremont's front were only Trimble's brigade and the Second Brigade, both small and both under the command of Brigadier General Isaac R. Trimble. His orders from Jackson were to hold his position as long as he could and, at the same time, to make as big a show as possible. If he were forced back, he should fight at every fence, wall, ditch, etc., and keep the enemy back as long as possible. If he could do this until 10 o'clock the following morning Jackson would be back to reinforce him. If he were forced back to the bridge, Trimble should burn it.

At the break of day on June 9, Jackson commenced his movement against Shields. With his troops he crossed the bridge over Middle River and marched through the town to South River, over which he made a bridge of wagons like the one on which we crossed at Bridgewater a few weeks before. Near the middle of the stream, where the planks running from one wagon to the next should have overlapped, only one of the planks did so, the others lacking a few inches of meeting. When the men in the front reached this place in crossing, those planks tilted and the men were thrown into the river. Seeing this, those who followed refused to cross on those planks and waited for each other as they crossed on the one. This caused a great delay in the crossing. When Jackson found his troops not coming up as quickly as they usually did, and learned the cause, he ordered the men to ford the river. This was a serious delay for Jackson, as time was most important to him. There is little doubt that this little incident ruined Jackson's plans and saved Fremont from utter rout.[33] After getting his troops over this stream, Jackson hastened them into position and launched an attack against Shields. After a severe battle Shields was utterly routed, and Jackson took many guns and prisoners. But time that waits for no man had been lost!

Fremont, hearing the heavy firing in the direction of Shields, knew that he and Jackson were engaged. He thought that Jackson's force was divided. He made a demonstration in his front, then made an attack on Trimble. But he could not drive him a foot. Fremont now

---

[32] On Oct. 25, 1866, Ashby was reinterred in Stonewall Cemetery, Winchester. Jackson, never one to mete out praise lavishly, nevertheless wrote of his fallen cavalryman: ". . . as a partisan officer I never knew his superior; his daring was proverbial; his powers of endurance almost incredible; his tone of character heroic, and his sagacity almost intuitive in divining the purposes and movements of the enemy." Douglas, *Stonewall*, p. 80; *OR*, XII, pt. 3, 712.

[33] See *SHSP*, VII (1879), 529-30; Chambers, *Stonewall Jackson*, I, 580.

brought up more troops, lengthened his line on both sides, and in this way forced him back. Late in the morning, after constant fighting, the Confederates were driven to the bridge, which they burned after crossing it.[34]

Jackson, recalling his troops from the pursuit of Shields, was hurrying across the battlefield to Trimble, whom he had not heard from, when his army was fiercely assailed by Fremont's artillery. Fremont was on the other side of the river and had placed his artillery on the high banks that overlooked Shields' battlefield. Jackson withdrew his men behind the hills for protection and there heard of Trimble's inability to keep the enemy back for a longer time. Without the accident at the bridge of wagons, there is not the least doubt of Jackson being able to carry out his plan to the very letter, and Fremont would have been wiped off the face of the earth. As it *was*, the campaign ended in a blaze of glory that was sounded from one end of the world to the other!

Jackson's loss with Shields was heavy and amounted to as much as he had previously lost in the campaign. The loss of Shields was also heavy, and Fremont's loss was in excess of Jackson's.[35]

Jackson stayed behind the hills in the neighborhood of Brown's Gap until June 12, when he marched up the Shenandoah to the neighborhood of Weyer's Gap and camped in a beautiful country. In the meantime, Fremont had become frightened and retreated toward Winchester. This ended the great Valley Campaign.

One of the Yankee prisoners marched at my side daily, talking about what he was going to do with me when they were retaken, and how he would take care of my gun. While we were uneasy all the time, for fear that the prisoners might make a break for liberty, we never had a thought of their being rescued except on one occasion. On June 5, after marching a short distance past Port Republic, we halted and were told that we would camp there for the night. While our lieutenant colonel was looking over the ground, an order came from General Jackson for us to move on. A few cavalry were ordered to

---

[34] Worsham's version of Trimble's actions on June 9 is largely inaccurate. In his official report Trimble stated that he held his old position that day until 9 A.M., when, with an enemy battery preparing to shell his men, he began a slow retirement to Port Republic. Two messages then came from Jackson, urging Trimble to hasten to the assistance of the Confederates enduring Shields' attack. Trimble accordingly burned the bridge and proceeded quickly to the new battle. No elements of Fremont's army gave pursuit. OR, XII, pt. 1, 798.

[35] Jackson lost 833 of 5,900 men (14% casualties). Shields' losses were 1,018 men (25% of his strength), while Fremont suffered 684 casualties (5% of his force). Chambers, *Stonewall Jackson*, I, 376, 385; G. F. R. Henderson, *Stonewall Jackson and the American Civil War* (New York, 1904), I, 578, 587. Hereafter cited as Henderson, *Jackson*.

report to Colonel Cunningham. This did not excite suspicion among the guard; but about 9 o'clock one of our officers came to me and whispered in my ear that the enemy were in Port Republic, and that I must keep the strictest watch and under no circumstances let a prisoner escape. I did not know what to think. The enemy in Port Republic meant that they were between us and Jackson, and the prisoners' expectation of release might be realized. We marched until about midnight, then went into camp near New Hope for a few hours' rest. The next morning we were up early and marched to Waynesboro.

The report of the enemy being in Port Republic on June 5 was untrue, but the advance of Shields did enter the village on the morning of the 6th and came near capturing General Jackson. There are several versions of his escape, but all agree that it was by the merest chance. Most of his staff with him at the time were captured. This body of the enemy, it is said, learned the direction in which the prisoners had been sent, and a part of them made an attempt to follow us. But they were driven back by some of our artillery, supported by a small body of infantry.

We remained in Waynesboro and heard the cannonading at Cross Keys and Port Republic. The prisoners were so excited that it would have taken very little to stampede them. Every man was on duty, and it was a great strain on our men. When more prisoners were brought us, with the information that Jackson had defeated Fremont, the relief was almost overpowering. Amongst a small squad of prisoners brought us here by some cavalry was an Englishman, calling himself Sir Percy Wyndham, captured on June 6.[36] He was a colonel in the Yankee army and, it is said, requested to be sent to the Valley, as he would capture the rebel Ashby the first time he got within striking distance of him. Ashby with some of his cavalry met Sir Percy near Harrisonburg, and almost the first man taken by Ashby was this same Sir Percy. He was made to march on foot with other prisoners from the place of his capture to Waynesboro. When he reached us, he was the most exasperated man I had seen for a long time. He said that, in his English army,

---

[36] Wyndham and 63 other members of the 1st N. J. Cavalry were captured in this action. Son of a British cavalry officer, Wyndham was a soldier of fortune who went wherever there was fighting. He was only fifteen when he participated in the revolution of 1848 in France; Victor Emmanuel II knighted him for his valor in the Italian wars; and when he came to America to fight in the Civil War, his close friend, Gen. George McClellan, got him command of the N. J. regiment. Both sides recognized his devil-may-care nature. Gen. Richard Taylor described him as a "stalwart man, with huge mustaches, cavalry boots adorned with spurs worthy of a *caballero,*" and a man who possessed "the nonchalant air of one who had wooed Dame Fortune too long to be cast down by her frown." On July 5, 1864, a leg wound forced Wyndham's retirement from military life. *OR,* XII, pt. 1, 712; Taylor, *Destruction and Reconstruction,* p. 26.

when an officer of his rank was captured, he was taken charge of by an officer of like rank and treated accordingly until exchanged or paroled. Here he was marched through mud and mire, and that too by a rebel private. It was enough to make a saint swear. We treated him as other prisoners; we made no distinction in his favor as he thought we should, since he had come all the way across the ocean to capture Ashby!

On the evening of June 8 we conducted our prisoners from Waynesboro across the Blue Ridge at Rockfish Gap. They did not give up hope of being retaken until they had crossed the mountains, when they became as meek as lambs and gave us very little trouble. On June 9 we reached North Garden depot on the Orange and Alexandria Railroad and went into camp. Here one of the prisoners made a break for liberty. The guard fired at him but missed, so the prisoner got away.

We took the cars on the 11th and went to Lynchburg, where we marched our prisoners through the town to the fairgrounds and there guarded them until the 18th. We then turned them over to the city guard and went by rail to Charlottesville, leaving the train, however, about a mile from the town. We camped on the side of the railroad until Jackson marched by on his way to Richmond, at which time we rejoined our brigade. It was the unanimous desire of the regiment never to have charge of prisoners again.

Chapter IV

"HIGH ON THE SCROLL OF HONOR"

On June 17, 1862, Jackson broke camp in the Valley and marched toward Gordonsville. As he passed through Charlottesville on the 21st, our regiment rejoined its brigade. We were plied with many questions as to the destination of the army, and we made as many inquiries of our comrades in the Second Brigade; but all agreed that we knew nothing. We guessed that on reaching Gordonsville we would file to the left and fall upon McDowell at Fredericksburg; or our destination was Washington, and this circuitous route was taken to mystify the enemy. None of us had a single thought of Richmond. Why then send W. H. Chase Whiting's division to the Valley to join Jackson?[1] When we reached Gordonsville, we kept on the same road. When we arrived at Louisa Court House, some cars came along on the Virginia Central Railroad, picked up the troops that were marching in the rear, and carried them to Beaver Dam Station. These cars returned, took those in the rear again, and carried them to the same place. In this way Jackson would use railroad cars to help his men on a march.

We now decided that we were going to Richmond to help Lee, and that the sending of Whiting to the Valley was a ruse to have two effects: one on General George B. McClellan at Richmond, and one on the enemy in the Valley. It is said that it was successful in both directions. Since we knew we could not stay in Richmond, Jackson's men realized that we would have to do some desperate fighting. The only way for us to leave was to attack McClellan and drive him away.

We reached Ashland on June 25 and received orders to cook three days' rations. The next morning, as soon as the column could be formed, we left the road we had been following and marched on one to the left that went in the direction of the Virginia Central Railroad crossing near Peak's turnout. After marching to the neighborhood of Pole Green Church, we stacked arms and rested for the night. Today we saw the first signs of the Yankees' presence in our march: the tele-

---

[1] Jackson wanted to strike down the Valley toward the Potomac and the North. Because Davis and Lee approved the plan, Whiting's troops were sent as reinforcements. The change of plans resulted with Lee's strategy to attack McClellan's exposed flank north of the swollen Chickahominy River.

graph wires were cut not far from Ashland. In the evening General "Jeb" Stuart's cavalry, which had joined us, had a brisk skirmish in our front and killed, wounded and captured some of the enemy.[2] Those prisoners were the first of McClellan's army that we saw.

We were up and moving early the next morning. At Pole Green church we found that Stuart's men needed the assistance of our infantry in order to clear the way. Some regiments were ordered forward and soon captured at Hundley's Corner nearly all the Bucktail Regiment of Pennsylvanians.[3] We did not know whether McClellan had learned that Jackson was in the neighborhood, or whether he thought the column was a part of Lee's force. We continued the march now without any obstruction. Soon we heard the musketry and artillery of Generals James Longstreet and A. P. Hill commencing the attack on McClellan at Gaines' Mill, and we learned that we were about to unite with them in an attack. Until now we had thought that they were on the south side of the Chickahominy River and that we were to make the attack alone from the north side.

Our march was kept up in quick time. The firing became heavier in our front and was the heaviest musketry I heard during the war. We marched on; toward evening we halted and retraced our steps until we came to a road we had passed some time before. This road was to the east, and we kept on it until our division was halted. We were ordered to load, formed a line of battle, and moved through a pine thicket so dense that a man ten yards in front could not be seen.

The Second Brigade was on the right of the division, the Stonewall Brigade in the middle, and the Third Brigade on the left. The division was about the center of General Lee's line of battle. In going through the thicket the division, having no guides, lost its way. Our orders were to press forward to the firing in front. The division obeyed; but, very singularly, the Stonewall Brigade crossed the line of march and, when it reached the firing line, it was on the left and came up just in time to help General D. H. Hill, whose line was giving way. The united force swept everything before it. The Third Brigade, maintaining nearly a straight line, came up to Whiting's line as it was falling back, and their united efforts drove the enemy at that point. When the Second Brigade emerged from the thicket, they had, like the Stonewall Brigade, taken

---

[2] Throughout June 26 sharpshooters of Capt. Connally T. Litchfield's company of the 1st Va. Cavalry cleared Federal pickets from the Confederate line of march. Their action evoked praise from Stuart. *OR*, XI, pt. 2, 514, 516.

[3] The "Bucktail Regiment" was the 1st Pa. Rifles of the 13th Pa. Reserve Regt. Its casualties at Mechanicsville were 2 killed, 18 wounded, and 75 captured. *Ibid.*, pt. 2, 38, 233, 553, 562, 621. See also Edwin A. Glover, *Bucktailed Wildcats* (New York, 1960), pp. 82-86.

a long swing, but toward the right. We entered an open field. Not far ahead we saw two men on horseback who seemed to be in consultation. As we approached them, we recognized at once our beloved leader, General Lee, on his well-remembered gray horse, and President Davis.[4] We passed them with a cheer, and they recognized it by raising their hats. Here were two of the most notable men of the Confederacy in close consultation on the battlefield and, from their appearance, no one would imagine that the fortunes of the war were on their shoulders.

President Davis looked calm and self-possessed and, it being the first time he had seen our brigade, he looked on us with interest. General Lee was as calm and dignified as ever in giving us the salute.

We went straight ahead and, not long afterward, we came in sight of some of our troops who seemed in confusion and were giving ground. Our brigade commander, Lieutenant Colonel Cunningham of the 21st Virginia, rode forward to the brigade commanded by Brigadier General Richard H. Anderson of Longstreet's division, which was on the extreme right of our line. I was told Colonel Cunningham said to General Anderson that his brigade was coming and that he would take the front. General Anderson thanked him and said that, because of the arrival of Jackson's men, he could finish what his brigade had commenced.[5] He moved his men to the right and made an attack on the enemy's flank while the Second Brigade kept them busy in front. When Anderson's men gave the yell, we went forward on a run, and the works were carried by Anderson in gallant style.

This was the strongest point I saw occupied by either army during the war. For half a mile in the enemy's front was an open field, with a hill gently sloping toward them. At the foot of the hill was a creek, eight to ten feet wide, that had washed banks about six to eight feet deep. When we jumped in, we could not get out without assistance. We threw our guns on the side next to the enemy. One comrade then helped another out; when he had scaled the bank, he stooped or lay down and pulled another out. It was almost level from this creek for about fifty to one hundred yards. Then there was a steep and high hill covered by a large and open wood. At its foot ran a rail fence

---

[4] This is the most glaring error in Worsham's entire narrative. Since Lee telegraphed Davis of the hard-won victory at Gaines's Mill (see *OR*, XI, pt. 2, 622), and since no other contemporary mentioned Davis being on the field (not even Davis himself), the President must have remained impatiently in the capital throughout June 27. Davis and an entourage, which Lee disapprovingly termed an "army," were with the Confederate forces the day before at Mechanicsville, but Worsham could not have seen them.

[5] This verbal exchange did not occur. Indeed, by the time Cunningham arrived with his troops, Anderson's South Carolinians had already attacked the Federals and driven them from their position. "We had only to secure about 40 prisoners who were trying to make their escape," Cunningham reported. *Ibid.*, 587.

which had been converted into an excellent breastwork. This was the enemy's first line of battle. About twenty-five yards up the hill was a second line of breastworks made of logs and dirt. About the same distance in its rear, on top of the hill, was another line behind similar breastworks. Behind this was their artillery, which had a full sweep at us as soon as we entered the clearing in their front.

Charging this point—Anderson on the flank, we in the front, we drove the enemy out and, on top of the hill, we entered a field that was filled with Yanks and Confederates. The line on the left of us having been carried too, every man was yelling and shooting into the mass of the enemy as fast as he could load. This was continued until it was so dark that we could not see.

The position taken by Jackson's division in this battle was rather remarkable. As before stated, our orders were to march right ahead to the firing. Not having guides, and in our moving about in the thicket, the brigades finally emerged apart; and in going to the front, each brigade moved, as was thought, in a straight line. But one went to the extreme right, another near the center, and the other to the extreme left. Yet each reached its destination when assistance was greatly needed. Thus it seems that the old division, which had such a bad start, put itself into a better place than "Old Jack" himself had ordered, and played no small part in the success of this great battle.

Late in the night we lay down on the hard-won field at Gaines' Mill to take some rest, but the cries and groans of the wounded kept many of us awake all night. In the morning we could see the result of the battle: the greatest slaughter of the enemy in the field, the dead and wounded numbering thousands. A large number of cannon were captured in this field; I don't know how many.[6] I counted fifteen on one hill, standing just as the enemy left them. On this same hill I saw the first machine gun, with its handle to turn out a bullet at every revolution.[7] I saw another which was captured during the Seven Days' fight. These were the only ones seen by the writer during the war.

During the night the enemy, destroying the bridge in our front, made good their escape across the Chickahominy. Replacing this, so

---

[6] At Gaines's Mill Gen. FitzJohn Porter lost 894 men killed, 3,107 wounded, and 2,836 missing. In addition, he left behind 22 of his 80 cannon. Confederate losses numbered about 8,000, and included two generals wounded and seven regimental colonels killed. *Ibid.,* 40-41, 973-84; E. Porter Alexander, *Military Memoirs of a Confederate* (New York, 1912), pp. 123, 131.

[7] The first Gatling (machine) guns appeared in small quantities in 1862. Mounted on wheels, the weapon "had little if any offensive value," one writer stated, "and made an inviting target for enemy artillery. . . . The Gatling gun became quite a different weapon after it was improved and smokeless powder was invented." Kenneth P. Williams, *Lincoln Finds A General* (New York, 1949-1959), II, 799-800.

that we could cross, delayed Jackson's command all of the next day. During the day the enemy sent up a large balloon for observation, and some of our guns fired at it. Whether or not it had any effect toward making the occupants retire I cannot say, but they were up only a short time.[8]

Longstreet and A. P. Hill crossed higher up the stream and went in pursuit of the enemy. General John B. Magruder's troops made an attack on the enemy in the evening near Savage Station.

The bridge being ready on the morning of June 30, Jackson's command crossed early to the south side of the Chickahominy. We marched past the house McClellan had used as his headquarters and thence on to the Williamsburg turnpike. Here we passed some of General Lee's troops, who had halted for us to take the front. As we were just from Jackson's brilliant valley campaign, we created much excitement and enthusiasm, and many remarks and cheers greeted us. I remember that our captain, William H. Morgan, had a saber but no scabbard, and the remark was made several times along the march: "See there, the officers don't even carry scabbards for their swords." Others said: "No wonder they march so; the men carry no baggage." (As a general thing, our knapsacks had been discarded long ago.)

We passed the field on which Magruder made the attack on the enemy the day before. We saw many of the enemy's dead along the road, and it was strange that nearly every one was shot near the heart.[9] Reaching the toll gate, we saw a man sitting on a box and leaning against the gate post. We soon discovered that he was dead. We passed Savage farm and saw hundreds of tents which were used by the enemy for hospitals. Nearly all were full of sick and wounded enemy soldiers. We marched to the vicinity of White Oak Swamp, where skirmishers were thrown forward. Some of our artillery was brought into position, and firing commenced. General Jackson ascertained that the enemy had made a stand here. We moved from place to place, looking for a ford where we could cross. At night we lay down on the ground for a little rest. Early in the morning we resumed the march. The enemy had left during the night. Crossing the swamp on a bridge of logs, we followed in hot pursuit and found the enemy in position at Malvern

---

[8] Worsham beheld one of seven balloons in the "armada" of a twenty-nine-year old scientist with the awesome name of Thaddeus Sobieski Constantine Lowe. His telegraphic reports, one authority has asserted, "especially those at Fair Oaks and Gaines's Mill in 1862, were of inestimable value to the Union army." Robert V. Bruce, *Lincoln and the Tools of War* (Indianapolis, 1956), pp. 85-88.

[9] Cpl. James E. Hall of the 31st Va. noted in his diary for June 29: "Passed over part of the battlefield today. Saw a few dead Yankees. Some were as black in the face as the Ace of Spades. Let lie and rot, I expect." Ruth Woods Dayton (ed.), *The Diary of a Confederate Soldier: James E. Hall* (Charleston, W. Va., 1961), p. 62.

Hill. General Jackson promptly formed his line of battle. Our division was in a wood on the right of the road in three lines, with the Second Brigade being the third line. The enemy shelled us terribly the whole time.

Just about dark the Second Brigade was ordered to march by the left flank. On entering the road we marched toward Malvern Hill, crossed a creek, and soon were in a field, at the edge of which we halted and stayed the remainder of the night. I sat down in a fence corner to get a little rest and had not been there long before one of our men, wounded, came along begging for water. Having some in my canteen, I stopped him and gave him a drink. He sat down and complained very much of being weak. I gave him something to eat from my scanty rations. He seemed very thankful and revived a little; but he soon complained of being cold. I unrolled my blanket, made him lie down, and covered him with it. A little while later, I got cold too, so I crept under the blanket with the wounded man, fell asleep, and did not awaken until morning. I then crawled from under the blanket as carefully as I could to avoid disturbing him. I went to the creek, took a wash, filled my canteen, and brought it to my friend. On trying to arouse him, I found that he was dead.

The enemy fled during the night, so my division was ordered back and stopped at Willis' Church the remainder of the day. It had commenced to rain and was very disagreeable. While we were here, I went to the spring for water and found a dead Yankee lying with his face in the spring. I suppose the poor fellow had been wounded in the fight at Frayser's Farm two days before with Longstreet's command and, going to the spring, had leaned down to drink when death overtook him.

The next morning we moved in pursuit of the enemy and found them busily fortifying at Harrison's Landing on the James River. Jackson's command, most of the time in line of battle, remained there until July 8, when our division was moved back one and one-half miles to a creek where General Jackson said he would like all of us to take a bath, and that he would give us several hours to do so. This was much needed; because of the constant duty and scarcity of water, some of the men had not washed their faces and hands for five or six days. We then marched from this place to White Oak Swamp, where we rested for the night. The next morning Jackson's command took up its march for Richmond, marching around the city on its northeast side. During this march we moved some distance along the York River Railroad. We saw many large warehouses in which the enemy had stores.

Some were burning, others were partially burned, and some had been captured before they were fired.

Jackson's division marched to the Morris farm on the Mechanics-ville turnpike and there, on July 11, went into camp. On the next day General Jackson gave F Company permission to spend the day in Richmond. To most of the company, many of whom had not been in the city since they left it a year ago, that was a great day. What changes had taken place in one year. We left Richmond a year ago in new uniforms, with the fair complexion of city men—some frail and spare, and none of us with one exception having seen anything of real war. Now we returned as veterans ruddy and brown, with the health and hardness that outdoor living creates. Our welcome was an ovation, and it made us feel our standing in public esteem. The only thing we regretted as our time closed was that the day did not last forever.[10]

We stayed at the Morris farm several days, taking a much-needed rest and the first we had had since April 30. During the time that ended now at the Morris farm, Jackson's men had marched over 550 miles, fought 9 battles and many skirmishes and captured several thousand prisoners plus large quantities of small arms, cannon, wagons, and stores.

At the commencement of the war the Southern army was as poorly armed as any body of men ever had been. Using my own regiment as an example, one company of infantry had springfield muskets, one had Enfields, one had Mississippi rifles, and the remainder had the old smoothbore flintlock musket that had been altered to a percussion gun. The cavalry was so badly equipped that hardly a company was uniform. Some men had sabers and nothing more, some had double-barreled guns, some had nothing but lances, and others had something of all. One man would have a saber, another a pistol, another a musket, and another a shotgun. Not half a dozen men in the company were armed alike. The artillery was better, but the guns were mostly smoothbore and some of the horses had on wagon and plow harnesses. It did not take long for the Army of Northern Virginia to arm itself with better material. When Jackson's troops marched from the Valley for Rich-mond to join Lee in his attack on McClellan, they had captured enough arms from the enemy to replace all that were inferior; and after the

---

[10] Richmond newspapers took no notice of F Company's presence in town. On the contrary, one issue of that period devoted its city column to the deplorable and unsanitary conditions of Richmond hospitals and to the untold number of Confederate stragglers who jammed Capitol Square "while the more conscientious and noble hearted troops" remained in their camps. Richmond *Enquirer*, July 25, 1862.

battles around Richmond, all departments of Lee's army were as well armed. After that time, the captures from the enemy kept us up to their standard. Yet our ammunition was always inferior to theirs.

Toward the close of the war, nearly all equipment in the Army of Northern Virginia were articles captured from the Yankees. All the wagons were captured; and to look at them on a march—with many of them having the name of the brigade, division, and corps of the Yankee army branded on them, one would not know that they belonged to the Confederacy. Nearly all the mules and horses had "US" branded on them; our ambulances were from the same generous provider; so also were our tents, many of them having the name of the company, etc., branded on them. Most of the blankets were those marked "US," and also the rubber blankets or cloths. The very clothing that the men wore was mostly captured, for we were allowed to wear their pants, underclothing, and overcoats. As for myself, I purchased only one hat, one pair of shoes, and one jacket after 1861. We captured immense quantities of provisions; nearly all the "hard tack" and pork issued to us was captured.

On July 16 we received orders to march to Richmond. We took the cars of the Richmond, Fredericksburg and Potomac Railroad to Beaver Dam Station, where we were transferred to the Virginia Central Railroad and conveyed to Louisa Court House. It was necessary to take this route because the enemy had destroyed a portion of the Central Railroad between Richmond and the junction (now known as Doswell), and the line had not been repaired at that time. We remained a day at Louisa Court House, then marched to Gordonsville, Liberty Mills and Mechanicsville, not far from Louisa Court House. We stayed two or three days at each place. On August 4 we marched again to Liberty Mills.

These movements were occasioned by reports from the enemy in our front, who had raised a new army. "The Army of Virginia" was commanded by Major General John Pope, who said he had been doing great things in the Western army. In an order to his troops on taking command, he said he had never seen anything "but the backs of the rebels." His headquarters were in the saddle, he said, and he wanted the talk of guarding the rear of his army stopped, as an invading army had no rear. It was useless, he said, to make provisions to look after communications in that direction.[11] In less than a month Pope found

---

[11] Pope's pompous order emanated from Washington on July 14, 1862, and stated in part: "I have come to you from the West, where we have always seen the backs of our enemies . . . The strongest position a soldier should desire to occupy is one from which he can most easily advance against the enemy. Let us study the probable lines

out that his army did not have any rear, as Jackson had quietly slipped into Manassas and gobbled it up. General "Jeb" Stuart with his cavalry had previously raided his headquarters at Catlett's Station, capturing his official papers and his military dress coat.[12]

On August 7 we left Liberty Mills and marched to Orange Court House. We were up early the next morning and on the march. During the day we were joined by A. P. Hill's division and Colonel Leroy A. Stafford's Louisiana brigade. Reaching Barnett's Ford on the Rapidan River, our advance guard found the enemy in their front and offering some resistance to our crossing. Near the ford we passed a "Quaker cannon" which our advance had rigged up. It was the hind part of a wagon with a black log on it. Our men ran this out on a hill in full sight of the Yanks and advanced at the same time with a cheer. The enemy left the ford in a hurry. They could not stand the sight of the cannon.[13]

On crossing the river we took the direct road to Culpeper Court House. We soon saw one of our cavalrymen whose ear had been nearly severed from his head by a saber. We forded Robertson River in the afternoon and about sunset went into camp in a wood near the road. About midnight we were awakened by the firing of muskets and the ting of balls falling amongst us. Each man rose and took his place in ranks more quickly than I ever saw it done. When the order was given to "take arms," every man had his gun ready for action. We marched to the road and halted to await orders from headquarters. The firing soon ceased. It resulted from the surprise of some Yankee cavalry on their way from Madison Court House to Culpeper Court House. They were ignorant of our advance. Being halted by our guard, they began to retreat; and after a brief skirmish, they made off as soon as they could extricate themselves. In this affair my regiment went into ranks directly from their beds. When we marched back to camp, the laughs began. Those old Confederates made the woods ring with

---

of retreat of our opponents, and leave our own to take care of themselves. . . . Success and glory are in the advance, disaster and shame lurk in the rear." *OR*, XII, pt. 3, 473-74. The "headquarters in the saddle" phrase was Pope's answer to a reporter's query as to the location of his base of operations. It was not a part of his address to the army.

[12] Worsham jumped ahead in his narrative to cite the Aug. 22 raid on Pope's headquarters at Catlett's Station. Gen. Fitzhugh Lee and two Confederate cavalry brigades skirted Warrenton and struck Pope's headquarters with such alacrity that they barely missed bagging the Federal commander. Yet they did capture Pope's supper, dispatch book, dress uniform (including a large plumed hat), and a chest containing $350,000 in Federal greenbacks.

[13] Elements of the 1st N. J. and 1st Pa. Cavalry of Gen. George D. Bayard's brigade were the Federal pickets routed by the Confederate advance. For reports of this and the midnight action described in the next paragraph, see *OR*, XII, pt. 2, 92, 129-30, 182.

shouts, for some of the men were in their shirt sleeves, some had on nothing but shirts, and some had on only one shoe. Hardly any man had a hat, but every man was in his place.

On the next morning, August 9, we resumed the march with Ewell's division in front, Jackson's next, and A. P. Hill bringing up the rear. About 1 o'clock we heard the boom of cannon in our front, and we knew that Pope had made a stand. The column hurried up, Ewell filing to the right and sending the first line of skirmishers forward.[14]

Our division was hurried along the road for some distance. The Second Brigade marched to the front of the column and halted. The roll was called, we were ordered to load and, after a few minutes of rest, we resumed the hurried march. Going a short distance, the men on the left of the road clear the way for a cannon ball that came bounding along like a boy's ball. To indicate the force with which it was traveling: the ball struck the stump of a tree, glanced up, and went out of sight. A little farther on we came to four of our men, lying dead in the road and killed by the same ball. The road was fairly alive now with shot and shell from the enemy. We filed to the left into the woods, went about 100 yards, then filed to the right and continued our march parallel to the road.

We passed an old Confederate who was standing beside a small sapling and had one hand resting on it. We asked him, "What is the matter?"

He said, "I don't want to fight. I ain't mad with anybody."

This put us all in a good humor, and amidst laughter and cheers we continued the march. After going several hundred yards we were halted and ordered to lie down. The enemy were shelling this wood terribly, and our Captain Morgan was killed by them.[15] After a short stay here we were ordered forward to the edge of the wood beside the main road that ran north and south. The woods we occupied extended northward about 150 yards to a field. This field continued along the road for about 200 yards to another wood.

The Second Brigade formed a line of battle in the corner or angle of the woods. The 21st Virginia was on the right, and the 48th Virginia was next. Both faced eastward. Next came the 42nd Virginia; and, at right angle to the road and facing northward, the Irish Battalion formed

---

[14] Following this paragraph in Worsham's original edition was a three-stanza poem relative to war in general. Because it has no connection with the Cedar Run campaign, it is omitted here.

[15] Capt. W. A. Witcher of the 21st Va. termed Morgan "a young officer of great merit." *OR*, XII, pt. 2, 202.

the left. The brigade thus formed a right angle. In front of the 21st and 48th Virginia was a large field surrounded by a rail fence. The road ran between the wood and fence. In the open, about 300 to 400 yards obliquely on our left, was a cornfield full of well-concealed Yankees. Another enemy line had formed at right angles to the main road and across it. Its right was concealed in the second wood, which was beyond the small field in front of the 42nd Virginia and the Irish Battalion. As soon as we reached the road, we saw a line of Yankees advancing from the cornfield. The 21st and 48th Virginia opened fire on them at once. The battle of Cedar Run had commenced in earnest.

After we caused the advancing enemy line to halt, the fighting was terrific. The Second Brigade was alone at this point, since Jackson had not had time to extend his line. The Yankees now made an advance with the line that had been concealed in front of the Irish Battalion and the 42nd Virginia. Their line being longer than ours, the Yankees swung around the Irish Battalion into our rear and occupied the position from which we had advanced only a few minutes before. The 21st and 48th Virginia were fighting the force at and near the corn field. Although this force had been strengthened by a second line, we still fought with such effect that we kept them back. Yet a part of the enemy force advancing against the left of the Second Brigade were firing directly into the flank of the 48th and 21st Virginia, and they were making terrible havoc in our ranks.[16]

Colonel Cunningham of the 21st Virginia, who was sick, came along the line, walking and leading his horse. He said to the men as he passed that the enemy were in our rear, that he desired to get us out of the position we were in, and that we must follow him. His voice was normally one of loud compass and great command. Yet he could hardly speak, and as he passed me he said, "John, help me get the men out of this. I can't talk loudly."

I induced all the men near me to face southward down the road, and we started. After a few steps I saw a Yankee sergeant step into the road about 50 or 75 yards ahead of us. At the same time I heard the firing of rapidly approaching enemy in our rear. A great dread filled me for Jackson, because I had seen him at this spot only a moment before. The Yankee sergeant, with his gun in his left hand and his sword in his right, turned up the road and approached us. A Yankee

---

[16] The Federals who assailed the 21st and 48th Va. were in Gen. Samuel W. Crawford's brigade, composed of the 5th Conn., 10th Maine, 28th N. Y. and 46th Pa. The bluecoats who crumbled the Virginians' left flank were in Gen. John W. Geary's brigade, made up of the 5th, 7th, 29th, and 66th Ohio. For an excellent account of this action from the Federal side, see Edwin E. Marvin, *The Fifth Regiment, Connecticut Volunteers* (Hartford, 1889), pp. 149-72.

private stepped into the road just ahead of him. As this was the road on which we marched to get to our position, this showed that the enemy were not only in our front, flank, and rear, but actually had the Second Brigade surrounded! The Yankee sergeant did not stop his advance toward us until he actually took hold of one of the men of our regiment, pulled him out of ranks, and started toward the rear with his prisoner. One of our men, who was in the act of capping his gun, raised it to his shoulder and fired. The sergeant fell dead, not ten feet away.

By this time the road was full of Yankees, and there was such a fight as was not witnessed during the war. Guns, bayonets, swords, pistols, fence rails, rocks, etc. were used all along the line. I have heard of a "hell spot" in some battles; this surely was one. Our color-bearer knocked down a Yankee with his flag staff—and was shot to death at once. One of the color guard took the flag, and he also was killed. Another, Roswell S. Lindsay of F Company, bayoneted a Yankee, then was immediately riddled with balls—three going through him. Four colorbearers were killed with the colors in their hands. The fifth man flung the riddled flag to the breeze, and went through the terrible battle unhurt.[17]

Leading his horse, Colonel Cunningham had crossed the road, pulled down the fence, and passed through the gap into the field. With a foot in the stirrups he had started to mount his horse when he was struck by a bullet and fell back dead.[18] His horse received a death wound at the same time.

It was a terrible time. The Second Brigade was overwhelmed; nearly half of the 21st Virginia lay on the ground, dead or wounded. F Company of Richmond had carried eighteen men into action. Twelve of them—six dead and six wounded—were lying on the ground. Many of the regiment were now prisoners. The remnant was still fighting hand to hand. Jackson now hurried men to our relief. The Stonewall Brigade came in our left, and the Third Brigade came in on the right. They succeeded in surrounding a part of the enemy command that had surrounded us, and they took nearly all of them prisoners, including

[17] Capt. W. A. Witcher, who succeeded temporarily to command of the 21st Va. after Cunningham's death, stated: "The adjutant was taken by the enemy, though afterward escaped; the sergeant-major was shot down; the flag-bearer was shot dead; a corporal of the color-guard, seizing the colors, shared the same fate; and a private who next raised them fell, wounded in three places." He concluded: "No troops, in my opinion, could have behaved with more daring and obstinacy than those of the Twenty-first. There were instances of individual heroism which I refrain from mentioning lest injustice should be done to others." OR, XII, pt. 2, 202.

[18] For sidelights on Cunningham's death and praise of his gallantry, see O. J. Hayes to Worsham, Mar. 2, 1895, Worsham Papers; OR, XII, pt. 2, 190, 201-02.

their brigadier general.[19] We released those of our men who had been captured in time for them to join the little band in the advance. Just at this moment the enemy hurled a line of cavalry against us from the cornfield, but our fire on them was so hot that those not unhorsed wheeled, and off to the rear they went on a run.

Our whole line now advanced; the enemy were in full retreat. We could plainly see Ewell with a part of his division on Slaughter Mountain, way off to the right of our line, advancing too. As the mountain at this point was free of woods, we could see his skirmish line in front advancing down the mountain, his line of battle following, and his cannon belching forth fire and smoke; and we could see the enemy's shells bursting on the mountain side. It was a magnificent and inspiring sight.

We kept up the pursuit until 9 or 10 o'clock that night, when we were halted and allowed to rest for the night.

The battle was fought and won. The 21st Virginia had written its name high on the scroll of honor, but at terrible cost. We went into battle with 284 men; now 39 of them lay dead on the field, and 92 were wounded.[20] Old F Company of Richmond lost Captain William Morgan, shot through the body by a piece of shell. He was a splendid soldier, and the best informed man on military matters that I knew during the war. Henry Anderson, Joe Nunnally, John Powell, William Pollard, and Roswell Lindsay were killed. Bob Gillian was shot through the leg, Clarence Redd through both wrists, Ned Tompkins in the body and through one arm, Porter Wren in the arm, Harrison Watkins through the body, and Clarence Taylor through the hip.

Nearly half of Jackson's loss in this battle was in the Second Brigade.[21] Amongst the killed were Brigadier General Charles S. Winder[22] of the Stonewall Brigade, who commanded the division, and

---

[19] Worsham erred here in his chronology. The Federals opposing the Virginians at this point were in Geary's Ohio brigade and a heterogeneous brigade of five battalions, a cavalry company, and an artillery battery under Gen. Henry Prince. At 7:45 P.M. when the battle was all but over, Prince was captured—"by losing his way in the dark while passing from one flank of his command to the other," Pope reported. Prince himself gave a more dramatic account of his capture, and he added that his command suffered 33% casualties in the day's fighting. The two Federal brigades involved suffered a combined loss of 928 men, including 102 missing. *Ibid.*, 134, 137, 160-61, 167-70.

[20] Surg. Gen. Lafayette Guild officially placed the regiment's casualties at 37 killed and 85 wounded. *Ibid.*, 179. Cf. an account by William Patterson of Co. E, 21st Va., in *Confederate Veteran*, XXIV (1916), 406.

[21] Jackson's losses at Cedar Run numbered about 1,300 men. The Second Brigade's casualties were 91 killed and 210 wounded. *OR*, XII, pt. 2, 179-80, 185.

[22] Maryland-born Charles S. Winder (1829-1862) was a Regular Army veteran noted for strict discipline. Individualistic members of the Stonewall Brigade never developed much affection for him, but Jackson considered him a highly capable and promising officer. See Robertson, *The Stonewall Brigade*, 79-81, 86-88.

Lieutenant Colonel Richard H. Cunningham, Jr. (an old F Company man), who commanded the 21st Virginia. These two men were as gallant as the cause ever lost, and they were a great loss to our command and the army. Both were conspicuous on every battlefield for brave deeds, and they gave promise of being great soldiers. I have always thought there was a similarity in their deaths. Both were on the sick list; each had been riding in an ambulance during the day; but, at the sound of the guns, each mounted his horse, came to the front, and took command of his men. Winder was posting his advance artillery in the open field just to our right when he was killed. Cunningham was killed a few minutes later at the same place. I also think that, if they had lived, each would have been promoted: Winder to major general and Cunningham to brigadier general—both commissions dating from this battle.

Major Robert L. Dabney of Jackson's staff, describing the position of the brigades that were already in line of battle to our right, came to that occupied by the Second Brigade and wrote: "The whole angle of forest was now filled with clamor and horrid rout. The left regiments of the second brigade were taken in reverse, intermingled with the enemy, broken, and massacred from front to rear. The regiments of the right, and especially the 21st Virginia, commanded by the brave Christian soldier, Colonel Cunningham, stood firm, and fought the enemy before them like lions, until the invading line had penetrated within twenty yards of their rear. For the terrific din of the musketry, the smoke, and the dense foliage, concealed friend from foe, until they were only separated from each other by this narrow interval. Their heroic Colonel was slain, the orders of officers were unheard amidst the shouts of the assailants, and all the vast uproar; yet the remnant of the second brigade fought on, man to man, without rank or method, with bayonet thrusts and muskets clubbed, but borne back like the angry foam on a mighty wave, toward the high road."[23]

Lieutenant Colonel Thomas S. Garnett, commanding the Second Brigade, gave the 21st Virginia special mention in his report of the battle.[24] Likewise does Brigadier General William Taliaferro of the Third Brigade.[25] Brigadier General Jubal Early of Ewell's division said

---

[23] Dabney, *Jackson*, p. 500.
[24] Garnett made no specific mention of the 21st Va. in his report. He merely stated that when the Federals first advanced against his brigade, "with coolness and determination the regiments on the right delivered their fire, keeping a superior number of the enemy at bay." *OR*, XII, pt. 2, 200.
[25] "The Twenty-first Virginia Regiment," Taliaferro wrote, "poured a destructive fire upon the enemy and exhibited a degree of heroic gallantry rarely ever witnessed." *Ibid.*, 189.

in his report that in the general advance his attention was directed toward a small band of the 21st Virginia with their colors, as every few minutes the colorbearer would shake out his colors, seemingly in defiance of the enemy.[26]

We remained on the battlefield all of the next day, gathering the wounded and burying the dead. During the day General J. E. B. Stuart, whom Jackson had ordered to take command of a reconnoitering expedition, reported to Jackson that Pope had been heavily reinforced. In consequence, Jackson would not renew the advance, and Pope, being so much surprised at seeing the *front* of a rebel, had not recovered sufficiently to attack Jackson.

About midday, Pope asked permission of General Jackson to bury his dead and to succor such of his wounded as had not already been treated by us. This General Jackson granted, putting the field of battle under the command of Brigadier General Early. Soon Yanks and Confederates were engaged in friendly converse, trading papers, tobacco, etc. When night came on, General Jackson thought it best to fall back behind the Rapidan. We crossed that stream the next day and went into camp between that river and Gordonsville. While we were there, Starke's Louisiana brigade was added to Jackson's Division. The division now consisted of the First (Stonewall), Second, Third, and Fourth (or Louisiana) Brigades.

We remained in this camp until August 16, when we marched a few miles and prepared for another advance against Pope.

---

[26] Worsham misread Early's report. The band of men to which the general referred were part of Col. Alfred H. Jackson's 31st Va. *Ibid.*, 233.

Chapter V

LOW WATER MARK IN MARYLAND

After Longstreet had joined Jackson and General Lee had completed his plans, the army broke camp on August 20 and marched in the direction of Pope's army. Jackson crossed the Rapidan River at Summerville Ford. Pope had retreated behind the Rappahannock River, and we made that river our objective point. After trying several fords with the seeming intention of crossing, the morning of August 25 found us near the village of Jeffersonton in Culpeper County. Here we received orders to cook three days' rations and to be ready to move as soon as possible. Soon afterward, orders came to fall in; but many of the men, for want of time, had not prepared their rations. The half-baked biscuit and the raw dough were left behind. This for many meant nothing to eat for some time, probably days! The wagon train left behind, and everything in light marching trim, indicated that something of importance was on hand.[1]

As soon as the column had formed, we hurried off on the march. We passed through the village of Amissville, crossed the Rappahannock at Hinson's Mill, and thence several miles right through the country—through fields, over ditches and fences, and through woods—until we came to a public road. This we took, passed the village of Orleans, and marched steadily until we passed Salem about 8 or 9 o'clock that night. Here we halted in the road and stacked arms. We were told we could lie down and rest, as we had marched about twenty-six miles. Early the next morning we were up and on the march again. We passed through Bull Run Mountain at Thoroughfare Gap, marched through Hay Market and Gainesville, and did not stop until 10 or 11 o'clock that night. We had marched about the same distance as the day before. Many of the men, so completely used up from the march and the heat as not to have energy to move to one side, lay down right where they were stopped in the road. We were near Bristoe

---

[1] On the night of Aug. 24 Lee and Jackson formulated a plan whereby Jackson would rush around Pope's right flank and either cut him off from Washington or force Pope's army to fall away from reinforcements moving up from Fredericksburg. Because speed was the essential factor for success, Jackson ordered his army into motion with "the utmost promptitude." *OR*, XII, pt. 2, 678.

Station, not far from Manassas Junction, and far in the rear of Pope, "the man that had no rear."

General Jackson now sent a force ahead to capture Manassas, which was done during the night with small loss to us. Immense quantities of stores were captured, as well as several trains of railroad cars, eight pieces of artillery (with caissons and horses, etc., complete), a number of wagons, several hundred prisoners, and several hundred Negroes who had been persuaded to run away from their owners.[2] Early the next morning Ewell's division marched in the direction of Bristoe. The remainder of the corps marched to Manassas Junction, which our division reached about 7 or 8 o'clock in the morning. The Second Brigade filed by regiments to the right of the road into an open field near the storehouses. Here we were ordered to stack arms, rest, and remain near our guns.

Not long after this it was rumored that an enemy force from Washington was approaching to drive us away. This force consisted of a brigade of infantry and some artillery that had been sent down to brush away a small raiding party, as they supposed us to be. A. P. Hill's division was sent forward to meet them, and soon put them to rout.[3]

A scene around the storehouses was now witnessed but cannot be described. When a boy, were you on some special occasion allowed to eat as much of everything as you wanted? Were you ever a soldier who had nothing but roasting ears of corn to eat for two days? Well, if you have ever been either, you may probably have some conception of what followed. Only those who participated can ever appreciate it. Remember that many of those men were hurried off on the march on the morning of August 25 with nothing to eat, that it was now August 27, and that we had marched in this time about sixty miles. The men who had prepared their rations did not have enough for two days, much less for three; and, after dividing food with such comrades as had none, everything had long been eaten.

Now here were vast storehouses filled with everything to eat, and sutlers' stores filled with all the delicacies: potted ham, lobster, tongue,

---

[2] Gen. Isaac Trimble, with the 21st Ga. and 21st N. C., seized the junction around 11 P.M., Aug. 26. Trimble reported the capture of 8 guns, 200 horses, 300 prisoners, 200 Negroes, a large quantity of stores, and a long train "loaded with promiscuous army supplies." *Ibid.*, 720-21.

[3] The Federal force was a new and spotlessly clean New Jersey brigade under Gen. George W. Taylor. Two Confederate batteries raked the blue lines to shreds; Hill's infantrymen then finished the work. At one point the slaughter became so one-sided that Jackson personally rode out under a white flag and called on the Federals to cease the sacrifice and surrender. They refused. In the end the bluecoats lost 135 men killed and wounded (including Gen. Taylor, who was mortally wounded), plus 300 of their number captured. *Ibid.*, 260, 401.

candy, cakes, nuts, oranges, lemons, pickles, catsup, mustard, etc. It makes an old soldier's mouth water now to think of the good things captured there. In the early part of the day a guard was placed over everything. Rations were issued to the men, but not by weight and measure to each man. A package or two of each article was given to each company. The first thing brought to F Company was a barrel of cakes; next came a bag of hams. We secured a camp kettle, made a fire, and put on a ham to boil. We had hardly gotten it underway before a barrel of sugar and coffee (the Yanks had it mixed) and a bag of beans were sent us. After a consultation we decided to empty the ham out of the kettle, as we could take that along raw. In its place we put the beans on the fire, as they were something we were fond of and had not had for a long time. About the time the beans commenced to get warm, a bag of potatoes was brought us. Over the kettle goes, and the potatoes take the place of the beans. As potatoes cook in a short time, we now think our kettle is all right. But here comes a package of desiccated vegetables. The kettle is again emptied and the vegetables are placed on the fire, as soup is so good. We were also given a barrel of syrup. This was a liberal and varied fare for our company, which was small then.

General Jackson's idea was to care for the stores, then turn the remainder over to General Lee when he came up. Hence, he placed a guard over them. Yet the enemy began to make such demonstrations that Jackson decided he could not hold the place. Therefore the houses were thrown open, and every man was told to help himself. Our kettle of soup was left to take care of itself. Men who were starving a few hours before, and who did not know when they would get another mouthful, were told to help themselves. Well, what do you think they did? Begin to eat? Oh, no. They discussed what they should eat and what they should take with them, as orders had been issued for us to take four days' rations with us.

It was hard to decide what to take. Some filled their haversacks with cakes, some with candy, and others with oranges, lemons, canned goods, etc. I know one man who took nothing but French mustard. He filled his haversack with it and was so greedy that he put one more bottle in his pocket. This was his four days' rations; but it turned out to be the best thing taken, because he traded it for meat and bread and it lasted him until we reached Frederick. All good things have an end. As night approached, preparations were made to burn everything that we could not carry. Not long after sunset the stores were set on fire. Taking up our march as soon as the fires got well underway, our division marched for several hours. Then our brigade was ordered to a road on our left for picket duty. At daybreak on August 28 we found ourselves on the Warrenton and Alexandria pike near Groveton.

At this time there was only one field officer in our brigade: Colonel Bradley T. Johnson,[4] whom Jackson had placed temporarily in command of the Second Brigade. The Irish Battalion was commanded by a major, John Seddon; the 48th Virginia by a lieutenant, Virginius Dabney; the 42nd Virginia by a captain, John E. Penn; and the 21st Virginia by a captain, William A. Witcher.[5]

The Second Brigade remained about Groveton all day of the 28th. Colonel Johnson had orders to make demonstrations and the biggest show he could so as to delay the enemy as long as possible from any advance in our direction. Well did he do this. At one time he had one regiment on top of a hill, with its colors under the next hill but just high enough to show over the top; a second regiment was on the next hill, with its colors so arranged. This thus gave the appearance of a long line of battle. We had two pieces of artillery. As one body of the enemy was seen, one or both pieces of artillery were brought into view; when the enemy moved, the cannon were limbered up, moved to some far hill, and the movement was repeated.[6]

Early in the morning of the 28th, while the 21st Virginia was lying down in line on one of these hills, the enemy ran a cannon out on a hill, unlimbered, and fired a shot at us. It struck one of the men of Company K, tore off the heel of his shoe, but did not injure him. This was the first cannon shot from either side at Second Manassas. It was the only one fired at that time, as the piece limbered up and withdrew in a trot. Soon afterward, when the 21st Virginia was deployed as skirmishers across the Warrenton pike, a Yankee artilleryman rode into our line, thinking that it was his. He was the first prisoner taken.

The inmates of the Groveton house now abandoned it. A bare-headed lady and her servant woman, holding between them a little girl who was crying loudly, ran out of the front door. They crossed the pike, climbed over the fence, went directly southward through the

---

[4] Bradley Johnson (1829-1903), a native of Frederick, Md., prior to the war had been a prominent attorney with no military experience. Yet he commanded the 1st Md. in its initial battles and, throughout his Civil War career, demonstrated high attributes for command. For reasons unknown, however, a brigadier's stars did not come to him until June, 1864.

[5] Witcher raised an infantry company in Pittsylvania County, entered Confederate service June 29, 1861, and served as captain until Dec. 1, 1862, when he was appointed colonel. Gen. Edward Johnson considered him "a most gallant officer." *OR*, XXIX, pt. 1, 848.

[6] Johnson made no mention of this maneuver in his official report. *OR*, XII, pt. 2, 664-65.

fields, and were soon lost to sight. In their excitement they did not even close the door to their deserted home.[7]

A Yankee wagon train on its way to Washington was seen on a road south of us. Our two pieces of artillery were run out; they commenced to fire at them and caused a great stampede. It was now about eleven or twelve o'clock. We retired to a wood north of the pike, formed the brigade into line of battle, stacked arms, and lay down in position.

None of the men had seen or heard anything of the remainder of our corps. We had no idea where they were, and it was singular that "Old Jack" had not made his accustomed appearance along the front—not even when the artillery fired. The men were much puzzled and mystified by this. Colonel Johnson sent word to the 21st Virginia for a lieutenant and six men to report at once to him with arms, etc. One of the men from F Company, the writer, was designated by name. On reporting, we were ordered to drive a squad of Yankees away from a house in sight. This we did in quick order, although we had to cross an open field and get over three fences before reaching the house. We remained at the house for awhile; then seeing that we were about to be cut off, we retired to the brigade without loss. This was the first musket fire of Second Manassas and, as the enemy had been seen in several directions toward our front, it may be said that the battle had commenced.

After the lieutenant made his report to Colonel Johnson, the colonel retained the "F" man (the writer) and ordered me to go out to the front as far as possible without being seen by the enemy. I was to keep a lookout and report to Colonel Johnson any body of the enemy seen approaching. In order to get along better, I left my arms behind. I crept to the front until I reached a bush on top of a slight elevation. Here I lay for several hours, observing the movements of several small enemy bodies, mostly cavalry.

While I was lying down behind the bush, an incident occurred that has always puzzled me. I heard the quick step of a horse to my right and rear. Looking around I saw a horseman in full gallop, coming from the north and going along a small country road that joined the Warrenton pike at Groveton House. Arriving at a gap in the fence along the road, he wheeled his horse and rode directly toward me as I lay in the field. It was done in such a deliberate way as to give me the impression that my presence was known before the horseman came

---

[7] These were possibly members of the Douglas family, whose home lay northwest of Groveton near the unfinished railroad. On the afternoon of Aug. 28 Johnson fell back to the woods near this residence. See Henderson, *Jackson,* II, 142-43.

along the road. He did not draw rein until he was almost on me; then he asked if I knew where General Jackson was. Receiving a negative reply, he wheeled his horse, rode back to the gap, turned into the road, and was off at a full gallop toward Groveton House. The man was riding a black mare and wore a long linen duster and dark pants. There was something so suspicious about his movements and dress that I would have taken him to Colonel Johnson if I had had his gun. A squad of Yankees was at the Groveton House. When the rider reached it, several of them ran from the front of the house and surrounded him. He dismounted and went with them to the front of the house while one of their number led the horse into the back yard and tied him. This was hardly done before a body of our cavalry charged up the Warrenton pike and captured the party. I had seen that detachment coming along the road a few minutes before, and I could also have warned the man riding the horse of the Yankees' presence. But a distrust came over me as soon as I saw him.[8]

About 4 o'clock in the afternoon I was startled by a long line of skirmishers advancing out of the woods in my front. Jumping to my feet, I started toward Colonel Johnson and had gone only a short distance when I looked back and saw their line of battle following. Now having been "dusted," I made my report to Colonel Johnson, who called the line to attention and gave the commands: "Right face! Double quick! March!" Away we went northward through the woods.

All of us were wondering what had become of Jackson; but when we moved out of the woods, the first man we saw was "Old Jack." Looking beyond, we could see that his command was massed in a large field, with arms stacked, batteries parked, and everything resting. Colonel Johnson rode up to him and made his report. General Jackson turned at once to his staff, gave each an order and, in a minute, the field was in a perfect hubbub—men riding in all directions, infantry rushing to arms, cannoneers running to their guns, and the drivers mounting. We saw the master hand now. In the time I am taking to tell this, one heard the sharp command of an officer: "Right face, forward march!" We saw a body of skirmishers march out of that confused mass and right up to "Old Jack," where the same officer gave the command to file right, and the next instant the command to deploy. The movement was done in the twinkling of an eye. Forward they went to meet the enemy.

[8] This mysterious rider was probably the Federal courier captured on the 28th by Capt. George R. Gaither's troop of the 1st Va. Cavalry. Found on the courier was a dispatch from Gen. Irvin McDowell that outlined the order of attack on Manassas Junction (where Jackson was presumed to be) by the troops of Gens. Franz Sigel and John Reynolds. See OR, XII, pt. 2, 664.

General Jackson had waited to see this. Now he turned to Colonel Johnson and told him to let his men stack arms and rest. As they had been on duty since the day before, he said, he would not call on them if he could avoid it. Then off he went with the advance skirmishers. In the meantime another body of skirmishers had marched out, filed to the left, and gone forward. A column of infantry unwound itself out of that mass, marched up to the point where the skirmishers had been filed to the right, fronted, and went forward. Another was now filing to the left, while the third column moved straight ahead. A part of the artillery followed each column of infantry. This was the most perfect movement of troops I saw during the war.

The crack of muskets and the bang of artillery told us that the lines had met, and the fire in a few minutes was terrific. An officer soon came and ordered the Second Brigade to report on the extreme left of Jackson's line, where the whole brigade was formed as skirmishers, ordered forward and, after going a certain distance, halted and ordered to lie down. We stayed there all night, sleeping on our arms. The enemy did not appear in our front, but our right had had a hard fight in which the enemy were defeated and retreated during the night. Brigadier General William B. Taliaferro, commanding Jackson's division, and Major General Ewell were amongst our wounded.

The next morning, August 29, the Second Brigade marched to the right of Jackson's line to the top of a large hill on which were several pieces of artillery. We stayed there about an hour and were shelled severely by the enemy, who made their appearance from another direction than that of the evening before. Jackson now took position behind an unfinished railroad which ran parallel to, and north of, the Warrenton pike and, I suppose, about a mile from it. Jackson's division was on the right, Ewell's next, and A. P. Hill's on the left. The Second Brigade marched from the hill to the left about half a mile, where we joined our division and formed two lines of battle near the edge of a wood and facing south.

In our front was a narrow neck of open land about 300 yards wide. On the west the woods ran along this field about 300 yards to a point where the field joined a larger field. A short distance around the angle of the wood was the hill which we occupied early in the morning. Jackson now had several batteries of artillery on it. On the east the woods ran along the field for 600 yards to a point where the field joined a large field. This large field ran east and west; at its far side was the Warrenton pike. About 200 yards in our front was a part of the abandoned railroad, running across the open neck from the woods on the east to near those of the west. The eastern end of the railroad was in a valley (where there was a fill for about 100 yards), then extended to a hill through which a cut ran out on the level ground just before it reached the west wood. The reader will notice now that in front of the railroad there was a short strip of woods on the west side and a long strip on the east. Our skirmishers were stationed at the railroad. We were ordered to lie down in line, guns in hand, and directed to rush for the railroad as soon as an order forward was given.

Colonel Johnson came along the line and stopped about ten yards in front of F Company. He took out his pipe, filled and lighted it, and then quietly sat on the ground, leaning against a small sapling.

Everything was perfectly quiet, but this did not last long. The stillness in our front was broken by a shot, and almost in the same instant a shell went crashing through the trees overhead. This was the signal for a severe shelling of our woods. One man fell wounded. Colonel Johnson immediately arose and went to him. He sent him to the rear, then stopped long enough to talk to the men around him and quiet their uneasiness. He then came back and resumed his seat. This was repeated several times.

The enemy now advanced and engaged our skirmishers at the railroad. Some of the balls aimed at our skirmishers occasionally reached our line and wounded some of the men. Colonel Johnson invited several of the men who were becoming uneasy to come and sit by him. He soon had a dozen around him, talking and laughing. Our skirmishers were now driven from the railroad, and they retired to our line of battle. The enemy were now some distance north of the railroad in our front. Being called to attention, the Second Brigade jumped instantly to its feet. When the order forward was given, we rushed to the front. On reaching the field we emptied our guns into the enemy and charged them with empty guns. They turned and ran, leaving many dead and wounded on our side of the railroad.

Approaching these men, who were lying on the ground about 100 yards from us, I noticed one man on his back who was gesticulating with his hands—raising them up and moving them violently backward and forward. I thought he was trying to attract our attention so that we might not injure him in our advance. When I reached him, I recognized from his shoulder-straps that he was a Yankee captain; and one of our captains, who was running on my left, said he was making the Masonic sign of distress. Arriving at the railroad, the 21st Virginia occupied the bank, and the remainder of the Second Brigade occupied the cut on our right. We loaded and fired at the retreating enemy, and soon cleared the field.

Expecting a renewal of the attack by the enemy, we remained at the railroad. After a short halt, the announcement, "Here they come!" was heard. A line of battle marched out of the far end of the east wood into the field, halted, dressed the line, and moved forward. We allowed them to come within about 100 yards of us before we opened fire. We could see them stagger, halt, stand a short time, then break and run. At this time another line made its appearance, coming from the same point. It came a little nearer. They too broke and ran. Still another line came nearer, broke and ran. The whole field seemed to be full of Yankees, and some of them advanced nearly to the railroad. We went over the bank at them, the remainder of the Second Brigade following our example. The enemy now broke and ran, and we pursued, firing as fast as we could.[9] We followed them into the woods and drove them out on the other side, where we halted and were ordered back to the railroad. We captured two pieces of artillery in the woods and carried them back with us.

As we returned, a Yankee battery of eight guns had full play on us in the field. Our line became a little confused; we halted, and every man instantly turned and faced the battery. As we did so, I heard a thud on my right, as if one had been struck with a heavy fist. Looking around, I saw a man at my side who was standing erect, with his head off and a stream of blood spurting a foot or more from his neck. He was Captain Nicholas Cabler of the 42nd Virginia, and his brains and blood bespattered the face and clothing of one of my company who was standing in my rear. As I turned farther around, I saw three others, all killed by this cannon shot, lying on the ground. This was the second time I saw four men killed by one shot. The other occurred a few weeks earlier in the battle of Cedar Run. Both times the shot struck as it was descending. The first man had his head taken off, the next was shot through the breast, the next through the stomach, and the fourth had all his bowels torn out.

We went back to our position in the woods, formed our old line of battle in two lines, and lay down as before. Immediately our atten-

---

[9] The brigades of Johnson and Starke attacked when the last of four Federal divisions (that of Gen. Joseph Hooker) attempted to break A. P. Hill's line on Jackson's left. When ordered to charge, Col. Johnson wrote, "with a yell the Second Brigade went through [the enemy], shattering, breaking, and routing them. The struggle was brief, but not a man faltered, and with closed ranks their rush was irresistible." The Federals who caught this onslaught belonged to Gen. Cuvier Grover's brigade, composed of the 1st, 11th and 16th Mass., 2nd N. H., and 26th Pa. Grover reported 486 casualties in twenty minutes' fighting. *OR*, XII, pt. 2, 439, 665.

tion was called to a line of battle filing into position in our front, but nearly at right angles to us. What did this mean? Were the enemy making preparations to storm us again? When General William E. Starke, our division commander, arrived, his attention was called to the line. He used his glass and, after a careful survey, called a courier and directed him to go to the right around the hill in our front and find out who they were. The Yankees were shelling our woods heavily, but the excitement was so great that the men, who had orders to lie down for protection, were all standing up watching the line, form and grow longer each moment. Our courier, after a short stay, was seen coming as fast as his horse could run. Before he reached General Starke, he cried out: "It is Longstreet!"

A great cry that Longstreet had come up was taken up by the men all down the line. The courier now told General Starke that the man whom we had noticed before sitting on a stump was General Lee, and that Longstreet said he had gotten up in time to witness our charge which, he said, was splendid!

This put new life into Jackson's men, who had heard nothing of Longstreet. They knew that if Pope with his large army would put forth energy, he could greatly damage us. But every thought was changed now. We only wished for a renewal of the attack, but we were afraid he would not attack us after his repulse that morning and now in the presence of Longstreet! Pope did attack A. P. Hill's division on the left, and he met with the same kind of repulse that we had given him. A part of Longstreet's command became heavily engaged also. This ended the second day's fighting, and the Second Brigade was jubilant over its share of Second Manassas so far.

The cannonading commenced early on the morning of August 30, with skirmishing in front that at times became active. About noon, expecting an attack, the Second Brigade moved to the railroad and took position as on the day before. About 2 or 3 o'clock we heard on our right the sound, "Here they come!" Almost instantly we saw a column march into the field from the point at which they appeared the day before. They dressed the line and advanced on us. Every man in our line shifted his cartridge box to the front, unstrapped it and his cap box, gave his gun a second look, and took his position to meet the enemy, who were rapidly approaching.

We allowed them to come about the same distance as on the day before; we then opened fire, with about the same result. Other lines advanced, each getting nearer to us. As on the day before, the field was filled with Yanks, but in much greater numbers. Their advance continued. At this moment every man in the Second Brigade remembered Cedar Run. Each one loaded his gun with care, raised it deliberately to his shoulder, took deadly aim, and pulled the trigger! We were fighting now as I never saw it done: we behind the railroad bank and in the cut, which made a splendid breastwork, and the enemy crowded in the field, their men falling fast, as we could plainly see. Our ammunition was running low, and our men began taking it from the boxes of dead and wounded comrades.

The advance of the enemy continued. By this time they were at the bank and mounting it. Our men were mounting it too—some with guns loaded, some with bayonets fixed, some with muskets clubbed, and some with large rocks in their hands.[10] (Colonel Johnson in his official report says he saw a man's skull crushed by a rock in the hands of one of our brigade.)[11] A short struggle on top of the bank, and in front of the cut, and the battle was ours! The enemy was running! Then went up that yell that only Confederates could make! Some men were wild with excitement—hats off, some in the air! It was right here that Lieutenant Rawlings, commanding F Company, was killed. He had his hat in one hand, his sword in the other, and was cheering his men to victory when he was struck in the head by a rifle ball and fell dead.

After the flying enemy we went! With our artillery firing over our heads, we ran through the field in our front to the woods on the left, and through that into the next field, where we could see our line advancing in all directions. Some of the artillery that was following in the pursuit ran up a hill, unlimbered, and fired rapidly through openings in our advancing line. Thousands of muskets fired, the men at the same time giving the old Rebel Yell! It was one of those inspiring scenes which its actors will never forget, and it made a staunch soldier of a recruit!

We kept up the pursuit until eight or nine o'clock that night. Then we halted and were allowed to rest until morning. The man "with headquarters in the saddle" who "had no rear" had been taught the second lesson of Jackson's tactics. Pope wished now that he had a rear, for he was putting forth all his efforts to find Washington and its fortifications, which were forty-five or fifty miles in his rear when we commenced our movement.

---

[10] Lt. E. E. England of Co. D, 21st Va., a bricklayer by trade, reputedly hurled the first stone at the Federals. Others of the regiment who soon gave out of ammunition followed the lieutenant's example with an unusual degree of accuracy. *SHSP*, XXV (1897), 264.

[11] Lt. Lewis Randolph of the Irish Battalion was the man who crushed the Federal's skull with a rock. *OR*, XII, pt. 2, 665. Opposing the Virginians in this fight were two brigades—mostly New York troops—under Gen. Daniel Butterfield.

The loss in our brigade was small. Among the killed was Lieutenant Edward G. Rawlings, Jr., commanding F Company. He was as good a soldier as the war produced—a magnificent specimen of manhood, tall and erect, over six feet in his stockings, weighing about 200 pounds, with endurance in proportion to his size. I have often heard him say he could march forever if his feet would not become sore. He was kind and gentle, and always at his post doing his duty.

To Jackson, as in the first battle of Manassas, belongs the chief honor of Second Manassas. The position held by the Second Brigade was one of the points on which the enemy made repeated and desperate assaults, in all of which they were repulsed with great loss. I saw more of their dead lying on the ground in our front than I saw in the same space during the war.

One of our company wrote home that he was shot all to pieces, having twenty-seven holes shot through his blanket. In his next letter he explained that his blanket had been folded, and that one shot went through it and made the twenty-seven holes!

I take pleasure in adding my mite of praise to our division and brigade commanders. Brigadier General Taliaferro, commanding the division the first evening (August 28), was wounded, and Brigadier General Starke of the Louisiana Brigade succeeded him. This was his first experience in handling a division, but he did it with great skill. He was conspicuous for gallantry, and seemed to be at the right spot at the right moment![12] His conduct was such as to endear him to this old command; and when he was killed at its head a few weeks later, many an eye was dimmed by tears!

It was the unanimous sentiment of the Second Brigade that it was never handled as well as it was by Colonel Bradley T. Johnson both during this battle and the rest of the time he was with us. His personal interest in the men went right to their hearts, and they showed their appreciation by obeying every order with cheerfulness and alacrity. And we made him a brigadier general. Writing to the Secretary of War, General Jackson stated of Colonel Johnson and the Second Brigade at Second Manassas: "The heroism with which the brigade fought, and its success in battle, but brightened my opinion of its commander."[13]

---

[12] William E. Starke (1814-1862) was born in Virginia but had become a successful cotton broker in Mobile and New Orleans when the Civil War began. His promotion to brigadier general was made retroactive to Aug. 6, 1862. For praise of his valor at Second Manassas, see *OR*, XII, pt. 2, 658, 668.

[13] No post-battle letter from Jackson to the Sec. of War regarding Johnson's conduct exists in published official sources. However, in the Maryland volume of *Confederate Military History*, which Johnson wrote, he cited a Sept. 4, 1862, letter of Jackson that stated in part:"The brilliant service of [Johnson's] brigade in the engagement on Saturday

It is not generally known that the ground occupied by the enemy in the battles of First and Second Manassas was almost the same. The junction of the Warrenton pike and Sudley Road was an important point in both battles. In the first battle the Yankees marched southward along Sudley Road to Stone House at the junction of the Warrenton pike, and thence moved to the southeast. In the second battle they marched northward along the same road to Stone House, and northwest from that point. Some of their guns occupied the same hills during both battles—in the first, firing to the southeast; and in the second, reversing and firing to the northwest.

The morning after the battle of Second Manassas, the pursuit of the enemy was resumed and continued all day. On the next morning, September 1, Jackson advanced by the Little River turnpike; about noon he learned that the enemy had made a stand near Chantilly, or Ox Hill. He immediately made arrangements to attack them. When we were ready to advance, it commenced to rain. It lasted but a short time, yet it came down in torrents! At its height the Yanks made an attack on us which was sudden and almost as furious as the rainstorm! We repulsed this attack and advanced, but night came on and put a stop to the fight. The enemy lost two generals killed in this battle; one of them was Phil Kearny.[14] During the battle, it is said, General Jackson was told by one of his officers that the rain had wet and ruined all the ammunition of the men, and the officer desired to know what he must do about it. General Jackson replied that the rain had ruined the enemy's, too![15]

We lay down in our wet clothes on the wet ground for rest, and we arose early the next morning feeling stiff and sore. We marched a short distance in pursuit of the enemy and heard that during the night they had retreated and sought protection in their fortifications around Washington. As night approached we made preparations for a good rest, for it was the first night we had had for a week out of sight of the enemy. We made good use of it and felt the next morning like new men. We resumed our march early on the morning of September 3. Soon it was passed from lip to lip along the line that we were going

last proved that it was under a superior leader, whose spirit was partaken of by his command." Clement A. Evans (ed.), *Confederate Military History* (Atlanta, 1899), II, 177.

[14] The other Federal general killed was Brig. Gen. Isaac I. Stevens, who commanded the First Division of the IX Corps.

[15] Some confusion still exists about this episode. At least two sources named A. P. Hill as the officer who sent the message to Jackson. *SHSP*, IX (1891), 311; XXV (1897), 99. That the dampness also hampered Federal firepower is borne out by Gen. Charles F. Walcott in *Papers of the Military Historical Society of Massachusetts*, II (1895), 158.

to Maryland. This created great excitement among the men, and they stepped off so briskly as to give no suggestion that they had had only one night's rest—and none during the day—for more than a week!

At night we were halted and allowed another good rest. During the night our wagons joined us. The next morning we were given time to prepare rations, the first that the men had cooked since August 25. It would have done one good to sit down by one of the fires and watch the men! As one "spider" of biscuits and one frying pan of meat was cooked, they were immediately divided and eaten; then another was cooked and eaten; and thus we disposed of most of the rations for the twenty-four hours.

After the cooking was done and the wagons were loaded, we resumed our march and halted that night in the neighborhood of Leesburg. The next morning, September 5, we marched again. About 9 or 10 o'clock in the morning the Second Brigade reached the Potomac River and forded it at White's Ford with great enthusiasm—bands playing, men singing and cheering! On reaching Maryland we marched up the tow path of the Washington Canal for a short distance to the locks. Here we crossed the canal on a bridge, then took a road and continued our march until night, when we camped in the neighborhood of the Three Springs. We resumed the march the next morning, the Second Brigade (with Colonel Bradley T. Johnson commanding) being given the advance of the army. Late in the evening we came to the Baltimore & Ohio Railroad depot near Frederick and saw several cars loaded with watermelons. The men broke ranks as they passed; many secured a melon and then hurried back to their places. Soon afterwards, with many of the men having watermelons in their arms, we entered Frederick.

We marched to the Fair Grounds, which had been fitted up as a large hospital for the enemy. Our brigade stacked arms and were told to make itself comfortable for the night. A guard was placed around our camp in order to prevent the men from straggling through the town. Yet a friend and I succeeded in passing the guard, and we took a stroll through Frederick. We were invited into several houses and entertained handsomely at supper. We ate enough for half a dozen men. After being absent for some time, we returned to our quarters. On reaching my company I was told to report to brigade headquarters at once. I thought something terrible was to pay now. I did not know whether I was to be shot or sent to prison, but I knew something was to be done with me.

I was soon ready, found headquarters, and reported to the adjutant general. He greeted me cheerfully, told me to go at once to the enemy's hospital, ask for the surgeon in charge, get a list from him of all the inmates, and write a parole for each according to the copy he furnished me. He said the surgeon in charge would give me all the information wanted and render me any assistance that was needed. I went back to my company with a light heart, made disposition of my gun and ammunition, and took my baggage with me.

I will take occasion to tell what that consisted of, and at the same time will say that it was rather above the average in our army in quality as well as in quantity. I had a very good oilcloth haversack in which to carry my rations, a tin cup, a splendid rubber cloth, a blanket, a pair of jeans drawers, and a pair of woolen socks—every article captured from the enemy! The socks and drawers were placed in the blanket, the blanket was rolled up with the rubber cloth on the outside, and the ends were drawn together and fastened with a short strap. To carry this, we put it over our head and let it hang from the shoulder.

Thus equipped, I reported to the surgeon. He treated me very politely, gave me a list of about 700 men who were in the hospital, conducted me into one of the dining rooms, gave me a lamp, pen, ink, and paper, and told me to use one of the tables. He thought the dining room the best place because I would have plenty of room and no one to disturb me. I prepared for action by cleaning the table, then sat down and commenced at once to write. I tell you it was a job, as I had to write every word of the paroles for those men in duplicate, one copy for the prisoner and one for us. I wrote until about twelve at night, when the doctor came in and brought me a nice lunch. He sat down and we had a pleasant talk for about an hour. He left and I continued my writing until nearly daybreak, when I lay down on one of the benches and had a good nap. I arose, went to the pump, washed myself, looked up my company, and had a little chat with them. I went back to the dining room and kept at my work until it was finished. The doctor sent me my meals. After I had finished I reported at headquarters to the adjutant general, who told me to stay there as I was wanted for special duty. Colonel Johnson was in command of the town and had the Second Brigade on guard duty. I stayed at headquarters until September 10, when Jackson's corps left the city, took the road to Hagerstown, and camped that night near Boonsboro.

I was marching at the head of the column and, on reaching Boonsboro the next morning, saw the advance cavalry enter and pass through the village. General Jackson followed a short distance after them. At a house near the corner of a cross street, he dismounted, tied his horse, and entered the house. He had hardly entered the house before a body of cavalry charged through the village on the cross street, in full sight of the head of our column. When we reached the village, we learned that they were a body of Yanks who had made a dash through our line. This was a narrow escape for Jackson, as he surely would have been captured if he had ridden on, or if he had delayed his going into the house! The god of battle took care of him; it was not destined that the Yanks should get him![16]

We turned to the left, marched to Williamsport, and crossed the Potomac into Virginia. I made a big speculation at Williamsport. My messmates asked me to get some soda, as we needed it to make our biscuits. I went to a drug store to get it and asked the salesman for a pound. The price was only eight cents. I gave him a Confederate note, which he took without hesitation, and gave me change. I then asked what he would sell a keg of soda for; his reply was six cents a pound. I paid him at once, shouldered the keg (120 pounds), and carried it to the river, where I induced a man with a wagon to carry it to camp for me. I sold soda that night for twenty-five cents per pound!

We marched to the neighborhood of North Mountain Depot on the Baltimore & Ohio Railroad and camped for the night. The next morning we continued our march, passing through Martinsburg, where we captured a good lot of stores from the enemy. They retreated to Harper's Ferry and we went into camp for the night not far from Martinsburg.

In the morning we marched to Harper's Ferry, where the enemy were fortified and awaiting us. We skirmished some, drove in the enemy and, after locating their position, we rested in our places for the night. The next morning a line of battle was formed. Jackson's division was on the left, with its left resting on the Potomac River. Ewell's division was next. A. P. Hill's division was on the right, with its right resting on the Shenandoah River. Our skirmishers drove those of the enemy all along the line, and the artillery on each side commenced firing. We were joined in the afternoon by artillery from Maryland and Shenandoah Heights, and learned through this that we had help from General Lafayette McLaws, who occupied the former, and from General John G. Walker, who occupied the latter. Both of these commands were sending shot into the doomed enemy. Firing was kept up this way until late in the evening, when we made several attacks on different enemy positions, capturing some men, gaining much advan-

---

[16] For the full story of this episode, see Freeman, *Lee's Lieutenants*, II, 163-64.

tage, and bringing our line closer to their fortifications. Night coming on, we rested in our places. Early the next morning (September 15) the guns all along our line opened fire. Our infantry was preparing for a general charge when the white flag was seen in several places along the enemy's fortifications. In a little while firing ceased; soon after, it was announced that the enemy had surrendered!

Some of the headquarters folks had offered to feed a horse for me if I would get one. My opportunity had come. Making my way to the fortifications, I clambered over them and saw that the Yankees had stacked their arms and were parking their artillery and wagons. I was surrounded at once and plied with all kinds of questions as to what Jackson would do with them. Since I did not know anything about the terms of surrender, I could tell them nothing. I took a Colt army pistol from one of them and, buckling it around my waist, went on my way looking for a horse. McLaws had not ceased firing, and every now and then a shot from his guns would drop near me. A Yankee major rode up to me and in a very rough manner asked, "Why do your people keep firing on us after we have surrendered?"

I told him very politely to ask General Jackson.

I approached a line of tents that looked as if they were abandoned. Going among these I was delighted by the sight of as fine a horse with equipment as I had ever seen. He was tied to a stake near a tent, and my heart fairly leaped to my throat as I went to him, untied and mounted him! As I started off, a Yankee colonel came from a tent, addressed me very politely, and inquired what I intended to do with his horse. I replied that I was very much obliged to him and would take good care of him for Harper's Ferry's sake. He asked me to stop, which I did. He came forward and told me that probably I did not know the terms of the surrender: General Jackson had allowed the officers to retain their arms, horses, equipment, and private baggage, and he added that he had no fear of my taking his horse after learning the terms. I sadly turned the horse's head toward the stake, rode him to it, and fastened him. The colonel invited me into his tent to take lunch, as he called it; yet it was a big dinner for an old Confederate. He also placed on the table several bottles, from which I might help myself. I disliked the losing of the horse but could not take him after the terms were made known to me. Indeed, the behavior of the officer so impressed me that it would have saved the horse if the terms had not been known!

I walked around and looked at the long lines of stacked muskets and the park of artillery and wagons. I gave up my notion of a horse

and soon wended my way back to our line over the route I had come.
While I was inside the enemy's fortification, I did not see a Confederate. We captured over 11,000 prisoners, 72 pieces of artillery with
caissons, horses, etc., about 10,000 muskets, several hundred wagons
and mules, and a large quantity of stores.[17] General A. P. Hill and his
division attended to the surrender. Jackson's and Ewell's divisions were
withdrawn from the line and, stacking arms, were allowed to rest. In
the afternoon we were ordered to cook rations and be ready to move as
soon as possible. As night approached we were under arms and marched
on the road to Shepherdstown.

Jackson's division marched all night, passed through Shepherdstown the next morning, and forded the Potomac at Boteler's Ford a
little below the town. We were in Maryland the second time. Marching
a short distance from the river, we came to the town of Sharpsburg.
Passing through it, we marched about a mile. We halted near the
Tunker or Dunkard church, stacked arms, and were told that we could
rest. We remained there several hours and were much refreshed. We
then marched up the Hagerstown road about half a mile when, in
passing through a field, we were heavily assailed by shot and shell
from the enemy.

We marched a short distance and formed a line of battle. Jackson's
division occupied the left of our line of battle. The division formed in
two lines on the left (or west) side of the Hagerstown road and at
nearly right angles to the road. The Second and Stonewall Brigades
formed the front line in a field, with the Stonewall Brigade resting on
the Hagerstown road and connecting with Ewell's division. This line
was under the command of Lieutenant Colonel A. J. Grigsby of the
Stonewall Brigade. Starke's and the Third Brigade, commanded by
Brigadier General Starke, formed in a wood about 200 or 300 yards
in our rear. We had been in position only a short time when the enemy
opened a heavy fire on us from guns in our front and on our right.
This was continued until late in the night. We then went to sleep in
line of battle.

On the morning of September 17 we saw that McClellan had
decidedly the advantage in position. His artillery in our front was on
higher ground, and on the right his guns on high hills beyond the
Antietam could enfilade us. Farther up the mountain side we saw his
signal flags at work. They seemed to overlook our entire line. We were

---

[17] Jackson reported the capture of over 11,000 men, 73 cannon, 13,000 small arms,
200 wagons, and "a large amount of camp and garrison equipage." The Federals
acknowledged only the loss of 12,520 men and 47 cannon (of which 7 had been spiked).
OR, XIX, pt. 1, 548-49, 951, 955.

not allowed to make much of an observation before the enemy's shells dropped in our midst from batteries in front and flank, and this soon became the fiercest artillery fire of the war. It seemed that the air was alive with shells! The fire continued a short time, then their infantry in dense masses attacked us. After stubborn fighting they were driven back with heavy loss, and the artillery commenced again, a fiercer fusilade than before!

General J. R. Jones,[18] commanding the division, left the field on account of injuries received from this fire. Brigadier General Starke, our commander in the battle of Second Manassas, assumed command of the division and ordered a charge by the entire division, which was promptly obeyed. While he was leading the division, Starke received three musket balls and fell dead.[19] We retired to a lane on the edge of the field, where the fighting was terrific! We were finally forced back into the woods by overwhelming numbers, but here we succeeded in driving back the enemy. We finally retired through the woods into a field, where we were allowed by the enemy to rest a short time.

Old F Company had reached low water mark! After Second Manassas there were only three men to answer roll call—Malcolm L. Hudgins,[20] Reuben J. Jordan,[21] and John H. Worsham.[22] As we had no officer, we were ordered to report to Captain Archer C. Page of D Company. When we did so, Captain Page called us young gentlemen and told us we might march and camp anywhere we chose in the regiment. We were to report to him once daily and, in the event of a fight, to report to him at once. He ended by saying we might call the

---

[18] Born at Harrisonburg and educated at VMI, John R. Jones (1827-1901) had few admirers in Jackson's division. At Sharpsburg he was stunned by shell concussion and borne to the rear. He left the fighting at Chancellorsville reportedly because of an ulcerated leg. The Confederate Senate never confirmed his promotion to brgiadier general; and when in 1863 Jones was captured and imprisoned on Johnson's Island, Confederate officials made no effort to effect his release. See John M. Patton to Worsham, Oct. 19, 1893, Worsham Papers; OR, XIX, pt. 1, 1008.

[19] During the bitter fighting on the Confederate left, Starke grabbed a flag and tried to rally a portion of his command. He was leading the men forward when shot (contemporary accounts state by four bullets) and instantly killed. Lee's praise of him is in OR, XIX, pt. 1, 149.

[20] Hudgins was a student in Hampton when in April, 1861, he journeyed to Richmond and joined F Company. He was 6'1" tall, with blue eyes and blond hair. Records of F Company, 21st Va., War Records Group 109, National Archives.

[21] Prior to his enlistment Jordan was a student in Goochland County. He was 5'7½" tall, with black hair, brown eyes, and dark complexion. Ibid.

[22] If only three men answered roll call, as Worsham stated, a majority of the company was either sick, wounded, or on furlough. The Dec., 1862, muster roll of F Company listed twenty-five men on active service. Ibid. See also B. T. Johnson to Worsham, Feb. 20, 1891, and J. E. Penn to Worsham, Aug. 23, 1895, Worsham Papers.

roll as often as we chose. This gallant and good man had to pay the penalty of commanding F Company, for he lost a leg in this battle.[23]

We were known during the Maryland Campaign as the guerillas of the 21st Virginia. At Harper's Ferry the company had Hudgins and Jordan to stand up for them; at Sharpsburg Hudgins got sick and Jordan was the only man with the company in that terrible battle. By a singular circumstance Jordan was detailed to the front as a skirmisher. When the line was deployed, he was on its left, and he was the soldier who held the extreme left of General Lee's line of battle. His position was on the edge of a wood. When the line in the field on his right was driven back, Jordan gathered a few of his comrades from the right and held back the line until he found he was outflanked on his left, and that the enemy's line was far in his rear. He made a run for safety, going back to our line of battle—only to find that it had retired and that he and his few comrades had been left behind! Hurrah for Jordan! Hurrah for F Company for having such a representative!

He passed along the lane and saw the great slaughter of friend and foe. He then passed through the woods into a field. Here he noticed a body of men in the field to his right; but he kept on until he reached the other side of the field, where he found General Jackson and his staff. Inquiring of one of the staff officers as to the whereabouts of his division, he was told that the body of men he had passed was the remnant.

At this moment Jackson was in the most critical position of his military career! His entire line had been driven back beyond the Dunkard church, and they were holding on now by a mere thread; but succor was at hand! Brigadier General Early and his brigade, which had been detached to assist General J. E. B. Stuart's cavalry on the extreme left, arrived, and McLaws' division was expected every minute.

Jordan, who had been retracing his steps in order to get to his command, now saw the first brigade of McLaws arrive on the field. He heard the commanding officer give his sharp commands: "On the right by file into line! Double quick! March!" In a run and under fire the line was formed.[24] Jordan stopped long enough to inquire who they were and to watch the line grow every moment. He then hurried to his

---

[23] Archer C. Page of Cumberland County enlisted in Co. D, 21st Va., July 6, 1861. He was elected lieutenant five days later, and elected captain in Apr., 1862. on the evening of Sept. 17, 1862, Surg. R. T. Coleman amputated his right leg above the knee. Page resigned from the army Dec. 11, 1862. Page's personal service file, War Records Group 109, National Archives.

[24] McLaws's lead brigade, commanded by Gen. Paul J. Semmes, managed to stunt the Federal attack but suffered exceedingly high losses in doing so. Three of four regimental colonels were wounded, and casualty percentages for Semmes' regiments were: 53rd Ga., 30%; 32nd Va., 45%; 10th Ga., 57%; 15th Va., 58%. OR, XIX, Pt. 1, 874.

command with the good news. On arriving, he saw General Early and Colonel Grigsby, the commander of our division, in consultation. It is said that Early directed Grigsby and his division to make an attack on the enemy, who were again advancing with a large force. Early would take his brigade to the left, pass swiftly around the brow of a hill, and attack the enemy in flank and rear. This attack, in which McLaws' troops joined, was a great success, and the enemy were driven back at this point with great slaughter!

Old Jack, who had been riding along the line, got his mettle up with this success and ordered an advance along his entire line. The men replied with the old yell and the bayonet! The enemy were hurriedly driven out of the woods and across the Hagerstown road. Jackson's old line was reestablished. The firing soon was confined to that of the sharpshooters. The enemy had suffered so much that they made no more attacks on Jackson's line.

Oh, for a few more men! With one good division we could have routed the enemy. But alas! General Lee had fought every man he had except one division on his right. This was soon attacked and driven back; but A. P. Hill, who had just marched upon the field from Harper's Ferry, saw the situation, wheeled his division into line, and attacked the enemy with such vigor that they were driven across the Antietam!

At night we lay down on our arms. The next morning, expecting a renewal of the battle, we were up bright and early. But the enemy was badly whipped and did not make any demonstration during the day. Feeble skirmish fire and an occasional shelling from his far-off guns were all that he attempted.

The loss in Jackson's command, in proportion to the men he had engaged, was larger than in any battle he fought during the war.[25] Captain John E. Penn,[26] commanding the Second Brigade, lost a leg. Captain Page of the 21st Virginia, commanding the skirmishers of the brigade, lost a leg also. Men and officers by hundreds were killed and wounded. Our brigade came out of the fight under the command of Lieutenant John A. Booker[27] of the 21st Virginia. The division, under

---

[25] Jackson himself placed his total loss in the battle at 2,438 men, including 351 killed. Henderson stated that Jackson's command numbered no more than 5,500 troops and suffered 2,034 casualties. *Ibid.*, 958; Henderson, *Jackson,* II, 235, 255.

[26] Penn had been named captain of Co. H, 42nd Va., in Oct., 1861. He was promoted to colonel Aug. 9, 1862. On Feb. 10, 1863, as a result of the amputation of his leg above the knee, he resigned from service. Penn's personal service file, War Records Group 109, National Archives.

[27] Booker enlisted July 1, 1861, in Co. D, 21st Va. He served as regimental ordnance officer through most of 1862, then was promoted to captain Feb. 6, 1863. At the Wilderness, May 5, 1864, he was shot in the knee; doctors did not extract the bullet

the command of Lieutenant Colonel Grigsby, was no larger than a good regiment! The little Dunkard church, situated in the nice grove on the Hagerstown road, had become famous. Around this church some of the fiercest fighting of the war had just taken place. Dead and wounded men lay in sight of it by the thousands.

During the night of September 18 we marched from our position to the Potomac River, which all of Lee's army forded into Virginia. My brigade crossed after sunrise on the morning of the 19th. All our army crossed in safety and without molestation. However, the enemy attempted to follow us on September 20. After a corps had crossed, General Jackson ordered A. P. Hill to attack them and drive them back. Hill attacked with his division and drove them back with great slaughter. He drove them into the Potomac, where most of them were drowned, and very few reached the Maryland shore.[28] This ended the Maryland Campaign.

---

until twenty-three days later. The wound and lack of prompt medical attention permanently disabled Booker. Booker's personal service file, *ibid.*

[28] This engagement took place on the morning of Sept. 20, 1862, at a point and time when the Potomac was respectively 300 yards wide and 3 feet deep. Like Worsham, most contemporary Confederate sources reported a severe and costly Federal defeat. However, only the 118th Pa. contested Hill, and it lost 269 men. See Freeman, *Lee's Lieutenants,* II, 233.

Chapter VI

A LOSS TO THE CONFEDERACY

After leaving Maryland, Jackson's troops marched to the neighborhood of Martinsburg. For several days here the men were busy destroying the Baltimore & Ohio Railroad. We tore up the track for about forty miles. We took up the rails and laid them aside, pulled up and stacked the ties, set them on fire, and then placed the rails on them. When the rails became hot they bent. Whenever there were trees or telegraph poles convenient, we easily twisted the rails, while they were hot in the center, around them.

We stayed several weeks in the lower Valley, mostly in Jefferson County. Every few days we moved our camp—sometimes because of an alarm from the enemy, and sometimes merely to be in a fresh place. General Jackson did not allow his men to camp in one place too long. New camps were more healthy. Consequently, we rarely stayed two weeks in the same place. Because we had by this time learned to live without tents, it was very easy for the men to move. The only shelter the men had were oil or rubber cloths and cotton flies. The latter were of cotton about four by six feet in size and hemmed around the borders. Button holes were worked around these borders and buttons sewed on at certain places. They were so arranged that three of them buttoned together made a very comfortable shelter for three men. We were dependent on the Yankees for them, as I never heard of our quartermaster issuing any.

The men who could not get these made a "shebang" by putting two forked sticks in the ground about six feet apart, laying a pole in the forks, and placing bushes with one end on the ground and the other end inclined to the pole. This enclosed one side and the ends and left the other side open. This would accommodate three or four men. With care the men could make them impervious to rain. They were very comfortable in warm weather. In moving, all that was needed was to roll up our fly or oilcloth to take with us, put our small lot of cooking utensils in the wagons, put on our accouterments, and take arms. Then we were ready for a march to another camp, or to meet the enemy.

While we were in one of these camps, a soldier one evening at regimental dress parade was conducted under guard along the front of the regiment. Attached to him was a large placard on which "Thief" was written, and two soldiers marched behind him with guns at charge bayonet. This was the first and only man I saw punished in that way during the war. We punished some by making them ride a wooden horse, by standing on a stump, or by putting over them a barrel on which was an inscription showing what they were guilty of.

On November 21 we took up our march to join General Lee at Fredericksburg, for it had been reported that he thought he would soon need us. We marched up the Valley pike to New Market, left the pike and crossed the Massanutton Mountain, then crossed the Blue Ridge Mountains at Fisher's Gap. My brigade was in front as we crossed the Blue Ridge, and we enjoyed one of the most inspiring views I saw during the war. It is said that the road leading over the mountain at this gap is six miles long from the Valley to the top, and seven miles from the top to the foot in Madison County. Near the top, in our line of march, was a large rock on the side of the road. Stepping on this rock and looking back and down the road, we could see six lines of our army—in one place infantry, in another artillery, in another ambulances and wagons. Some seemed to be coming toward us, some going to the right, some to the left, and some going away from us. However, they were all climbing the winding mountain road and following us.

We passed through Madison Court House, Orange Court House, the Wilderness, Chancellorsville (which became famous and full of grief before we left it!), and on to the neighborhood of Guinea's Station on the Richmond, Fredericksburg and Potomac Railroad. There we went into camp on December 2, having marched from fifteen to twenty-three miles each day since we left Winchester.

Winter had come, and many of the men were shoeless. They could not obtain shoes, and finally orders were issued in Jackson's division that the men should get the hides of cattle we killed daily and make moccasins of them.[1] It became such a serious matter that a list of shoemakers in the division was made, and I was sent to Richmond to get leather, etc., in order to enable these men to make shoes in camp for their comrades.

I went to Richmond and attended to orders. On the morning of December 11, I read a telegram that the enemy, now under Major General Ambrose E. Burnside, was crossing the Rappahannock River at Fredericksburg. I at once went to the Provost Marshal's office to get a pass to leave the city by the first train. No one could leave without this

---

[1] William H. Morgan of the 11th Va. also mentioned this incident in his *Personal Reminiscences of the War of 1861-5* (Lynchburg, Va., 1911), p. 144.

permission. Yet I was told that I must report to a Sergeant Crow,[2] who would carry me under guard and turn me over to my proper command. I did not intend to submit to this indignity, and I so informed the officer. I explained to him why I had been sent to Richmond, and I showed him my papers. I did not ask for transportation, as I was willing to pay my own railroad fare. I only wanted the necessary permission to leave the city in order to join my command and take my post in the expected battle. Yet the only answer I received was: "You must report to Sergeant Crow."

I left and went back three times during the day with the hope that I would find another man in command who would be more civil and accommodating. But I had no success. The next morning I went again very early. When one of the men there threatened to take me into custody, I left very quickly. I returned about an hour later, and an old comrade, who had witnessed the way in which I was treated the day before, quietly slipped a pass into my hand. This comrade was an old member of our regiment who had lost a leg in battle and was at this time employed in the provost office. This is mentioned to show how far red tape went.

Going at once to the depot, I boarded a train that was pulling out and reached Guinea's Station about 1 or 2 a.m. on December 12. Making inquiries, I learned that Jackson's corps had gone to the front. After tiresome walking, I found his command at Hamilton's Crossing, awaiting orders to take its place in line of battle. On the morning of December 13, Jackson's division was assigned to Jackson's second line of battle and was lying down on the ground awaiting the movements of the enemy. General Jackson soon made his appearance along the line with a cavalcade of officers following him. He was dressed in a brand-new uniform, with the usual gold lace trimmings for a lieutenant general. He even had exchanged the old gray cap for a new bespangled one. He looked so unlike our "Old Jack" that very few noticed him and none recognized him until after he had passed. Then the old accustomed cheer to him went up with unusual vigor!

About 10 o'clock in the morning the fog lifted, and the cannonading from the enemy commenced. It was awfully terrific, as, it is said,

---

[2] A careful search of personal service files in the National Archives failed to reveal anyone serving as sergeant by the name of "Crow," "Crowe," "Croe," or "Crough" in the Provost Marshal's office. However, John B. Jones, in his *A Rebel War Clerk's Diary at the Confederate States Capital* (Philadelphia, 1866), I, 124, made contemptuous mention of a "Sgt. Crow" from Maryland in the Provost Marshal's headquarters. Since extant records of Maryland Confederate soldiers give no clue as to the identity of this man, it is reasonable to assume that he was a civilian.

they had 250 or 300 guns sending shot and shell at us![3] Soon afterward
the Yankees in our front made their advance. We were in the woods
on a slight hill that overlooked an immense open field. The number of
the enemy visible to us gave the impression that the whole of the
Yankee army was in our front! A battery to our right and front was
pouring shot and shell into them as they advanced. We learned after
the fight that it was John Pelham's! What a grand and heroic stand
he maintained during the battle![4]

Jackson's artillery was posted along our front, but it did not fire
a shot at the advancing lines until they got within easy range. All of
it opened at once and sent its hail of iron into the dense masses. They
staggered, stopped, then retreated to a road where they were protected
by its banks and fences. An hour or so afterward they made another
advance, this time with so much determination that they broke the first
of our lines and commenced the advance more vigorously. Our second
line was then ordered forward, and charged! After some stubborn
fighting at several points, they were driven back along their entire line
with great loss.[5] They continued their retreat to the road and river
bank. Their skirmishers and batteries kept up a fire during the whole
day.

A splendid line of breastworks had been made around Marye's
Hill and extended along the line of Generals Longstreet and D. H.
Hill. They did not extend as far east as the position occupied by
Jackson during the December 13 battle of Fredericksburg. The fight
in Jackson's front was a regular stand-up one. The only protection we
had was such as the woods afforded. As evening advanced, Jackson
arranged his lines; the Second Brigade moved up and occupied the
railroad in the first line of battle. Here we awaited the expected
advance of the enemy, and only wished they would come. During the
14th skirmish fire and fire from their far guns was kept up at intervals.
The next day the enemy asked permission to look after their wounded
who were in the field in Jackson's front. This was granted, and the
pickets and sharpshooters of each army ceased firing, entered into
friendly converse, and traded tobacco, coffee, and sugar. Night

---

[3] At Burnside's disposal in this battle were 325 guns. Involved in the artillery action
described by Worsham were 22 batteries with a total of 116 guns. A reserve group of
42 guns was also in that sector. L. Van Loan Naisawald, *Grape and Canister: The Story
of the Field Artillery of the Army of the Potomac* (New York, 1960), pp. 236-37, 246.

[4] For additional praise of the twenty-four-year-old artilleryman's action at Fredericksburg, see *OR,* XXI, 547, 553, 631, 638, 645.

[5] In this assault the first wave of Federals were the Pennsylvanians of Gen. George
G. Meade's brigade. Reinforcing them in the second charge was Gen. John Gibbon's
brigade of New Yorkers and Pennsylvanians.

approached and put a stop to this, and each man took his place in line, ready to shoot the man in his front on sight! The next morning we learned that the enemy had taken advantage of the night and had crossed the Rappahannock. The fight on the left of Lee's line, at Marye's Hill, had been terrific, and the enemy had been slaughtered by thousands. The loss in Jackson's corps was not large.[6] Brigadier General Maxcy Gregg was among the killed.[7] There were a larger number of cannon used in this battle than in any previous battle, for the situation was such as to give them fine positions.

On December 17 Jackson's corps left the battlefield of Fredericksburg and marched down the Rappahannock River to get a better location for protection against the weather and the observation of the enemy. About this time the 1st Virginia, or Irish, Battalion was detached from our brigade and made provost guard for the Army of Northern Virginia. The 44th and 50th Virginia were added to our brigade. About January 1, 1863, Major General Isaac R. Trimble was assigned to the command of Jackson's division.[8] He remained with us until about March 1, when he was ordered to another command. About this time Brigadier General J. R. Jones left the Second Brigade.

Jackson's division went into camp and made winter quarters at Moss Neck. Huts were made of any material that could be gotten, and in any way the architect of the party thought best. The greater number were of logs. A few men had tents. The men soon made themselves very comfortable. A large picket was required along the river, which was several miles from our camp. A brigade was usually sent and stayed there several days. The picket guard was sent to the front from the brigade by companies and, as each company arrived at its destination, it was divided into squads. These squads stationed themselves near the picket post, erected a shelter of cloth, brush, etc., built a fire

---

[6] The 21st Va. had four men wounded in the battle. Gen. John R. Jones, commanding the Second Brigade, concluded his official report of the campaign thus: "I can only say that the gallant little brigade, which has fought so gallantly and lost so heavily in the great battles of the past summer and fall, was ready to do its duty, and bear its part in making the shortest and most direct route to Richmond a hard road to travel." OR, XXI, 562, 685.

[7] Maxcy Gregg (1814-1862) was a South Carolina officer known for courtesy and courage. During the fighting at Fredericksburg, a young officer shouted that Federals were firing at him. "Yes, sir, thank you," Gregg replied softly, "they have been doing so all day." A few moments later, a bullet pierced his side and arched into his spine. He died that night. Freeman, Lee's Lieutenants, II, 374-75.

[8] Trimble (1802-1888), a former railroad developer, was promoted to major general and given command of Jackson's division on Jan. 19, 1863. A recurring attack of osteomyelitis forced his transfer in March. Seriously wounded the previous summer at Second Manassas, he lost a leg at Gettysburg and was a prisoner of war thereafter. Of him Kyd Douglas wrote admiringly: "There was fight enough in old man Trimble to satisfy a herd of tigers." OR, XXI, 1099; XXV, pt. 2, 801-02; Douglas, Stonewall, p. 212.

in front of the shelter, and tried to be comfortable while not on duty as sentinels on the picket line. But in snow and cold rains, the weather tried men's souls! While they were on this outpost picket duty, a soldier's nerves too were tried! Far to the front he stood on his lonely beat, only occasionally moving because he feared he might attract the attention of the enemy's sentinel on similar duty, who might shoot him from a distance, or else creep up later and shoot him! Or a party of the enemy might steal up on him and take him prisoner! Knowledge of this created an uneasy feeling that could not be gotten rid of, and the man on outpost guard was uneasy until he was again in camp with his comrades.

Occasionally some of the men went down to the river's edge and had a talk with the Yanks on the other side. Sometimes a little boat was made of bark or a piece of rail. With the assistance of the wind and tide, it now and then crossed to the other shore. In this manner papers and tobacco were exchanged.[9]

After getting back to camp, the brigade had its daily drills, camp guard duty, inspections, etc. The daily roll calls and cooking left very little idle time for the Confederate soldier. Notwithstanding this, one could always hear someone singing, laughing, whistling, or in some way indicating that the camp was not dead. We indulged in games of all kinds: ball, marbles, drafts, chess, cards, etc. When the snow was on the ground, we had great fun snowballing. Several times I have seen more than 2,500 men engaged in a game of snowball!

No one who has not had the experience knows what a soldier undergoes on a march. We start off on a march some beautiful morning in spring. At midday slight clouds are seen floating about; these thicken with the appearance of a heavy storm soon to come. The instinct of home comes over us and, instead of the merry chatter of the morning, stillness pervades the ranks. Each man is thinking of home and some place to shelter himself from the storm. The command "Close up!" awakens him from his reverie, and he is made to think of his place in ranks. A flash of lightning and a loud peal of thunder cause him to realize his position all the more. Now the rain commences and soon pours down. Poor fellow! He pulls down his hat, buttons up his jacket, pulls up his collar, and tries to protect his gun. In a short while he feels the water running down his arms and legs; but he is

_____

[9] During this same period, a Federal picket yelled to his foes: "You Rebels are mighty ragged and dirty, but you fight well." With a pleasant air the Confederate shouted back: "By next winter we will be naked, and then we will give you thunder!" Worsham to his mother, Dec. 30, 1862, Worsham Papers. For another account of this fraternization, see Wayland F. Dunaway, *Reminiscences of a Rebel* (New York, 1913), pp. 59-60.

defiant yet, and the same good old Confederate! Now the water is slowly feeling its way down his back. As it gradually covers him, the courage goes out; and when his back gets *completely* wet, he for a few minutes forgets that he is a Confederate soldier! The thought only lasts a few minutes; yet the storm within him breaks loose, resulting in his cursing the Confederacy, the generals, everything in the army, and even himself! Then, with a new inspiration, he commences on the Yankees, is himself carried away, and is once more the good old Confederate soldier, marching along at a brisk rate in the pelting rain. He is all right now; conversation commences; and when he reaches camp, he builds his fire and has something to eat. When he lies down to rest, it makes very little difference whether it is raining or not!

We went through equal trials in very *dusty* marches—when our eyes, noses, mouths, ears, and, in fact, our whole person became soiled with dirt, and dust found its way all over one. Besides, we had muddy days to march in! We would soon get our shoes full and our pants wet to the knees. Some comrade, stepping into a mud hole, would throw it all over someone! Ask Tom Ellett[10] what he thinks of marching in the mud, and be sure to do so when he is in a good humor! Then think of the marches in hot weather, when we became so hot and tired that we could hardly put one foot before the other. But on we went, the command "Close up!" being always in our ears! In winter, too—amid sleet and snow, and sometimes when it was so cold that with an overcoat on we could not keep warm—when ordered to fall in, a soldier takes his place in ranks, ready to face whatever may come. Indeed, any season makes no difference to a soldier.

At the commencement of the war, we were usually given the route step soon after starting on a march. On passing a village or town we were called to attention and marched through with military precision. Yet toward the close of the war we generally kept the route step throughout the march, for all had learned that the men got along so much better and could march much farther by being allowed to take their natural step and to carry their guns as they chose.

One thing the government managed well, and that was the mail for the soldiers.[11] In my brigade we had a man who was the mail

---

[10] Thomas Ellet was one of the original members of F Company. In 1862 he transferred to the artillery; two years later, he was a captain in command of Crenshaw's Battery. Ellet's personal file, War Records Group 109, National Archives.

[11] Confederate mail service was undependable in the war's first days, and it grew worse as the struggle progressed. See Wiley, *The Life of Johnny Reb,* pp. 200-01. During the war Worsham himself made strongly critical remarks about mail delivery. See his letters to his mother, Mar. 25, 1862, and to his sister, July 27, 1864, Worsham Papers. In a letter to his father, Mar. 21, 1862, F Company's Tucker Randolph stated: "The mail is very much in disorder." Randolph Papers.

carrier, and the government furnished a horse for this purpose. Letters written by the soldiers were delivered at regimental headquarters. Our carrier would come for them (and also take all that were handed him by the soldiers), and then he would start for the nearest post office at some depot or village. There he delivered the mail. If he found there any mail directed to the men of his command, he brought it to us at once. If there were none, he would go to the next place, and to the next, until he found it, after which he brought it to us. His arrival was a great event in camp. Because he had no regular hour for returning, some of the men were always on the lookout for him both day and night, and heralded his coming. On his arrival, men from each company gathered at regimental headquarters, got their company's mail, took it to the company's quarters and looked it over, and called out the names of the men to whom it was addressed. It made no difference to the hour—whether it was day or 1 or 2 o'clock at night. When a man's name was called for a letter, unless on duty he was generally on hand to get it in person.

It was interesting to watch those fellows as they gathered for their mail. Those who received letters went off with radiant countenances. If it was night, each built a fire for light and, sitting down on the ground, read his letter over and over. Those unfortunates who got none went off looking as if they had not a friend on earth!

In the beginning of the war, postage was not required to be prepaid on a letter from soldiers in the field. The postage was collected on the delivery of the mail. In directing a letter to soldiers, it was necessary to write name, company, regiment, brigade, division, and command. This was the rule in Jackson's command, and I suppose in the army generally. There was no post office or location mentioned, because we moved about so much our post office was continually changing. Notwithstanding this roundabout way for letters to travel, I never heard of one being lost either going to or from the army.

Sometimes, for two or three weeks regularly, we would receive mail daily. Then it would be several days, sometimes a week, before another came. But the letters always turned up. If the carrier overtook us while we were on a march, the mail was distributed and collected. I have seen it delivered in this way just before a battle.

It is surprising how the Confederacy got along with such a small variety of medicines, which consisted in the field almost entirely of blue powders,[12] one kind of pills, and quinine. Go back with me to the

---

[12] Blue powders (or "blue mass") was a popular medication administered to soldiers suffering from intestinal disorders. For the reaction of Confederate soldiers to the primitive medical practices of that day, see Wiley, *The Life of Johnny Reb*, pp. 244-69.

"sick call" or "doctor's call" one morning. Reaching the surgeon's quarters, the sick were lined up. The surgeon and his hospital steward passed along the line. The first man accosted was asked, "What is the matter with you?"

The answer is something like this: "I don't know, Doctor, but I have a terrible misery here." He designates the locality by placing his hands on his stomach.

"Put out your tongue," says the doctor. After an examination the doctor says to Ira Blunt, the hospital steward of my regiment, "Give him a blue powder."

The next is examined in about the same manner, and Blunt is instructed to give him two pills. The next is given ten grains of quinine. Then the treatment is varied by giving the next one pill and five grains of quinine, and to the next a blue powder and quinine. The treatment varied as the supply of pills, blue powder, and quinine held out. Occasionally some favored one was given a gill of whiskey. Nearly every man thereafter developed the same symptoms!

Probably one of the men had an aching tooth. The doctor would tell him to take a seat on some nearby log, that he would make an examination presently. The poor fellow seats himself and waits his turn. The doctor soon comes to him, looks his mouth over, and says, "It must come out."

He goes to his tent and gets a pair of forceps. On his return he straddles the log, inserts the instrument in the man's mouth, takes hold of a tooth and, by main strength and after a lengthy struggle, succeeds in pulling the wrong and an excellent tooth! But he cures the ache.

This was about the daily medical routine in camp, and it was surprising how many cures were effected with this limited supply of medicines. Surgeon Robert Coleman[13] and Hospital Steward Blunt of my regiment were always kind and considerate to the sick, and they did all in their power for them. I will mention the treatment used on the first man of my company whom I saw after he was wounded. The surgeon gave the nurse a bottle of whiskey and instructions to put a spoonful in the water each time he dressed the wound.

By January, 1863, old F Company of Richmond had become so small that three or four men in it were ordered to Camp Lee in Richmond to recruit new members. They enlisted a few men as soon as they reached the camp, and commenced squad drill. Subsequently, as soon as they had enlisted enough to call it a company, they commenced com-

---

[13] Robert T. Coleman, a native of Richmond, served as regimental surgeon of the 21st Va. through most of the war. Two assistant surgeons generally served under him.

pany drill. They entered upon camp guard, policing, and other duties at once. The old members of the company did all in their power to make efficient soldiers of the recruits, who were conscripts of boyhood and middle age, as well as some old substitutes. On June 21 we received orders to get ready to leave Camp Lee the next day and rejoin our regiment in Lee's army. All the old members were allowed to go into the city to bid family and friends goodbye—to take a last look at some bright eyes. It somehow took longer to bid that pair of eyes farewell than it did to take leave of a whole family. This consumed the larger part of the day; the remainder we diligently devoted to preparations for moving promptly the next morning. As night came on, each man, instead of going to bed, stole off quietly to the city to look once again into those eyes to which he had already bidden farewell. He returned in time to get a short nap before day. After breakfast we marched from Camp Lee to the Virginia Central depot, where we took the cars for Staunton.

The following are the names of the members of F. Company who left for Staunton on June 22, 1863:

Captain William A. Pegram
Second Lieutenant Reuben J. Jordan
Jr. Second Lieutenant Malcolm L. Hudgins
First Sergeant William S. Archer
Second Sergeant John H. Worsham
Third Sergeant J. Porter Wren
Fourth Sergeant Thomas B. Walker
First Corporal E. Gouldman
Second Corporal W. C. Tiney
Third Corporal George J. Floyd
Fourth Corporal Henry F. Munt

Anderson, Joseph H.	Cumbia, W. S.
Barber, Nathaniel	Dillard, R. H.
Bates, W.	Divers, W. H.
Bowe, H. C.	Dowdy, Nathaniel A.
Brown, A. D.	Fox, Henry C.
Brown, A. H.	Gentry, M. G.
Brown, George W.	Griffin, J.
Brown, Henry	Hawkins, L. A.
Brown, James R.	Houston, George W.
Callis, G.	Johnston, J. W.
Coleman, Nicholas	Kayton, P. W.
Couch, J. M.	Kidd, J. A.

Mason, J. M.

Merriman, J. T.

Nance, J. L.

Richeson, P. S.

Richeson, William R.

Rutledge, William

Searles, Samuel

Seay, Morton

Simpson, F. J.

Smith, J. T.

Smith, Thomas

Soles, Peter D.

Trainum, Charles

Tyree, William C.

Wallace, R. H.

Wilkins, J. M.

Wood, S. E.

We were joined afterward by a few of the old members and the following new ones:

Bates, Edward

Legg, A. C.

Seay, W. C.

Smith, Henry

In exchange for R. H. Wallace, W. E. Cumbie was transferred to our company from the 24th Virginia Battalion.

During the summer of 1862, Colonel John M. Patton of the 21st Virginia had been transferred to Major General Anderson's division of Longstreet's corps. Lieutenant Colonel Cunningham had been killed. During the fall Major John B. Moseley left the regiment. This left the 21st Virginia without a field officer. While the regiment was in camp at Moss Neck, the following appointments were made:

William A. Witcher, Colonel

William R. Berkeley, Lieutenant Colonel[14]

William P. Moseley, Major[15]

Lieutenant Colonel Berkeley remained with the regiment only a short time, after which William P. Moseley became lieutenant colonel and A. D. Kelley[16] became major. Those three officers remained with the regiment until the surrender of Lee's army.

---

[14] A lawyer by trade, William Berkeley was twenty-two when he enlisted May 28, 1861, at Meherrin in Co. B of the 21st Va. Appointed captain of the company at its muster, he received promotion to major in Apr., 1863. He resigned from service when W. A. Witcher was promoted over him. Berkeley's personal service file, War Records Group 109, National Archives; Page Mann to Worsham, July 15, 1893, Worsham Papers.

[15] At his June 19, 1861, enlistment in Co. E, 21st Va., Moseley was eighteen, stood 5'7½" tall, and had light hair and blue eyes. Elected lieutenant of his company a month after enlistment, the Buckingham County native moved up to captain in Apr., 1862. He subsequently received wounds in the left hip at Cold Harbor and in the left shoulder at Winchester. Moseley's personal service file, War Records Group 109, National Archives; Worsham to his mother, Sept. 25, 1863, Worsham Papers.

[16] Alfred Kelley enlisted July 2, 1861, as a lieutenant in Co. G, 21st Va. He was elected captain of the company in Apr., 1862. Wounded at Cedar Run, he continued with the regiment until his resignation from service, Mar. 7, 1865. Kelley's personal service file, War Records Group 109, National Archives.

The battle of Chancellorsville was fought May 1-3, 1863.[17] General Jackson's great flank movement against General Joseph Hooker was managed with skill and success. Jackson was wounded, unfortunately by his own men, and died on May 10 in the height of his fame. When this news became known in the Army of Northern Virginia, the men of Jackson's old division were prostrated with grief. Nearly every man in it shed tears.

On hearing of the wounding and then the death of Jackson, General Lee's conduct caused the old division to love him even more. What a loss to the Confederacy! What a loss to the Army of Northern Virginia, and to its commander, Lee, who said he had "lost his right arm." What a loss to his corps. Never more will his sword flash in the enemy's rear, nor will he see his banner floating in one of his fierce attacks on their flank, nor will he hear the wild cheers of his men as they drive everything before them. In my humble opinion, the army never recovered from the loss of Jackson.

There was something about Jackson that always attracted his men. It must have been faith. He was the idol of his old soldiers, and they would follow him anywhere. The very sight of him was the signal for cheers. It made no difference where he was—in camp, on the battle-field, or on a march; when the men were so thoroughly used up that they could hardly put one foot before the other, or when they were lying down resting on the roadside, the sight of Jackson riding by caused each man to jump to his feet, pull off his hat, and cheer him. This was done with but one exception. One evening, while we were marching around Pope to get in his rear at Manassas, we came upon General Jackson and his staff. They were dismounted and, while Jackson's little sorrel lay down nibbling at the grass, the group of officers stood in a field a few yards from the road. As soon as the men recognized "Old Jack," hats came off and the usual cheer broke forth. One of his staff standing near the road said to the troops, "No cheering, men; the enemy will hear you. General Jackson requests that you do not cheer."

This was repeated by the men all down the marching column and, as they passed their beloved commander, they took off their hats —some waving them at the General, others flinging them in the air. Not one cheer was given, but some of the fellows nearly busted from

---

[17] Worsham was not a participant in this battle and therefore failed to mention that the 21st Va. lost 4 killed, 40 wounded, and its flag. *OR*, XXV, pt. 1, 478, 809.

keeping it back. It was here that General Jackson said, "With such soldiers, who could keep from winning battles?"[18]

What shall I say of Jackson's wonderful marches? His men have long since been known as "Jackson's Foot Cavalry" because of his long and rapid marches. We have often marched daily for a week—on some occasions for three weeks—and twenty-five miles on many days. I do not think my brigade ever marched over thirty miles without stopping for a rest of several hours. Yet some of the regiments of the old division have marched over forty miles, only stopping occasionally for ten minutes' rest. We have often marched and fought all day and, in case of a pursuit of the enemy, kept up the march all night and a part of the next day.

It was in battle that the men showed their great love for, and confidence in, General Jackson. His old soldiers had implicit confidence in him. How many times his old command wished him back to lead one of his furious attacks on the enemy. The South produced many generals of great ability; but for brilliancy and dash, the world never saw Stonewall Jackson's equal.

Our company arrived at Staunton on June 22, 1863, and received orders to take charge of about 100 stragglers from Lee's army. They had been collected there so that we could march them to the Army of Northern Virginia and deliver them to the provost guard. We left Staunton on the 24th with stragglers and nothing else: no baggage wagon, no cooking utensils, no rations—"No nothing," as the men expressed it. On account of those stragglers (who gave us a great deal of trouble), we made short marches and generally stopped for the night at barns. As it was necessary to guard our stragglers, the company could do better when they were placed in buildings. Whenever we stopped, we induced someone in the neighborhood to let us have rations. Generally they would also cook them for us. In this manner we reached the Potomac River opposite Williamsport, Maryland, on the morning of July 4, without rations or cooking utensils.

After some of the officers had visited Williamsport and found no rations, a detail was made and sent to a mill not far off to "press" flour, if it could not be gotten otherwise. This detail went to the mill, seized two barrels of flour, secured a wagon for hauling it, and then went to a hog pen in the neighborhood for a hog. The owner told them that bacon could be gotten at a certain store in Williamsport, where they found as much as they wanted. Having no cooking utensils, but with a

---

[18] Maj. R. L. Dabney of Jackson's staff first related this incident in his *Jackson,* p. 517. Worsham's version differs slightly from Dabney's account.

baker in the company, the men decided to bring into service one of the "Dutch ovens" found in nearly all houses in that part of the country. It was now late in the evening. We decided to do the best we could for the night and to use the oven in the morning. A sergeant with a file of men went into town early the next morning, took possession of an excellent oven, and went to work. During the day of July 5, F Company disposed of the stragglers and crossed the Potomac into Williamsport. We marched through the town to the northeast side, stacked arms, and there received the cooked rations.

A Confederate officer soon found us and said that he had orders from General Lee to stop all men here, as the battle of Gettysburg had been fought and General Lee intended to fall back into Virginia by this route.[19] Many of his wagons had already arrived, and others were coming in every moment in large numbers. Because of recent rains the river was too high to be forded; therefore, the wagons were being parked along the river under the bluff near the town. This officer asked our captain to remain with his company, as it was thought that a raiding party of the Yankees might make an attempt to capture or destroy the train. Since there was only one organized regiment at the place,[20] he thought it the duty of our company to stay. During the afternoon and night of July 5, there was much talk of Yankee cavalry coming.

On the morning of July 6, the company formed a line and stacked arms in a field overlooking two roads that ran into Williamsport. While the rest of the men were ordered to stay near their arms, a picket guard under a sergeant went out on the road that the enemy would use. They had orders to allow no one to go outside. Soon after the picket was posted, a young lady and a boy on horseback passed the picket on their way into town. She was a fine looking woman and, as she passed, she gave me a bow and a smile. She stayed in town an hour or two; on her way out, she was stopped by a sentinel. I was called, and the lady stated to me that she was returning home after being in town on business, and that she had no idea we would prevent her return. I told her my orders, but she tried unsuccessfully to induce me to let her pass. I told her I would go with her to see our captain, and that he probably might let her pass. I did this, and the officers consulted and agreed to it.

---

[19] At Gettysburg the other companies of the 21st Va. lost 6 killed, 34 wounded, and 10 missing. *OR*, XXVII, pt. 2, 535. Cf. p. 331.

[20] This was Col. John S. Hoffman's 31st Va. His report of the July 6 engagement is in *ibid.*, 489-90.

Yet a little Georgian,[21] who overheard the conversation, said to Captain Pegram, "You ain't going to let that young woman pass, are you? She is a spy, come in here to find out all she can, and now she is going back to tell the Yankees."

It was then decided not to let her pass. She asked me where the commanding officer was. I told her who he was and where his office was located in town. She asked me to go with her to see the officer. I could not leave my picket post, so I turned the duty over to our handsome orderly sergeant, Willie Archer.[22] She did not get the permission; and from what we heard afterward, it was well she did not.

The day passed quietly. The wheat and hay that had recently been cut was shocked in the fields around the town. Most of it, however, was on the two roads in our front and beyond our picket post. The teamsters were quietly getting it for feed. Some were putting it in wagons, while others placed it on the backs of mules. About 4 or 5 o'clock in the afternoon a pistol shot was heard, and a great commotion was seen amongst the teamsters farthest from us. Soon the field was full of Yankee cavalry, whooping, yelling, and firing pistols.[23] They rode up to the wagons containing hay and wheat, and ordered them to halt. They quietly pulled out matches, fired the provender, and then let them go. Mules were seen flying across the field with a flame of fire leaping from them. This would last only a few seconds before the rider would have it off, and in many instances have himself off too as he tried to remove the burning hay and wheat. Many wagons were burned.

During the day all the broken-down artillery that had been sent along with the wagon train was placed in some prominent place around the town. The guns made a formidable appearance. I have been told that twenty-two pieces were in clear view. Yet some had no ammunition, some had no chests, some had only a few shots, and some were disabled. But they made a show.

---

[21] Pvt. Michael Ward, Co. I, 3rd Ga., was the soldier whose conduct Worsham described throughout his narrative of the battle. Lillian Henderson (comp.), *Roster of the Confederate Soldiers of Georgia, 1861-1865* (Hapeville, Ga., 1951-1961), I, 531.

[22] Only nineteen when the war began, though more than six feet tall, Archer eventually won promotion to lieutenant and command of Sullivan's Virginia Battery.

[23] In an effort to bag Lee's ambulance train, Federal Gen. John Buford, with three brigades of cavalry and a battery of artillery, struck the meager Confederate defenders of Williamsport on July 6. Fighting was critical for the Southerners until "Jeb" Stuart arrived and sent the Federals "in hasty discomfiture" to the rear. "The enemy was too strong for me," Buford reported, "but he was severely punished for his obstinacy. His casualties were more than quadruple mine." Federal losses were 72 men; the Confederates suffered 300 casualties. *OR*, XXVII, pt. 1, 337, 715; pt. 2, 928, 931. See also Garland Quarles *et al.* (eds.), *Diaries, Letters, and Recollections of the War between the States* (Winchester, Va., 1955), pp. 98-99. Hereafter cited as Quarles, *Diaries*.

Out of the woods, into a field in full view of us, the enemy had now brought eight pieces or artillery and a large body of mounted cavalry. They formed a line of battle, while a body of dismounted men with mounted officers busily leveled fences. The dismounted men approached a lot of farm buildings about 400 yards from our company. Our picket post had been called in; our company had loaded guns and formed as skirmishers. Captain Pegram[24] took in the situation at once and acted promptly. He knew we could not hold our position in the open field against these large odds. He remarked to some of the old members of the company that there were only two things for him to do: attack or retreat. Captain Pegram then said he was going to charge the enemy. He gave the order, "Forward! Double quick!" and to the farm buildings we went in a run.

We had fifty-two men present in our company, and nearly all of them were substitutes and conscripts. One of them fainted when he saw the enemy; another got a terrible ache and had to lie down on the ground. We could hear him groaning after firing commenced. This reduced us to fifty. A few stragglers, including the little Georgian of A. R. Wright's brigade, volunteered to go with us. All told, this made about sixty who went into action.

About fifty yards in our front it was necessary to climb over the first fence. There the Yankees opened fire on us. About halfway to the farm buildings we encountered a second fence. A lane ran from the buildings toward the town. A fence ran on each side of it, and at the end of the lane a gate opened into the barnyard. Our advance was oblique to this lane. Soon after we passed the second fence, the left of our line came to the lane fence. I was on the left and went over the fence into the lane. I ordered three or four men to follow me. Among them was the little Georgian, who was wearing a red Zouave cap. We ran up the lane to the gate, which I threw open, and rushed into the barnyard. The little Georgian followed me, and I think old man Callis[25] was next.

In the yard was a mounted officer, cursing and flourishing a pistol. I told the men to shoot him; but he leveled his pistol at us and fired— and the little Georgian, as gallant a fellow as I ever saw, fell dead. I

---

[24] A native of Surry, Pegram had blue eyes and dark hair. He jumped from 3rd Sgt. to captain on May 20, 1863, and appeared to be on his way toward an illustrious military career until his death at the age of twenty-five. Pegram's personal service file, War Records Group 109, National Archives.

[25] Worsham was referring to G. Callis of F Company, an apparently aged and infirm soldier. From Aug., 1863, at least through Dec., 1864, he was hospitalized with a malady diagnosed as "abcess of the leg with great debility." Callis's personal service file, War Records Group 109, National Archives.

cannot say that the officer killed him, for the enemy were firing briskly at us from several points in the yard. My men fired at the officer, who rode off bowed down on his horse. A citizen told me a few days after the battle that this officer was a major and was wounded.[26] I can truly say he was a gallant gentleman.

In the barnyard, on the right side of the lane, was a small house facing away from us. It was occupied by some of the enemy, who were firing at us. As I ran around to the door I met some of my company who by this time had gotten into the yard from the other side. We brought out five Yankee cavalrymen and sent them to the rear.

We had now cleared the yard and buildings of all opponents, but the fight was on in earnest. The enemy had opened with artillery; some were firing at us, others at our guns on the hills. We took up a position along a rail fence beyond the buildings. The fence was about halfway between the two roads mentioned before, and it ran parallel to them. We kept up our fire on any of the enemy we could see within range. Our right had suffered more than our left. Lying dead in the barnyard were Sergeant Thomas B. Walker[27] and Corporal W. C. Tiney.[28] Both were splendid soldiers. We captured, wounded, and killed fifteen of the enemy in the barnyard.

We now found that the enemy were advancing on the road in our rear, and we fell back to that road. We were joined there by a company of about thirty men, mostly stragglers. In order to protect our flank, we placed a few of our company along a cross fence while we kept up a fierce fire in front. Soon Captain Pegram was killed, another one of old F Company to join Jackson "under the shade of the trees." The Yankees were shelling us very heavily. Their dismounted men, now largely increased, had possession of the fence we had relinquished and were firing heavily at us. A regiment of our men,[29] that had been at the river with our train, now made its appearance and drove the Yanks from the fence. A large body of armed wagoners lengthened

---

[26] If the citizen's story was correct, the mounted officer was Maj. William H. Medill of the 8th Ill. Cavalry, who was mortally wounded in the fighting. *OR*, XXVII, pt. 2, 194, 935. See also *Report of the Adjutant General of the State of Illinois* (Springfield, 1867), III, 76.

[27] Walker had been in the army only five months at the time of his death. He was a native of Franklin County.

[28] Prince George County's W. C. Tiney, who enlisted Feb. 16, 1863, had barely seen four months of military service.

[29] This was the 54th N. C. and a large contingent of stragglers. In command of the regiment was Col. Kenneth M. Murchison, whose report is in *OR*, XXVII, pt. 2, 488. See also Walter Clark (ed.), *Histories of the Several Regiments and Battalions from North Carolina in the Great War, 1861-65* (Raleigh and Goldsboro, N. C., 1901), III, 270-71. Hereafter cited as Clark, *N. C. Regiments.*

our left, and enabled our company to move farther to the right. We kept up our fire until night, when the enemy disappeared.

This I consider the best fight of F Company during the war. With only six or eight of the old company and nearly all new men, we attacked, drove the enemy, and held our position against tremendous odds. General John Buford, who made the attack, had present 12 regiments of cavalry and 12 pieces of artillery.[30] When he made his appearance in front of our company, no armed body of men except our small company stood between him and General Lee's entire wagon train. We fought nearly half an hour before a company of thirty men came to our assistance, and we fought an hour before a regiment reinforced us. I repeat that it was the best fight the company ever made; and, in its results, it was one of the best battles of the war. The new men, except those two noted, behaved like veterans. Everyone did his duty, and they covered themselves with glory.

As before stated, our loss was four killed, including the Georgian. One of the substitutes became frightened when the enemy opened their artillery and ran toward the wagons. As he approached a fence, one of the enemy's shells burst in front of him and tore the fence to pieces. This so "conflumuxed" the man that he ran back to us, saying, "No whar is safe!" He stayed with us during the remainder of the fight. With the loss of a piece of skin knocked from his shin, he was the only one wounded.

In the death of Captain William A. Pegram, we suffered a great loss. Young, unassuming, but a true soldier, he was noted for his gallantry on many a battlefield. The next day we buried him and the three other men in the cemetery at Williamsport—a city they had given their lives to win. In the afternoon we marched to Hagerstown. We slept that night on the brick pavement at the market house. Early the next morning, July 8, 1863, we resumed our march and joined our regiment in their bivouac two miles from Hagerstown.

During the absence of F Company from the army, several changes had been made in officers. Lieutenant General Richard S. Ewell now commanded the Second Corps; Major General Edward Johnson was commander of Jackson's Division; and Brigadier General J. M. Jones commanded the Second Brigade. The battles of Chancellorsville, Winchester, and Gettysburg had been fought. On reuniting with our regiment, we learned of these battles, and we told them of Williamsport.

When General Lee arrived in the neighborhood of Williamsport and found that his army could not cross the Potomac on account of a

---

[30] Buford actually had ten full regiments and segments of three others, plus two batteries of artillery. *OR*, XXVII, pt. 1, 166.

rise in the river, he promptly turned his army back and formed a line of battle near Hagerstown. Here he awaited an attack from General George G. Meade, who marched his army up in front of Lee's and began to fortify. We followed his example. General Lee had thrown a pontoon bridge across the Potomac at Falling Waters, about four or five miles below Williamsport. This had been partially destroyed after Gettysburg by an enemy raiding party from Harper's Ferry. While we were in line at Hagerstown, General Lee had the bridge repaired, and the wagons passed over it. In the meantime, the river had fallen enough for the men to ford it. On the night of July 13 General Ewell withdrew his corps from the line. We marched all night and reached the Potomac a short distance above Williamsport about daybreak. We at once marched across the river. The water came up to our breasts. It was necessary that a comrade and I help little W. Bates; yet every time we stumbled on some of the large rocks at the bottom of the stream, his head went under the water. The remainder of our army crossed at the same time on the pontoon bridge.

At this time our army was in a sad plight as to clothing. Hundreds had no shoes. Thousands were as ragged as they could be—some with the bottoms of their pants in long frazzles; others with their knees out, others out at the elbows, and their hair sticking through holes in their hats. Some of the men patched their clothing, and it was usually done with any material they could get. One man had the seat of his pants patched with bright red, and his knees patched with black. Another had used a piece of gray or brown blanket. There were, however, so few patches and so many holes that, when a Pennsylvania girl on the side of the road saw us pass and asked her mother how the officers were distinguished from the privates, the mother replied that it was easy enough: the officers' pants were patched, and the privates' pants were not.

Chapter VII

CAMP LIFE

By July 14, the Army of Northern Virginia had returned to Virginia from the Pennsylvania campaign. General Lee crossed the Blue Ridge Mountains into Orange County with all of his troops except Ewell's corps, which was left in the Valley to destroy the Baltimore & Ohio Railroad. On July 20 Ewell's corps took up the march to join General Lee. We marched through Winchester to Manassas Gap, where we learned that the enemy had advanced into the Gap from the other side of the Blue Ridge and were trying to effect an entrance into the Luray Valley. We had some heavy skirmishing with them that lasted until late in the night, when they withdrew. In the morning we marched up the Luray Valley to Thornton's Gap, where we crossed the mountain and marched to Orange County. On August 1 we joined General Lee and went into camp at Montpelier, the old home of President James Madison. This last day's march was the hottest I ever experienced. More than half the men, overcome by the heat, fell out of ranks on the march. Every tree we came to along the roadside had a squad of men, officers as well as men, under its shade.

While in this camp, that splendid regiment, the 25th Virginia,[1] was added to our brigade. We remained in camp at Montpelier until August 14, when we marched to Liberty Mills to meet some movement of the enemy. We remained there until the 16th, at which time we returned to Montpelier. One evening while we were at Liberty Mills, it was reported that a small body of Yankees was at the Madison County Poor House. A detail of men and an officer were sent there to capture them. I was one of the party. We started as soon as we could get ready, which was a little after sunset. Soon after we left camp, a severe thunderstorm arose. I do not know that I ever saw one more severe. It rained in torrents, the thunder roared, the lightning flashed and, in the midst of it all, we trudged along an unknown road without

---

[1] The 25th Va., under Col. J. A. Robinson (its regular commander, Col. John C. Higginbotham having been wounded at Gettysburg), gained a measure of fame by checking a Federal probe of Lee's lines on July 12, 1863. This accounts in part for Worsham's praise of the depleted unit, which sustained forty casualties at Gettysburg. *OR*, XXVII, pt. 2, 331, 536.

a guide. No one in the party had ever been over the road before. At times it was so dark that we could not see our hands before us. We halted several times to let a passing cloud empty itself on us, or to let the sky clear so that we might see how to march. The dogs along the road proved to be great friends that night, since it was so dark that we could not see the houses. When we heard a dog bark, someone would go toward him and thus find the house, awake the inmates, and get directions for our march.

By this time the little branches and creeks running across the road had become small rivers, and the water of some came up to our waists as we forded. Just before reaching the poor house village, the moon came out, and we entered the village about midnight. No lights were visible and not a soul was stirring. However, we surrounded the largest and best-looking house and knocked at the door. After some delay an old man who had on the veritable nightcap poked his head out of an upper window and informed us that a squad of Yankee cavalry had been there that afternoon and had left about sunset. We then marched to the church, which was open, went in and, after posting a sentinel, lay down on the benches in our wet clothes. Thoroughly broken down, we slept the rest of the night.

On our return the next morning, one of the streams we crossed the night before had risen so high that we could not recross it. While we were waiting, an old gentleman in the neighborhood gave us a breakfast which was so good that it paid us for our trip. This night-time march was as trying an experience as I had during the war. We reached camp about 10 o'clock in the morning, having marched about twenty-four miles.

Soon after we returned to Montpelier, a detail of men was assigned to make soap. These men gathered the ashes from our fires, put them into several barrels, and commenced making lye. They also gathered the offal from the slaughter pens and, with the use of several old-fashioned dinner pots (in which the soap was made), they soon had some excellent and pure soap. This was issued at once, and the men of our brigade soon presented a very clean appearance. All the work of these men was done out of doors. They were so successful in their work that, when we left camp, we carried a large quantity of soap with us.

This was a very busy week for us. First, our regiment, the 21st Virginia Infantry, was presented with a battle flag; the next day we had brigade inspection; the next day, a brigade review; and the next day, a division review. Quite a charming story is connected with our flag. At the battle of Chancellorsville our colorbearer was shot down. One of the color guard caught the flag and waved it aloft. In a few minutes he was shot and taken to the rear, where his left arm was amputated above the elbow. When he recovered, he reported to this camp for duty, saying he could carry the flag with one arm as well as before. General Johnson, our division commander, on hearing this determined to present the flag in person to our one-armed colorbearer. It was received at division headquarters, and Friday, August 20, was the day announced for the presentation. On that day the Second Brigade was drawn up in line. In the presence of many spectators, including a number of ladies, General Johnson, in patriotic and thrilling words, presented to our regiment its first battle flag. The occasion was very impressive and enthusiastic. Our flag had the following battles inscribed on it: Kernstown, McDowell, Winchester, Second Manassas, Harper's Ferry, Sharpsburg, Fredericksburg, Chancellorsville, and Gettysburg. Through an oversight these were omitted: Gaines' Mill, Malvern Hill, and Cedar Run. This flag was carried with distinction in all of our battles to the end.

On September 3 we received orders to clean our arms and accouterments, to cook one day's rations, and to be ready to march early the next morning, when a grand review of the Second Corps would take place. This created a great stir in our regiment, since we had never been to a review on such a grand scale and we all wanted to participate in it. We were up betimes on the morning of the 4th, soon had our breakfast, and then were ordered to fall in. We marched through Orange Court House to a large field about one mile east of that village, arriving there at about 10 a.m. About midway in this field our division formed a line facing east, stacked arms and rested. Early's and Rodes's divisions soon joined us, the former taking position about 200 yards in our front, and the latter about the same distance in our rear. This made three lines, each about half a mile long.

About a quarter of a mile in our front was the reviewing stand, where the corps headquarters flag was waving. The officers and visitors who were to witness the review arrived and took their positions near that flag. Many ladies were present on horseback and in carriages. Among these were two of General Lee's daughters, who received much attention from everyone.[2] The scene was very gay and brilliant around the flag.

[2] The two ladies with Lee were not his daughters; rather, they were Misses Margaret and Carrie Stuart, two cousins of whom Lee was very fond. See Clifford Dowdey and Louis Manarin (eds.), *The Wartime Papers of R. E. Lee* (Boston, 1961), p. 598. In his original narrative, Worsham erroneously had the review occurring on Sept. 4 rather than Sept. 9.

We were to be reviewed by General Lee in person. About noon he made his appearance, mounted on Traveler. He joined the throng around the flag and seemed to enjoy himself highly with the visitors. Soon the bugle sounded and announced that all was ready. General Lee, accompanied by his staff, rode to the front; then came General Ewell and his staff, followed by the generals of the several divisions and their staffs in their respective order of rank. General Lee rode to the right of the front division, which had taken its place. With bands playing and drums beating, the General dashed along the line, followed by the large cavalcade of generals and their staffs. The men presented arms, flags were lowered, the officers saluted with their swords, and all the pomp of war that could be shown by these old Confederates was brought into view. Reaching the left of the line, the generals wheeled to the left and passed in the rear of the same line until they reached its end. Then they wheeled to the right, went to the second line, and reviewed them in the same manner as the first. Then they went to the third line, after which they went back to the flag and took their respective positions near it.

The three lines now marched forward several hundred yards while the bands played. Then we left-wheeled into column of regiments, the regiment at the head guiding us to a line with the flag, where the corps marched past the stand in column of regiments. As each regiment arrived in front of General Lee, the men came to shoulder arms, the flags dipped, the officers saluted, and the bands played. General Lee raised his hat in recognition; the ladies waved their handkerchiefs and clapped their hands and cheered us. We answered with a Confederate yell. After passing some distance beyond the reviewing stand, the regiments filed to the right, again formed a line, and waited until the review ended. We then took up our march for camp, which we reached about 9 or 10 o'clock at night.

This was said to be the grandest review of our troops during the war. The movements of the men were excellent, and our marching was splendid. Jackson's old division, commanded by General Johnson, attracted special attention, and the one-armed colorbearer of the 21st Virginia was loudly cheered by all the officers and visitors as he passed the reviewing stand.

It was at Montpelier that the great religious revival commenced which spread so rapidly through the entire army.[3] The converts were so

---

[3] That winter the Confederates built more than forty chapels along the Rapidan River. For references to the revival in Lee's army during the fall of 1863, see J. William Jones, *Christ in the Camp, or Religion in the Confederate Army* (Atlanta, 1904), pp. 245-55, 260-63, 318-52.

numerous that they were numbered not by tens and hundreds but by thousands. In our camp the place selected for preaching was on a hillside in a large wood. A road ran on one side of the place, a small branch on the other. The ground was slightly inclined. Trees were cut from the adjoining woods, rolled to this spot, and arranged for seating at least 2,000 people. At the lower end a platform was raised with logs, rough boards were placed on them, and a bench was made at the far side for the seating of the preachers. In front was a pulpit, or desk, made from a box. Around this platform and around the seats, stakes were driven into the ground about ten or fifteen feet apart. On top of them were placed baskets of iron wire, iron hoops, etc. Into these baskets were placed chunks of lightwood, and at night they were lighted and threw a red glare far beyond the confines of the place of worship.

The gathering each night of bronzed and grizzly warriors devoutly worshiping was a wonderful picture in the army, and when some old familiar hymn was given out, those thousands of warriors would make hill and dell ring. For several weeks thousands gathered in this crude place of worship. The interest manifested was so great that the seats were taken in the afternoon by such men as were not on duty. When night relieved from duty those who had been drilling, the men stood up in immense numbers around those who were seated. I think I can say that the order was perfect—no disturbance of any kind was ever known to occur—and the attention to the words of the preacher was never more faithful.

In this camp we enjoyed the longest rest of the war, and it was much needed. After the review we were disturbed only by regular drills and the usual camp duties. The men enjoyed this rest more than any we ever had. The camp was located in one of the healthiest spots to be found. In full view of the Blue Ridge Mountains and Monticello, it was a beautiful place; also, it was on a magnificent farm.

Our rest ended on September 16, when we commenced a series of marches and movements which culminated in General Lee crossing the Rapidan River and offering battle to the enemy. They, however, preferred to retire. We followed as far as Bristoe Station, where their rear guard was overtaken and promptly attacked by a part of A. P. Hill's division, which suffered some loss.[4] When our division arrived on the field, the Second Brigade was formed in line of battle near the railroad

---

[4] On Oct. 14, 1863, while attempting to turn the flank of the Federal army, Powell Hill impetuously attacked the V Corps at Bristoe Station. He quickly found himself caught in a vise between the Federal veterans of the V and II Corps. Hill lost over 1,800 men, including 323 of 416 troops in the 27th N. C. OR, XXIX, pt. 1, 433; Clark, N. C. Regiments, II, 443.

and perpendicular to it. Skirmishers were thrown forward, and we were ordered forward through a thin pine thicket for about half a mile. The men were cautioned to keep perfectly quiet, as the enemy was supposed to be in this thicket. We halted and were ordered to lie down in place with guns in hand. Everything so far had been done very quietly; but when an old hare came running to our line, the boys could not restrain themselves. Some sprang to their feet, grabbing at the hare as it went by the line of battle. Yet it was captured by one of the men who was lying down. A wild yell burst from the men, and the silence of that day was broken.

Our skirmishers pushed on to Broad Run, and it was soon reported that General George G. Meade had taken refuge in the fortifications around Centreville. We quietly took up our march and returned to camp. The Second Corps followed the Orange & Alexandria Railroad, destroying the track from the bridge over Broad Run to the Rappahannock River. Part of the Second Corps stayed at the river; Johnson's division crossed the stream and went into camp about three miles from it.

We remained in this camp until the night of November 7, when we marched to Kelly's Ford to meet the enemy who, it was reported, had crossed there. Near the ford, at about 2 or 3 a.m., we halted and sent scouts ahead. They learned that a large body of the enemy had crossed, but had stayed only a short time and then recrossed the stream. One of our regiment captured a prisoner; he was the only enemy seen by my Corps as far as I know. This man stayed with the regiment two or three days before he was turned over to the provost guard.

On the following morning we marched to Culpeper Courthouse. We went around the town to the Rapidan River, which we crossed at Raccoon Ford about 8 or 9 o'clock at night. It was the coldest water I ever forded. Oh, how cold! I can feel it now. As the water at this time was about knee deep, we were ordered to take off our shoes and roll up our breeches. As we stepped into the water, it was so cold that it felt as if a knife had taken one's foot off. At each step the depth of the water increased. This feeling continued until we reached the middle of the river, where the water came to the knee. One then felt as if the leg was off from the knee down. Reaching the opposite shore, we were ordered to put on shoes and let pants down. Many of the men were so cold they could not do it. This was true of myself. I put on one shoe, but I could not tie it; nor could I roll my pants down. In this condition we marched about a mile. When we halted in a large wood, we soon built immense fires and became warm. The next morning we marched and went into camp at Mt. Pisgah Church in Orange County. Thence our division went on picket at Morton's Ford, eight miles away on the Rappahannock River. A brigade would go to the ford, stay three days and, relieved by another brigade, return to camp at Mt. Pisgah.

During the winter of 1863-1864, the subject of taking care of the widows and orphans of soldiers who had been killed was agitated by some of the prominent citizens of the Confederacy. An organization was formed for that purpose; committees were appointed to make collections, etc.; and agents of the society were sent to the armies in the field to ask assistance from the soldiers. While we were in this camp, one of these agents visited our company. He was received most cordially, as the cause was one that appealed to the sympathy of every soldier. When the company was assembled, the following sums were subscribed by its members, to be paid at the next pay day or as soon thereafter as the collector could visit us:

Lt. R. J. Jordan	$ 20.00	J. Griffin	2.00
Sgt. J. H. Worsham	10.00	J. W. Johnston	2.00
Sgt. W. S. Robertson	10.00	P. W. Kayton	5.00
Sgt. E. Gouldman	2.00	J. A. Kidd	5.00
Cpl. H. F. Munt	5.00	A. C. Legg	2.00
Cpl. N. A. Dowdy	2.00	J. M. Mason	2.00
Cpl. H. C. Tyree	5.00	J. T. Merryman	2.00
Pvts.: N. Barber	2.50	H. Peaster	5.00
A. D. Brown	2.00	P. S. Richeson	2.00
G. W. Brown	2.50	W. R. Richeson	2.00
J. R. Brown	2.50	S. Searles	5.00
L. M. Couch	2.00	W. C. Seay	2.00
W. E. Cumbie	5.00	J. T. Smith	5.00
W. S. Cumbie	1.00	S. E. Wood	5.00
W. B. Edmunds	5.00		
H. C. Fox	5.00		$127.50

This was a liberal contribution from men whose pay was eleven dollars a month, especially since a majority of them had families who needed all their income. It is a pleasure to me to add that, when the collector came, every one present paid his subscription. Those who were absent left the amount with me, and it was duly handed over. Every man present at the first visit subscribed. A few who were not present then but were present when the collector came gave him what they could spare. They are included in the list.

General Bradley T. Johnson was commanding our brigade again, and his wife visited him here.[5] On the day of her arrival she visited the camp of the brigade and went to each company, asking after the health of the men, how we were getting along, etc. This she continued to do daily as long as we were in this camp. She was a beautiful woman with charming manners, and she always had a pleasant word and good cheer for the sick. The personal interest she took in us so impressed the men that they looked forward to her daily visits with great pleasure. The good she did in this camp was never forgotten.

On November 27, 1863, it was reported that Meade had crossed the Rappahannock and was advancing. Johnson's division broke camp and marched toward Mine Run on a road north of that taken by the remainder of the Second Corps. We were quietly marching along a road that ran through a wood; we were listening to the distant cannon in our front and speculating as to the location of the expected battle. Suddenly a part of our column was assailed on the flank by a Yankee skirmish line. It was a complete surprise to us, since no one thought the enemy was in the vicinity. Regimental officers cut off companies from their regiments, formed them as skirmishers right in the road, and ordered them forward. I must say this was the promptest movement I saw during the war.

Our skirmishers drove the enemy back on their line of battle. By this time General Edward Johnson had formed our division in line of battle, and we were moving forward. The left of our line became heavily engaged at once. The Second Brigade was on the right. We swung around until we came to a field where we could see the enemy behind a rail fence on the edge of a wood at the far side of this field. Continuing our wheeling, we soon came to a swampy bottom, the most miry place I ever entered. How the men crossed it, I do not know. Many left one or both shoes in the mud; as the horses could not cross, the officers were compelled to dismount and also to take the mud. However, we crossed, halted a few moments under a hill, reformed our line, and went forward. As soon as we advanced up the hill sufficiently for the enemy to see us, the action became general and heavy. We fought until night put an end to the battle.

[5] Worsham was slightly in error on Bradley Johnson's status. While the Marylander did command the Second Brigade for a brief period immediately after Gettysburg, he was on a recruiting mission for Maryland troops during the period of the Mine Run campaign. His duties might have caused his presence in camp at that time. Johnson's wife, the former Jane Claudia Saunders (1832-1899), was the daughter of a North Carolina congressman and one-time minister to Spain. She married Bradley Johnson in 1851. She was known throughout the Confederacy for her zealous work on behalf of soldiers. See *SHSP*, XXIX (1901), 33-43; *Confederate Veteran*, IX (1901), 321-25.

I will mention a gallant action which I saw here. Captain John C. Johnson of the 50th Virginia was a large and stout man of about fifty years of age. Thinking that some of his men were not doing as well as they ought, he walked out to the brow of the hill, lay down on its top—broadside to the enemy, and then called to some of his men to come up. If they were afraid, he said, they could use him as a breastwork. Several of them very promptly accepted his challenge. They lay down behind him, rested their guns on him, and fired steadily from this position until the fight was over. I am happy to say that the gallant captain was not injured.[6]

This action was known as the battle of Payne's Farm, or Mine Run. It was fought by Johnson's division alone and against one of the wings of the Army of the Potomac that had crossed the Rappahannock at a small ford to make a flank attack on Lee's army. But for the promptness with which the attack was met, it might have been very disastrous to Lee's army. Our division suffered greatly. In F Company, L. M. Couch, J. A. Kidd, Henry Peaster, and Porter Wren were wounded.[7]

During the night we withdrew across Mine Run. On the next morning we joined Lee, took our position in line of battle with our corps, and threw up breastworks along the hills of Mine Run. Meade occupied the hills in our front. Skirmishers had been thrown out in our front all along the Run. We heard the continuous crack of their guns; occasionally a brisk cannonade occurred. Thus matters went on all that day. At night all became still, and we lay down on the breastworks to rest. When we arose the next morning, we saw that the hills in our front had a line of fortifications from one end to the other of the enemy's line. They were more formidable than our own. The skirmishing was as heavy as on the day before, and at one time we endured heavy cannonading from the enemy. Night put an end to the firing. In the morning we saw that Meade had strengthened his works and had brought up additional cannon.

I went a few yards in back of our fortifications, built a small fire of twigs, put my cup on it to warm something for breakfast, and quietly took a seat on the ground nearby to wait until it was heated. Two members of the 21st Virginia joined me and put their cups beside mine. Enemy shells from a battery on our right occasionally dropped

---

[6] Johnson, a resident of Lee County, was mustered into service as a lieutenant on June 27, 1861. Shot in the chest and taken prisoner at Monocacy, Md., July 10, 1864, he spent the remainder of the war at Elmira. Johnson's personal service file, War Records Group 109, National Archives.

[7] In this battle the 21st Va. was engaged from 3 P. M. until sundown. It lost 1 killed, 9 wounded, and 7 missing. OR, XXIX, pt. 1, 856-57.

in our vicinity. Soon after my friends put their cups on the fire, a shell dropped into it and burst, wounding one of the men on the head. When the smoke and ashes cleared, our cups and fire had disappeared. Without breakfast, I went sadly back and took my place in line. Once during the day the cannonading from the enemy was the most severe we had from them. Anticipating an attack, a sergeant from F Company and two men of the 21st Virginia were ordered to go back to our rear and, finding the ammunition wagon, bring two boxes of ammunition to the line of battle. They were to keep the boxes within 100 yards of the regiment. If we were attacked, they were to issue ammunition to the men as fast as they might need it.

That night A. P. Hill's corps, which occupied the right of Lee's line, moved out of the breastworks and took a position on the flank and rear of Meade in order to attack him at daybreak. Our corps remained in the breastworks and extended its line so as to occupy the whole fortifications. In my regiment the men were not much closer together than a skirmish line. In case of attack, the men were told to hold the line at all hazards.

About midnight the men lay down in their places for some rest. Aroused at the break of day, we sprang to our feet promptly and listened for the expected attack by Hill. Not a gun was heard. We became very anxious because we had no tidings from him. Soon after sunrise Johnson's division formed in column and marched along the breastworks until we reached a country road, where we filed to the left and marched over the Run into the Yankee fortifications. Everything was perfectly still; not a Yankee was seen, for they had left during the night. We gave pursuit until we knew that they had recrossed the Rapidan River.

The men suffered a great deal at Mine Run from the cold winds. We were on a high hill, were kept in the breastworks all the time, and were not allowed to make fires. Early in December Johnson's division marched to Morton's Ford and, on the next day, to Raccoon Ford, where we remained until December 19. We then marched to the neighborhood of Orange Courthouse. On December 24 we returned to our old camp near Mt. Pisgah Church. The next day we had a regular old-time Christmas, since a good many boxes had been received from home. In some of them were all the ingredients for egg-nog.

Before leaving our camp near Mt. Pisgah Church for the march to Mine Run, some of the men had built huts. When we returned to camp, huts were built for all, and soon we were comfortable. The Second Brigade also built a commodious log church. There we gathered every Sunday for regular religious services. Sometimes a preacher expounded the gospel; at other times a soldier would lead the meetings, which were largely attended and much enjoyed by the men.

One afternoon the whole division was ordered out to witness the execution of three Confederate soldiers from another division.[8] They were to be shot for some violation of the laws of the army. The division formed three sides of a hollow square, the fourth side being open. Three stakes were fixed in the ground about the center of this open side. Soon after our formation, an officer and a guard appeared with the prisoners. The condemned were made to kneel with their backs to the stakes, to which they were securely tied. Cloths were fastened over their eyes. Twelve men then picked up the twelve guns lying on the ground in front of the prisoners. The guns had already been loaded. It is said that six had balls and six did not—so that no man would know whether he killed one of the prisoners. The twelve men took their places about thirty feet in front of the three prisoners. The order to fire was given and, at the report of the guns, two men were killed— the balls going though each. The third man, while shot, was not killed. One of the detail was ordered to place another gun against the man's breast and to fire. This shot killed him instantly. This was the only execution I witnessed; if I live a thousand years, I will never be willing to see another.

We remained in this camp a long time. During good weather we drilled, and we went regularly on picket to Morton's Ford. On February 5, 1864, the whole Second Corps was called to the ford. Indications were that the enemy was moving and had sent a column to the ford with the intention of crossing. They did not make their appearance on the other side of the river; rather, they sent skirmishers to the ford, and they became engaged with ours. Some of their artillery went into action and shelled our lines. We remained at the ford until February 8, when we left the usual brigade on picket and returned to camp. Before we moved the enemy had disappeared and gone back to their camps. In the Yankee army this was known as the "Mud Campaign."

---

[8] Owing to a frightful increase in the rate of desertion, a large number of executions took place in Lee's army that winter. Not even Johnson's division, of which the 21st Va. was a part, was exempt from this evil. On Feb. 18, 1864, Lee himself expressed deep concern to the Sec. of War over the number of deserters in Stafford's Louisiana brigade of that division. *OR*, XXXIII, 1187-88. See also Casler, *Stonewall Brigade*, pp. 188-90; H. M. Wagstaff (ed.), *The James A. Graham Papers, 1861-1864* (Chapel Hill, 1928), pp. 177-78; McHenry Howard, *Recollections of a Maryland Confederate Soldier* . . . (Baltimore, 1914), pp. 258-61. Hereafter cited as Howard, *Recollections*.

They said that, if their artillery and wagons had not stuck in the mud, they would have made things lively for us.[9]

On March 1 the enemy made a movement in our front and, at the same time, sent a body of cavalry on a raid in our rear. About sunset of the 2nd the long roll sounded in the camp of Johnson's division. As soon as we had fallen in, we marched to the stone road. There the division was formed, and we marched at a quick step in the direction of Fredericksburg. Arriving at Mine Run, we camped there for the remainder of the night. The roads were full of mud and the marching was bad. At one place we forded a branch and then ascended a steep clay hill. The wet shoes of the soldiers treading on the clay made it perfectly slick, and many a fall was the consequence. We had a boy recruit just from home, and this was his first march. He wore wooden bottom shoes. Poor fellow, he slipped back into the branch so often after taking a step or two that some of his comrades finally undertook to help him. Frequently they went with him two or three yards from the branch; then he would commence to slip and pull them all back together into the water. He was finally told to sit down on the roadside until daybreak, then he would be able to see his way and could then join us.

This he did. Yet some of the boys, to have a little fun, told him that the Yankee cavalry was marching behind us and, as soon as we got a little way from him, they would come along and take him prisoner. Poor little fellow, he began to cry as if his heart would break. However, this recruit made his mark a few weeks later at the battle of the Wilderness. During the attack the enemy made on us, I saw him blow a hole through a Yankee who was at the muzzle of his gun.

Early the next morning we continued the march. We halted at the crossing of the Germanna Road, formed a line of battle across the road, and stacked arms. We were told that we might rest, but that we must remain near our guns. It was rumored that the Yankee cavalry raiders were expected to return this way to their army, and we were there to intercept them. We remained there several hours; we then marched to Chancellorsville and, forming a line across the road leading to one of the fords, stayed there several hours. We then marched back to the Germanna Road, where we remained all night. The next morning we again marched to Chancellorsville and stayed there all day and night.

---

[9] Lee and others felt that the Federal movement was merely a probe to ascertain the Confederate position and strength. *OR*, XXXIII, 114-18, 140-42. This maneuver by Meade should not be confused with Burnside's well-known "Mud March" after the battle of Fredericksburg.

On the afternoon of March 2, we were called out of camp very suddenly, and we did not carry any rations with us. (Some of the men were left behind in camp to cook them and then bring them to us.) During the day we had eaten everything in camp and were drawing rations for supper when we were ordered off on the march. The men with the rations joined us at Chancellorsville on the morning of the 4th. During all this time, very few of us had anything to eat. I had nothing, and it was the longest time I went without eating during the war. As soon as we finished eating what the men brought, we took our places in line. The raiders having returned to their army by another route, we returned to Mt. Pisgah the next morning.

We saw at Chancellorsville that a year's time had not healed the scars of the bloody battle fought there. The ground where we were was literally covered with human bones that had been scattered about since the shallow burial of those who fell there. It was an awful experience, even for soldiers, to scrape the bones away before lying down for rest at night.

The night of March 5 found us back in our old quarters. We were glad, very glad, to return to them, and we were soon comfortable. For a long time we received short rations. It being hard to divide them equally among the members of the messes, the majority of the messes adopted a system that gave general satisfaction. After the rations were cooked, they were divided into as many parts as there were members of the mess. Each of these parts was piled on a log or on the ground in a row. One member of the mess was selected to turn his back to the piles of rations while another member pointed his finger toward one of the piles and asked, "Who has this?"

The man with his back toward the piles designated one of the mess by name, and he immediately took it. Then another pile was disposed of in a similar way, until all the piles were taken. Coffee was not included in this method of distribution, because it was given to us in the grain and in quantity so small that the grains were counted out to each man. None but the Confederate soldier knows how they lived. For months we had not had a full ration. The rations became more scanty as the war continued; and after this time, we never received as much as we wanted to eat—unless we captured it from the enemy.

The regular rations allowed by army regulations were insufficient; yet we did not get the regular allowance even at the beginning of the war, when everything was plentiful. Here is the daily ration allowance for each man in the field: a half-pound of bacon or beef; one and a half pounds of flour or corn meal, or one pound of hard bread. For every 100 men the following rations were issued: eight quarts of peas or ten pounds of rice, four quarts of vinegar, one and a half pounds of tallow candles, four pounds of soap, two quarts of salt, and six pounds of sugar.

While we were in this camp, we received some of the Telescope rifles,[10] which were entrusted to a select body of men. On suitable occasions the men practiced shooting with them. At one of these practices they stood on one hill and shot at a target about half a mile off on another hill. The bottom between those hills was used as a grazing place for horses and mules belonging to our wagon train. During the shooting, the men accidentally killed one of the mules. That mule was very fat. Not long after it was killed, some of the men cut chunks of meat from him and carried them into camp to be cooked and eaten. When an officer learned of this, he stationed a guard during the day near the mule to prevent it. That night, however, many had mule steak for supper.[11]

We were now in a bad plight for cooking utensils. Spiders and frying pans were scarce. Hardly a boiler existed, and all the pans for making bread were gone. We made bread in spiders, frying pans, and oilcloths. During the time of year that the bark of trees would slip, we got an excellent tray by peeling the bark from a tree.

We enjoyed this camp, as the quarters were the most comfortable we had during the war. The men really enjoyed the rest—the longest ever spent. There was more sociability here than I ever saw in camp. I enjoyed visiting Clark's Mountain, a mound rising several hundred feet above the surrounding country and immediately on the Rapidan River. From its top, which was about three miles from our camp, I could see the camps of many of the enemy in Culpeper County. I also had an extensive view of the surrounding country. We had a signal station on its top, and sometimes I had an opportunity to look through the glass at the Yankee camps.

One of the incidents I witnessed while in this camp was changing the clothing of a handcuffed man confined in the guardhouse. He desired to put on a clean shirt. As he was not allowed to take off the cuffs, he went to work, took off his soiled shirt and put on the clean one without the handcuffs being removed. However, it took him about two hours to do it.

---

[10] "Telescope rifles" generally referred to the heavy target weapons used by sharpshooters. Since such weapons weighed from between 15 to 30 pounds, Worsham apparently was describing a new-issue musket equipped with a telescopic sight.

[11] For other observations on the palatability of mule meat, see Wiley, *The Life of Johnny Reb*, pp. 93-94.

During the war the Negroes who accompanied their masters were a source of much merriment as well as comfort to us. I recollect the experience of two of our Negro cooks in battle. On one occasion we were in line of battle when Archer, a cook in one of our companies, came to the front with his master's haversack of rations. We were taking things easy at the time—some lying on the ground, others sitting or standing up and engaged in talking over the impending battle. At the sight of Archer we gave him a hurrah as a welcome. He had been with us only a few minutes when the enemy made an advance along our front and turned our flank. Fighting became warm, and we had a hot time before we succeeded in driving them back. Following up our success, we drove the enemy from the field of battle. Archer was caught in the fight and, when night came and we were joined by the cooks, he had a splendid account to tell his companions of the part he took in the battle. He told them that he took the gun of one of our dead and fought side by side with "Marse Jim," who "knows I killed a dozen Yankees. Oh, you ought just to have see me in the charge! Me and 'Marse Jim' just whipped them clean out!"

This account of Archer's made a hero of him in the estimation of his friends, and it so impressed them that one of their number, Ned, made up his mind then and there to go into the next battle and see if he could eclipse Archer's account! Ned did not have long to wait, as we met our old enemy some weeks later when a line of battle was formed in a wood. Ned was in it, with gun in hand. He had a large knapsack strapped to his back; it was filled to overflowing with articles from many a battlefield, which he had been carrying for a month or more with the hope of sending it to his wife by some soldier who was going to his neighborhood. Besides the knapsack, he had one or more haversacks, and his canteen, filled in the same manner!

When we received orders to move forward, Ned marched boldly in our midst. When we reached the edge of the woods, the enemy opened on us. A spent ball hit Ned squarely in the forehead, and in a few minutes it had raised a knot as large as a hen's egg! As soon as Ned was struck, he halted; his mouth flew open, his eyes bulged, and he made a movement as if he were going to run. Yet the men steadied him by telling him that Archer was knocked down several times by balls, and that he got up and killed the man that shot him!

In our advance we crossed a fence and started across a field. A man at Ned's side was shot down. Ned started and stopped at the sight. His gun fell from his hand. A ball went over his shoulder, cutting the strap on his knapsack; and as it turned, Ned slipped out of it and let it fall to the ground. At the same time, he disengaged his haversack and canteen. He pulled off his coat, dropped it too, brushed off his hat, wheeled and broke for the rear like a quarter horse—and amidst the yells of our men!

This was a sore subject ever after for Ned. Not that he ran away —but that he lost all those things he had been saving to send to Sally! And he would not believe a word of Archer's tale!

Here is a tale of a Negro that shows the feeling the Southerner had for him. My mess of about a dozen men had built for winter quarters a log pen about two feet high. On this we erected our tent, and at one end we built an excellent log chimney. This made us very comfortable. As cook we had a Negro slave who stayed about our tent during the day but who slept in a cabin at night with other Negroes. He was taken sick with measles. We made him leave his quarters and come and stay in our tent, where we cooked for him and nursed him until he was well.

I tried to keep clean while in the army, and I made it a rule to take a bath once a week and oftener when convenient. This included winter as well as summer. It looked very formidable to take a bath on some of those cold and stormy days which we had in the army, but it was more in looks than in reality. Here is a winter day's experience in this camp. One day about noon, with the sun shining brightly and little wind stirring, I thought I would take my bath. I walked over to Madison Run, a large stream about half a mile from camp. I found the stream frozen over solid. I got a large rock, walked to the middle of the stream, raised the rock over my head and hurled it with all my force on the ice. But it made no impression. I repeated this eight or ten times without breaking the ice. I then returned to camp, got an axe, went back to the Run, and cut a hole in the ice, which was about seven inches thick. I cleared the hole of all floating ice, undressed, took a good bath, dressed, and was in fine condition when I returned to camp.

Chapter VIII

FROM THE WILDERNESS TO COLD HARBOR

For several weeks it had been rumored in camp that General U. S. Grant had command of our old enemy, the Army of the Potomac. From indications in his camp, it was supposed Grant intended to make a move soon. In anticipation of this, Johnson's division broke up winter quarters on May 2 and marched to Bartley's Mill on the Rapidan for better observation and to be in a better place to guard our line. On the morning of May 4, Johnson's division left Bartley's Mill and marched to Locust Grove, from where we proceeded nearly all night along the Stone Road toward Fredericksburg. We then halted and rested on the side of the road, General Ewell, who had been riding at the head of the column, lay down beside a log not more than ten yards from me.

As the streaks of day were just beginning to show themselves, we fell into ranks and resumed our march. We had gone only a short distance when the stillness in our front was broken by the sound of a drum and the sweet notes of music from a band. Every man clutched his gun more tightly, as the direction of the music told him that the enemy were in front. There was no need of urging us to hurry, no need to inquire what it meant. All knew now that Grant had crossed the Rapidan, and that soon the tumult of battle would begin. The march continued; the command was "Close up!" Soon came the order, "Halt! Load your guns!" Then came "Shoulder arms! March!" The Second Brigade, which was in front of the division, soon formed a line of battle. The 21st Virginia was on the left of the Stone Road, the remainder of the Brigade on the right of that road. When the order "Forward!" came, we moved forward through wood and brush. We were in the Wilderness!

With a tumult that seemed to come from the infernal regions, we were assailed by the enemy! As soon as the lifting of the smoke enabled us to see, we discovered that the portion of our brigade on the right side of the road had been swept away. There were no Confederates in sight except our regiment. We broke the enemy's line in our front and made no halt in our advance. On we went, shooting as fast as we could load![1]

Suddenly I was confronted by a gun resting on a big stump, and behind the stump we saw a Yank! Several of us took aim at him and hallooed to him to throw down his gun. He started to rise; but before he could do so, a little boy on my left who had also taken aim at him pulled the trigger of his musket. At the crack of the gun the Yankee fell dead. This was the little fellow who was wearing wooden bottom shoes, and the one we had left crying on the road a few weeks before because he could not keep up with us on the march.

We captured many prisoners. Behind every tree and stump were several who seemed to remain there in preference to running the gauntlet of our fire. We advanced to a dense pine thicket and halted, every man falling flat on the ground at once for protection! We could see troops coming to our assistance.[2] The Third Brigade then extended the line on our left. One of its regiments halted directly in our rear, and its members lay down too! On the right the woods were large and open; for some reason the enemy had disappeared from it. Major Meret C. Walsh of the 7th Indiana gave an explanation of this in his report by stating: "We charged the rebel line, capturing the colors of the Fiftieth Virginia (rebel) Regiment and nearly 200 prisoners, but being flanked on the right were forced to retire from the field."[3]

The force on the right was the 21st Virginia! We not only drove those in front, but we also cleared the enemy from the field on the right of the road. The pine thicket in our front was so dense that we could not see twenty feet in it, yet we heard the enemy talking. My company was near the road. Wishing to see what was going on in front, I ran across the road to the top of an elevation. What a sight met my gaze! Obliquely across the road and just behind the pine thicket, the enemy was massed in a small field. I looked down the road and saw two pieces of artillery coming up in a run. At this time I realized that I in turn had been seen, and that the guns were leveled at me! I took shelter behind a big tree just as W. E. Cumbie of our company came

---

[1] The Federals involved in this fighting were the Indiana, New York, Pennsylvania, and Wisconsin troops of Gen. James S. Wadsworth's division, V Corps. One of the better Union accounts of this action, by Maj. B. F. Wright of the 146th N. Y., is in *Glimpses of the Nation's Struggle: A Series of Papers Read before the Minnesota Commandery of the Military Order of the Loyal Legion of the United States,* II, (1890), 7-15.

[2] These reinforcements were the brigades of Gens. Junius Daniel and John B. Gordon. The latter, wrote Ewell, made "a dashing charge" and captured "several hundred prisoners." *OR,* XXXVI, pt. 1, 1070. See also John B. Gordon, *Reminiscences of the Civil War* (New York, 1904), pp. 237-42. Hereafter cited as Gordon, *Reminiscences.*

[3] *OR,* XXXVI, pt. 1, 617.

running to me. The enemy fired a hundred shots, and Cumbie fell dead, shot through the body.[4] He was as gallant a soldier as any in our army.

I ran back to my company. Seeing the colonel of the regiment of the Third Brigade who was with us, I informed him of the condition of affairs in our front. At once he gave the order: "Forward, men!" The two regiments jumped to their feet and advanced, with the whole of the Third Brigade taking part. We went through the thicket and came upon the mass of the enemy. The battle raged again more fiercely than before. With a yell we were on them, front and flank! They gave ground and then ran! The yell that then went up fairly shook the ground! Hurrah! The cannon were ours, we having captured both pieces.[5] The enemy in their flight had crossed to the right of the road, and we followed them through the field and about 200 yards into the woods. Here we were halted and ordered back.

In retiring through the field, we discovered a body of the enemy in the woods on our left. The 21st Virginia immediately wheeled and poured a hot fire into them. They disappeared in great disorder. We resumed our march across the field and halted as soon as we reached the woods on the east side. Taking position there and on the right of the Stone Road, the 21st Virginia commenced to fire slowly at the enemy, who had taken position on the west side of this field. The remainder of the Second Brigade soon joined us.

We were then treated to a rare sight! Running midway across the little field was a gully that had been washed by the rains. In their retreat many of the enemy went into this gully for protection from our fire. When we advanced to it, we ordered them out and to the rear. All came out except one, who had hidden under an overhanging bank and was overlooked. When we fell back across the field, the Yankees who followed us to the edge of the woods shot at us as we crossed. One of our men, thinking the fire too warm, dropped into the gully for protection. Now there was a Yankee and a Confederate in the gully—and each was ignorant of the presence of the other!

After awhile they commenced to move about in the gully, there being no danger so long as they did not show themselves. Soon they came in view of each other, and they commenced to banter. Then they

---

[4] A resident of Mecklenberg County, Cumbie had joined the 22nd Va. Battn. in Jan., 1862, but had transferred to the 21st Va. on Sept. 4, 1863. Cumbie did not die instantly, as Worsham stated; rather, he succumbed to gangrene on May 24. Cumbie's personal service file, War Records Group 109, National Archives.

[5] The Confederate elements in this assault were the brigades of George H. Steuart and Cullen A. Battle. The Southerners captured the two 24-pounder howitzers of Capt. George B. Winslow's Co. D, 1st N. Y. Artillery, after a charge of 800 yards across broken ground. Winslow fell severely wounded; his lieutenant was captured, and almost all the horses for the two guns were slain. *OR*, XXXVI, pt. 1, 640, 1070.

decided that they would go into the road and have a regular fist and skull fight, the best man to have the other as his prisoner. While both sides were firing, the two men came into the road about midway between the lines of battle, and in full view of both sides around the field. They surely created a commotion, because both sides ceased firing! When the two men took off their coats and commenced to fight with their fists, a yell went up along each line, and men rushed to the edge of the opening for a better view! The "Johnny" soon had the "Yank" down; the Yank surrendered, and both quietly rolled into the gully. Here they remained until nightfall, when the "Johnny" brought the Yankee into our line. In the meantime, the disappearance of the two men into the gully was the signal for the resumption of firing. Such is war!

We remained in this position for two or three hours. We then marched across the road and took position immediately on its left and about 200 yards in the rear of the line of breastworks occupied by the Third Brigade. Slight firing continued all day; as night approached, everything became quiet. We were ordered to rest for the night on our arms.

About midnight I was aroused to take a verbal order to the officer on our skirmish line, which was on the outskirts of the pine thicket. I was instructed to leave my arms, etc., behind, to take my time, and to make as little noise as possible. The night was dark, and the pine thicket was so black that I could almost feel the darkness. Moving carefully, and thinking that I was moving splendidly and in perfect silence, I was suddenly thrown to the ground amid a rattling noise that awakened everybody in the neighborhood! The Yankees commenced shooting at once! They fired hundreds of shots into the thicket, and I lay perfectly still until quiet was restored.

When I sat up and felt around to see what caused me to fall, my hand came in contact with a saber which I found belted to a dead man. The saber had caught between my legs and had thrown me. It rattling against the man's canteen, as well as my falling amongst the pine twigs, was the big noise in the night. Fully reassured, I proceeded, found the officer, and delivered the order. He was an old friend and inquired why I had made so much noise! My explanation brought a laugh and a caution not to repeat it. After giving a good-night, I started to our line, shaping my course as well as I could so as to find my dead man again.

Fortune favored me. I found him, removed his sword, and then felt in his pockets to see what he had. I found a knife, a pipe, and a piece of string. In every pocket—even the one in his shirt, he had smoking tobacco. I had to take an order to the front again at daybreak. On my return I looked for my man again and saw that he was a Yankee lieutenant. Soon after this, the enemy assailed our position furiously with shot and shell for a short time. Then quiet was restored and lasted in our front the remainder of the day, except for an occasional skirmish fire.

On the morning of May 7 the Second Brigade marched by the flank to the extreme left of General Lee's line. There we took a small country road through the woods toward one of the fords at which Grant crossed the Rapidan. After going some distance, we halted and formed a line of battle. A few pieces of artillery that had accompanied us unlimbered, loaded, and fired through the woods in the direction of the ford. For a short time the firing was fast. The artillery then limbered up, and we returned by the same road and resumed our place in line with our division. We did not know until a few days later that this movement was a feint on Grant's communications. It is said that it made a great commotion in his army.

The giants had met, and Grant was badly worsted in his first encounter! His loss was great.[6] All along Lee's line he had been repulsed. The ground in the little field in our front was literally covered with enemy dead! Our loss was severe; nearly all of that splendid regiment, the 25th Virginia of our brigade, was captured.[7] F Company lost W. E. Cumbie killed, and G. W. Brown, L. M. Couch, N. A. Dowdy, A. C. Legg, and Henry Smith wounded. Among the killed in the division were those splendid soldiers, Brigadier General Leroy A. Stafford of the Louisiana Brigade and Brigadier General John M. Jones of our brigade.[8]

General Jones was a strict disciplinarian and inaugurated several plans for the benefit of his men. According to my information, he was the only officer who made the men take care of themselves as far as

---

[6] Grant's losses in the three-day battle were indeed staggering. His army suffered 2.175 killed, 9,840 wounded, and 4,016 missing—a total of 16,031 casualties. *OR, XXXVI*, pt. 1, 219, 907.

[7] For more on the 25th Va. in the Wilderness, see *ibid.*, 672, and Lt. McHenry Howard's narrative in *Papers of the Military Historical Society of Massachusetts*, IV (1905), 99.

[8] Exceptional gallantry at Gettysburg had brought Stafford (1822-1864) a brigadier's commission. He was mortally wounded on May 5, wrote Lee, "while leading his command with conspicuous valor." Stafford died three days later in Richmond. *OR, XXXVI*, pt. 1, 1028. A staff officer wrote after the war that John Marshall Jones (1820-1864), refusing to retreat with his men, was killed "while sitting on his horse gazing at the approaching enemy." However, Ewell reported that Jones and his aide, Capt. R. D. Early, both fell dead "in a desperate effort to rally their brigade." Howard, *Recollections*, p. 273; *OR, XXXVI*, pt. 1, 1070.

they could. He allowed no straggling; even the musicians had to march in their places. If he saw the men becoming weary or fagged, he would order every musician to the head of the brigade. One of the regiments had a very good band, while the others had small drum corps. All together they were a considerable company of musicians. The general would direct the band to play a short time, and then the drum corps would play. With four or five bass drums, ten to twelve kettle drums, and twelve to fifteen fifes, they made a big noise and always received the hearty approval of the men! It was noticeable that the men, feeling refreshed, would close up, take step with the music, and march several miles in this way.

On a march we would often reach a stream that had to be forded. If the water came below the knee, every man and officer who was walking was required to take off his shoes and socks and roll up his pants above his knees. If the water was deep enough to reach above the knees, all were required to strip. Thus, when we crossed the stream we had dry clothes. This was a great comfort to the men, but none of them would do it unless compelled. The men of our brigade sometimes tried to evade it. General Jones usually caught them and, whether officer or private, woe unto the man who was caught! He received a severe reprimand, and one of his staff marched him back across the stream and saw that he stripped and then forded according to orders.

Well do I remember a laughable occurrence at Front Royal. In one of our marches through the town, after the bridges over the Shenandoah River had been burned, the citizens desired to see the soldiers ford the river. Our brigade was in the front of the army that day, and when we reached the river, the hill around the ford was covered with citizens, mostly women and children. General Jones and his staff had ridden into the water to allow their horses to drink. The colonel at the head of the marching column gave the order to halt. He looked at the hill, then at General Jones, and then at the men. The men did the same thing. The General looked up. Not seeing the men making preparations for fording, he called to the colonel and asked why the men did not strip and come along. The colonel looked again at the hill and the men. Then, in a loud voice, he gave the command: "Strip, men, and be ready to ford!"

The men hesitated, but the general hallooed to them to strip at once. This we commenced to do, and several of the men had their pants off before the citizens were aware of what was going on. Then over the hill they went, pell mell, amidst a general yell from the men. They did not see us ford the river that day!

On the morning of May 8, the Second Corps, with the Second Brigade in front, marched from the left to the right of Lee's line in the Wilderness. As we passed along the rear of the army, an occasional Yankee cannon shot or musket ball flew over us. On reaching the right of Lee's line we continued our march in the same direction until we came to woods on fire. Our course was several miles through this fire. At times the heat was intense, and the smoke suffocating![9] The men, fearing an explosion of their cartridges, were very uneasy all the time. We finally emerged from the woods onto a fair road, which carried us by Todd's tavern and a mill. Several miles after we left the mill, we overtook some of our cavalry who, since it was then 2 or 3 o'clock in the afternoon, informed us that they were mighty glad to see us. All day long they had been fighting Yankees, who were not far ahead.

We heard the musketry, and the order, "Close up," was given. We marched along the road for about half a mile. We then filed to the left and marched in various directions, sometimes at a snail's pace and then in a run. After standing seemingly for hours, we finally moved off at double quick and went into line of battle at Spotsylvania Court House. This was just about sunset. We did not become engaged, but we heard the enemy, like us, taking position. About 8 or 9 o'clock our line was moved about thirty or forty feet to the front. As we were in the presence of the enemy, it was necessary to use strategy. The markers were taken to the new line, and the officers in forming an alignment called out to "John" or "Bob," who would answer, "Where are you?"

In replying, the officer indicated a step or two to his right or left as the direction and distance he wished the marker to go. The marker then made the necessary change of position, and the line quietly dressed on him. In this way the line was finally formed, and we lay on our arms for the night.

Early on the morning of May 9 we moved farther to our right. Johnson's division occupied the right of Lee's line. The Stonewall Brigade was on the left of the division, the Louisiana Brigade on its right, the Second Brigade next, and the Third Brigade, occupying the right of the division and also of the army, on its right. The Second Brigade occupied what became known as the "Bloody Angle." My regiment, the 21st Virginia, was near the toe of the horseshoe, as it is often called. As soon as we formed our line, we began to throw up breastworks. After our brigade finished its works, our regiment secured a few axes and commenced to cut down the pine bushes that ran at

_____

[9] Ewell himself stated that his men had "a very distressing march through intense heat and thick dust and smoke from burning woods." *Ibid.*, 1071.

this point nearly up to our line. While we were thus engaged, several Yankee batteries opened fire on our lines. We took refuge at once in our breastworks—which the 21st Virginia found to be of no protection, since the angle was so abrupt that the enemy threw their shells in our rear as well as in our front!

As soon as the enemy ceased firing, we went to work and made regular pens large enough to hold eight to ten men each. We thus protected ourselves in all directions. The 21st Virginia had just finished the pens, and the men were taking places in them, when an order came from General Johnson, our division commander, for us to report to Brigadier General George H. Steuart, who commanded the Third Brigade of our division. All the men and officers of our regiment protested against this order. We had never fired a gun from behind a breastwork, and these were made so much better than any we had ever made that we desired to have the honor of defending them! Nevertheless, we were compelled to go.[10] We left our pens with many a grumble and reported to General Steuart, who sent us about three-quarters of a mile to the front.

We halted in a large wood on the south side of a small branch and formed a skirmish line along this branch. The left of the line ran a short distance along the border of a field; the remainder of the line ran straight through the wood and ended along the border of another field. About one-third of the regiment was placed on the line. The remainder took a position about 200 yards in the rear of the center. It was held as a reserve and a relief. One of F Company was detailed to take orders along the line and to the regiment. As yet no enemy had been seen; but about half an hour after the line had been formed, along the line came a message: "The Yankees have made their appearance and are moving to the left" (our right).

Late in the evening their skirmishers advanced within range on our left, and skirmishing continued until night. During the night other companies from our regiment relieved those on the skirmish line. When morning came we found that the enemy had moved far enough to their left to come into contact with our right. Here skirmishing was kept up all day, with an occasional shot on our left. The enemy had not made their appearance before our center. During the day heavy fighting occurred along the line of breastworks to our left. The breastworks occupied by Brigadier General George Doles' Georgia brigade, and a

---

[10] D. S. Freeman analyzed the merits of this withdrawal in *Lee's Lieutenants*, III, 394, 444-46. For a description of the terrain in front of Jones' and the Louisiana brigades, see Percy G. Hamlin, *"Old Bald Head"* (General R. S. Ewell) (Strasburg, Va., 1940), p. 177.

company of Richmond Howitzers just to the left of the Stonewall Brigade, were captured by the enemy. But troops nearby were hurried to that point. As soon as they could be formed in line, the order was given to charge and drive the Yanks out! This was done quickly, and our line was re-established.[11] A portion of the Second Brigade participated in this charge. Its members were among the first to replant our standards on our works.

On May 11 occasional firing occurred between their extreme left and the right of our regimental skirmish line. We could hear some heavy fighting along the line of battle on our left. Soon after dark the Yankees commenced to move in front of our skirmish line. We could hear the rumble of wheels, the noise of marching, and the command to "close up." It was far in the night before the sounds ceased.

This was the prelude to an attack such as was not witnessed during the war, and I expect that it was the heaviest attack ever made at a single point by any army in the world! Major General Winfield S. Hancock's Second Corps of 25,000 men (consisting of 4 divisions, 79 infantry regiments, and 10 batteries of artillery), assisted by 15,000 men in Major General Horatio G. Wright's Sixth Corps, were ordered to break our line on the right. During the night of May 11, General Hancock moved this force to the front of the skirmish line of the 21st Virginia and formed a line of attack—two divisions front, the regiments massed in double columns on center, thus making ten or twelve lines of battle. At the firing of the signal gun at 4:30 a.m.—the time was later changed to 4:35, they were to move ahead and not to fire a shot until they were inside our works.

Day broke on May 12 with a heavy fog. Drops of water dripped from the trees as if it had rained. I had started with an order from the reserve of our regiment to the skirmish line when a cannon shot and the screaming of a shell broke the stillness. I put my hands instantly to my head to see if it was still on my shoulders. The shell seemed to come near enough to take off my head! (Such feelings as this often come to a soldier!) Recovering from my dazed condition, I proceeded on my mission. Before I reached our line, I could hear the sound of 40,000 men marching, and soon a few shots from our skirmish line on the left put us all on the watch. I saw the line approaching to my left. I ran back and reported to Colonel William Witcher, who

[11] The Federals attacked in three waves starting at 6:10 P.M. The ensuing battle was short but bitter. Even though partially flanked on both sides the Richmond Howitzers continued to pour shot into the blue ranks. A strong counterattack by three Confederate brigades finally restored the line. While the Federals lost about 100 men, they in turn captured around 500 Confederates. Freeman, *Lee's Lieutenants*, III, 394-96.

immediately called the regiment to attention. By this time the enemy had approached so near that the men of the 21st Virginia could see them and their immense numbers.

Some of the skirmish officers appeared and reported to the colonel that the enemy had run over our men without paying any attention to them, and that the enemy force was the largest they had ever seen! I was immediately sent out on the line to recall all the skirmishers I could find. As soon as this was done, we faced about and marched to our line of battle. We made a circuit to the left so as to avoid the enemy, who had now passed between us and our breastworks. At once we heard heavy fighting in our front. As soon as we came in sight of a field, the regiment halted. Colonel Witcher sent me forward to reconnoiter. Running to the field, I saw that the far end of it was perfectly blue with Yankees, and farther off I could see the smoke of the terrible fighting that was going on! I ran back and made my report to Colonel Witcher. He called the regiment to attention and made a circuit farther to the left. This was the second and last time during the war that a feeling of dread came over me that I would be captured, and I said to myself, "Well, old fellow, you are gone this time, and I will not give ten cents for your chances of getting away!"

I was sent forward as a pilot. In a short time an old, ragged, dirty Confederate rode up from behind a bush in my front and took deliberate aim at me with his musket.

"Don't shoot!" I cried. "We are friends!"

I saw an expression of doubt on the old fellow's face, for he knew I came from the direction in which the enemy was momentarily expected. I made haste to exclaim again that we were skirmishers of the 21st Virginia who had been driven in. Men rose up all along the line, and I knew we were in front of a Confederate skirmish line. How my heart jumped! I felt so good that I could have hugged every one of them! We passed through their line and soon reached the breastworks occupied by Brigadier General Joseph R. Davis's brigade.[12] While our regiment was at the front, troops from A. P. Hill's corps extended their line of battle into our sector on the right. We went to the rear and reported to General Ewell, who informed us that our division had been captured and that he thought we had been captured too.

The capture of Johnson's division was a terrible blow to the army! This was Jackson's old division, and those were the men who had done

[12] The brigade of J. R. Davis, nephew of the Confederate President, consisted of the 2nd, 11th, and 42nd Miss., plus the 55th N. C. This unit had been badly mauled at Gettysburg and was but a skeleton force at Spotsylvania, where it held a rear position on the eastern end of The Salient.

so much fighting and who had made those wonderful marches for him. They were now prisoners in the hands of the Yankees. It is true that, for a division, their numbers were small, but they were such trained soldiers that they counted as many in a fight. Jackson's old division was annihilated, and from that date it ceased to be a division. The Old Stonewall, Second, Third, and Louisiana Brigades also lost their organizations.

After striking and rushing over the breastworks, Hancock's men had turned to the right and left and had taken our division in the rear. During the preceding night, the artillery supporting our line had been withdrawn. It had just gotten back when the attack was made. Only one piece had time to get into position and fire a shot. Its captain then heard someone in his rear say, "Don't you fire that piece!"

On looking around, he was confronted by hundreds of Yankees, who captured all sixteen guns.

The situation seemed so critical at this time that "Marse Robert" came to the front to look after it. He sent for Brigadier General John B. Gordon, in command of the reserves, and gave him directions for bringing them up, placing them in line, etc. Gordon soon had the men in line. When General Lee's presence was noticed by the troops, they showed their devotion to him a third time. A great cry went up from them: "General Lee to the rear! General Lee to the rear! If General Lee will go to the rear, we promise to drive the enemy back!"

But the old hero did not stir.

General Gordon then rode up to him, took his bridle, and gently led him to the rear, saying, "Those are Virginians and Georgians, General Lee, and they will do their duty!"

"Yes! Yes!" shouted the men, many of whom were in tears. "We will drive the Yankees back, if General Lee will go to the rear!"[13]

And well did they redeem their word! As soon as the order was given, forward the men went. It was one of the most terrible battles of the war. The slaughter of Hancock's men, hemmed in this angle, was so great that it received the name "Bloody Angle." The enemy were finally driven back and sought refuge in a part of our captured breastworks. Here they were compelled to stay. The men of our

---

[13] This is but one of several versions of the now-famous "Lee to the rear" incident. As customarily told, Gordon looked at the troops standing around his and Lee's horses and then said to his commander: "These men are Virginians and Georgians. They have never failed. They never will. Will you, boys?" A chorus of shouts came back: "No! No!" For other accounts of this third "Lee to the rear" incident, see Freeman, *R. E. Lee*, III, 319n.; *SHSP*, XXIV (1896), 81-82.

reserve covered themselves with glory, and the troops who helped them shared in the praise! Gordon was made a major general at once![14]

All this had taken place while my regiment was being driven in, and while it was in the rear. We were given fresh ammunition and ordered to the front. A staff officer went with us to show us our position. On arriving at the designated point, we formed a line and advanced through a large wood. Soon we were under fire; yet the undergrowth prevented us from seeing the enemy. We advanced until we came to a small bottom. Going through that, we reached the rise and plainly saw the Yankees about 150 yards from us. They were in the pens made by our regiment. They were standing in those pens as thick as herring in a barrel, and as far back behind them as the smoke would allow us to see. Such a mass of men I never saw!

We found one Confederate soldier, an Alabamian, standing behind a large pine tree. He was loading and firing his musket with as much deliberation as if he were firing at a target. At this point he was keeping back the whole of Hancock's force. He said he was a sharpshooter, and that his line was on each side of him! There certainly was no other Confederate in front of our regiment line, nor could we see one either on the right or on the left. We lay down, taking advantage of everything that offered protection, and opened on the enemy. Musket balls were fairly raining. Great limbs of trees were cut off by bullets as if by an ax. The men seemed more uneasy about the limbs than about the balls. No cannon were used here, yet this was the heaviest rifle fire the world ever saw at a single point! The fire from those 40,000 men was so heavy that they literally shot trees to pieces. On exhibition at the War Department in Washington is an oak tree about fourteen inches in diameter. It was severed at this time by minie balls. The enemy used mules to bring ammunition on the field, and some of their men fired over 400 rounds.

Colonel Witcher and Lieutenant Colonel Moseley were wounded here early in the action. Many in the regiment were also wounded. After staying here about two or three hours, we were ordered to the rear where we spent the remainder of the day gathering up the stragglers and those of our division who had escaped capture. That night we lay down on the ground for rest with truly great hearts that our regiment had been ordered out of the breastworks—even against our protest— and sent to the front on special service, thus escaping capture.

---

[14] Gordon was not promoted to major general until after the battle, and his promotion stemmed from his May 6 fighting in the Wilderness as well as from his gallantry at Spotsylvania. Freeman, *Lee's Lieutenants*, III, 434.

We remained in the rear until the morning of May 15. In the open field in the middle of our camp we found an old hare's bed containing four little ones. The mammy had run away on our approach! I do not know that I ever saw men more solicitous for the welfare of anything than were those grizzly warriors for those little bunnies. It was raining; some of the men wanted to make a house for them, while others wanted to hold their oilcloths over them. No one was allowed to touch them. One might look as much as he chose, but hands off! When we left, it was a sad parting.

Hancock's attack, formidable and intended to cut Lee's lines, was one of the most terrible battles of the war. It ended in a miserable failure. That night our line was straightened across the bend; breastworks were thrown up; and we had a much better line than before, both as to direction and position. While we were in the rear, we collected about 600 men of the division, marched to the front, and took position in this new line. The day was quiet in our front. On the 16th we had some skirmishing. On the 17th General Robert E. Rodes' skirmishers and our regiment made an attack on the enemy.[15] On the 18th the enemy, having been heavily reinforced, made an attack on our front. They were easily repulsed with heavy loss.[16] On the night of the 19th the enemy moved to their left and disappeared from our front. The Second Corps followed them and came up with them late in the evening. We made a fierce attack that lasted until late in the night.[17] We then marched back to our old position in the breastworks and rested there.

About the coolest thing I saw during the war was under that terrific fire from the Yankees who were in our breastworks. It should be remembered that, when we took our position in their front, we found one lone Confederate who was keeping up a steady fire on them. This man had captured a Yankee knapsack, which he had strapped on his back. Soon after our arrival he stopped firing and said that, as he needed a change of underclothing very badly, he wanted to see what he had in the knapsack. He took off the knapsack and opened it; from

[15] Worsham erred here; no engagement of any consequence occurred on May 17.

[16] At 8 A.M., May 18, Gen. W. S. Hancock attacked the Confederates with his II Corps. The Southerners countered with one of the most severe artillery barrages of the war. Twenty-nine guns hurled round shot at those Federals in the woods, and shell and case shot at those in the open. By 10 A.M. the battle was over, and Hancock's corps had been badly battered. OR, XXXVI, pt. 1, 337-38, 431-32, 1046, 1073, 1087-88; SHSP, XXXIII (1905), 333.

[17] On the 19th, in an effort to check the Federal move to the east, Ewell with 6,000 men assailed Gen. R. O. Tyler's division. Heavy Federal reinforcements soon forced Ewell to retire from the field. His losses numbered 900; those of the Federals were about 1,000. This engagement ended the fighting around Spotsylvania. OR, XXXVI, pt. 1, 140, 338, 1073, 1082-83.

the remarks he made as he took out each article and inspected it, he seemed to have gotten possession of a big clothing store with a notion store thrown in! He selected a suit of underclothing and laid it aside. He then replaced the remainder in the knapsack and fastened that, after which he deliberately undressed—taking off each piece of his clothing, even his socks. He put on the clean underclothes, donned his old uniform, and quietly took his gun. Bringing it up to his shoulder, he took deliberate aim and fired, and he loaded and fired as long as we were there!

In writing of this battle, Brigadier General James A. Walker, the commander of the Stonewall Brigade, stated:

"Before it became light enough to distinguish objects, the rapid firing of our skirmishers in the wooded ravine in front of the centre of Johnson's line gave notice that the enemy was advancing, and the heavy tramp of a large body of infantry and the sharp words of command could be distinctly heard. . . . Our men were all up and ready for them with their muskets cocked, peering through the gloom for the first glimpse of their foes. . . .

"The enemy . . . had emerged from the ravine and advanced about one-third of the way across the open plateau before they could be seen, or could themselves see our works on account of the fog. All at once the slowly-lifting fog showed them our heavily fortified position, some four or five hundred yards in their front. At this expected but unwelcome sight the advancing columns paused and wavered and hesitated, and seemed to refuse the task before them. Their mounted officers rode in front and urged them on, while many officers on foot and horseback shouted: 'Forward! men, forward!' and repeated the words again and again. Then the moment for the Confederate fire had come, and the men, rising to full height, leveled their trusty muskets deliberately at the halted column, with a practiced aim which would have carried havoc into their ranks. But the searching damp had disarmed them, and instead of the leaping line of fire and the sharp crack of the muskets came the pop! pop! pop! of exploding caps as the hammers fell upon them. A few, very few, pieces fired clear; but fresh caps on most of them only produced another failure. . . .

"As the enemy received no fire from our lines they took heart and again moved forward with rapid strides. On they came unopposed, and in a few moments had torn our well constructed abattis away and were over our works taking prisoners of our unarmed troops. . . .

"This statement as to the failure of the muskets of our men to fire is true as to that portion of our line between the Stonewall Brigade and the salient, which was far as my vision extended, but I have been informed by officers of Jones' Brigade that the right of that brigade had been more careful or more fortunate, and their muskets were in good order, and that the enemy was repulsed in front of that portion of our lines with great loss, and that they held their position until the enemy's troops, who had crossed to their left, had swung round in the rear and came up behind our lines."[18]

Major David W. Anderson of the 44th Virginia of the Second Brigade was officer of the day on May 11, at 4 a.m. on May 12, he stated, Captain Willam H. H. Clary of General Johnson's staff came to him with instructions from Johnson for the regimental commanders to awaken their men, have them in their trenches, and see that their guns were in good order. This order was promptly obeyed. Major Anderson further said that when the enemy advanced they were repulsed with great slaughter. Not one of them got to the breastworks until they crossed to the left and came up in the Confederate rear. Anderson and many of his regiment were taken prisoners and marched back some two or three miles to Provost Marshal Marsena Patrick's headquarters where, he said, one of General Patrick's staff said to him that they charged us "with only 45,000 this morning!"[19]

Among those lost in our division were Major General Johnson and Brigadier General Steuart, captured; Brigadier General Walker and Colonel Witcher (who commanded the Second Brigade in this battle), wounded. F Company lost W. C. Seay, who died of wounds a few hours after the battle, and W. B. Edmunds and P. S. Richeson, wounded.

While we were engaged in these battles, General Philip Sheridan with his cavalry left Grant's army May 9, 1864, on a raid to cut Lee's communications and capture Richmond. On the morning of the 12th he arrived at Brook Schoolhouse, on the Brook turnpike about three and a quarter miles from Richmond. At that time my grandmother, the widow of Captain John Goddin,[20] lived on the west side of that road, two and a quarter miles from Richmond, and her house fronted south. In front of it, several hundred yards off, was a fort situated on the turnpike at Laburnam. On the Hermitage road was a similar fort, and the two were connected by breastworks.

---

[18] *SHSP*, XXI (1893), 235-36.
[19] *Ibid.*, 251-54.
[20] John and Roxanna Ford Goddin were Worsham's maternal grandparents. Capt. Goddin, an officer in the War of 1812, was for a time sheriff of the Richmond area. He died in Feb., 1865, lacking three days of being eighty-five. His wife died five months later at the age of eighty.

On the morning of May 12 Grandmother got up early to do the churning (she preferred to do it herself), and she took her position on the front porch. When the butter "had come," she went to the well at the side of the house to cool the churn dasher and to get some cold water to take the butter up. At the same moment a squad of Yankee cavalry came around the other side of the house. Perceiving the churn, they helped themselves to buttermilk. When the old lady came back she found the Yankees on the porch, and one was drinking from the churn!

It made the old lady hot. She whacked him as hard as she could with the dasher, and she said some very plain words to the party. They ran off in good humor, saying they would see if our breastworks were manned. Going down a dividing fence until they reached the Laburnam fence, they fired a few shots. At once they discovered the breastworks were manned! They ran back to the house and went to the barnyard, where they took possession of a mule and cart, filled the cart with corn, and drove off toward the main body of Yankees at Brook schoolhouse. All at Grandmother's home lamented the loss of the fine mule and cart; but about two hours later, the mule came back with the empty cart!

That party of Yankees went nearer to Richmond than any raiders during the war. I should say the distance by the Brook turnpike was about two miles and 100 yards.[21]

On May 19 the Second Corps singularly occupied the left of Lee's line of battle at Spotsylvania Court House. When the line was first formed we were on the right. But Grant made all his movements to our right, and General Lee, in withdrawing men from the left to strengthen his right, had taken all except our corps. On the 21st we were aroused at daybreak. As soon as we formed ranks, we marched out of our breastworks toward the right of our line. As we passed, an occasional cannon shot and minie ball from the enemy passed over us. We marched past our right a short distance and took a road leading in the direction of Richmond. We continued this march until night, when we stopped to rest.

It will be remembered that Edward Johnson's division was nearly all captured on May 12. This was Jackson's old division and consisted of the Stonewall (First), Second, and Third Brigades—all Virginians, except two North Carolina regiments in the Third, plus the Fourth Brigade, which consisted of Louisianians. After bringing together the Virginia stragglers and such as were not captured, and putting regi-

21 Sheridan's report of this campaign is in *OR*, XXXVI, pt. 1, 776-78.

ments into companies and brigades into regiments, we found we had about 600 men. These were organized and called a brigade. Colonel William Terry of the 4th Virginia, Stonewall Brigade, was made brigadier general and appointed its commander. It was known to the end of the war as Terry's Brigade. The Louisiana Brigade was consolidated with another from that state in Early's division and was put under the command of Brigadier General Zebulon York. The North Carolinians joined some brigade from that state.[22]

When our brigade marched out onto the road on the morning of May 21, the brigades of York and Clement A. Evans joined us. We were told that Brigadier General Gordon had been made major general and had been put in command of these three brigades. We were afterwards known as Gordon's division of the Second Corps, and the division took a prominent part in all operations until the end came at Appomattox. While our brigade was known officially as Terry's, its members continued to designate the different bodies as the Stonewall, Second, and Third Brigades. In speaking or writing of them, I use these names. Thus, the Stonewall Brigade consisted in our view of its old members who were present, however few. We spoke of other brigades in the same way. We did this instead of using regiments to designate portions of this multiform brigade.

General Gordon soon rode by, and we filed into the road and followed him. We reached Hanover Junction in the night and ahead of Grant, who was marching for the same point. The next morning we formed a line of battle in a wood across the road on which he was marching. When his advance guard approached, it found Lee in their front again. We remained in our position, momentarily expecting an attack. Grant moved some of his troops across the South Anna River and made a demonstration in front of our line. During the day and night the remainder of Lee's army joined us and took position on our right and left. The next morning our division hurried at a double quick to the left of Lee's line and at once formed a line of battle. The hurry and the firing in our front caused us to expect to become heavily engaged. We waited several hours, then marched to the right of the line and stayed there all night. The following morning we took position on the east of the Richmond, Fredericksburg & Potomac Railroad and threw up breastworks. We continued in that position until the morning of May 27.

---

[22] The 1st and 3rd N. C. joined Gen. William R. Cox's brigade of Rodes' division. The thrice-wounded Terry (1824-1888) had first gained fame as colonel of the 4th Va., Stonewall Brigade.

Grant, after making a slight attack, left our front during the night of the 26th and swung around to our right. Early on the morning of the 27th the Second Corps was on the march to oppose him again. We marched to Pole Green Church, the place where Jackson first struck McClellan's outposts in 1862. On the morning of the 29th we formed a line of battle not far from Bethesda Church and threw up breastworks. When Grant came along the road that evening, he found our division across the road in his front and again ready for him! After slight skirmishing he drew off without making an attack. On the next morning the Second Corps made an attack and drove Grant about one and a half miles. We then returned to our line and resumed our position in the breastworks.[23]

Tucker Randolph, the gallant boy soldier in old F Company, was killed in this fight. He deserves more than a passing notice. Entering the service at the age of seventeen, he took an active part in the company from the first, and he was one of the first men promoted in the field. A sergeant when wounded at Kernstown, he soon after was promoted to lieutenant and appointed an aide on Brigadier General John Pegram's staff. He was killed while displaying conspicuous gallantry.

On May 31 we moved to the right and again threw up breastworks. On June 1 the Second Corps marched to the front to make an attack on the enemy, but for some reason it was not made. After sharp skirmishing lasting until sunset, we returned to our breastworks. On the next morning we moved out again, made the attack, took three lines of fortifications, and captured about 700 prisoners.[24] We remained in the enemy's line and next to them until about midnight of June 3, when we withdrew and took our old position in the breastworks. While we were in the enemy's works, they made several slight attacks on us. They fired their artillery through the woods. Once they fired two rammers of their cannon, and the rammers stuck in the ground a little in the rear of the 21st Virginia. Corporal James H. Anderson was wounded in those fortifications on June 3, and Captain Reuben Jordan was severely wounded while he was on the skirmish line in front of them.

---

[23] On May 30, in another effort to check Grant's movement, Gen. Early launched a heavy attack with two brigades. Insufficient reconnaissance by Early and improper coordination with A. P. Hill doomed the assault. Entrenched Federals easily repulsed the attack and, in the process, inflicted high casualties. See Clifford Dowdey, *Lee's Last Campaign* (Boston, 1960), pp. 278-80.

[24] Early was not ordered by Lee to make a June 1 assault against the heavy concentration of Federals in his front. On the afternoon of the 2nd, as Grant's army continued eastward, Early's three divisions attacked and carried part of the Federal line, capturing "several hundred prisoners," Early stated. Near 4 P.M. a heavy downpour of rain put an end to the battle. J. A. Early, *War Memoirs*, edited by Frank E. Vandiver (Bloomington, Ind., 1960), pp. 362-63.

During the night of June 5 the enemy left the front of our corps. We followed them the next morning and found them fortified about one and a half miles to our right. On the 7th the skirmishers were ordered forward, and our division was ordered to support them. On the 9th the Second Corps moved to the right and rear of General Lee's line. We stacked arms and went into camp, having been on active duty for thirty-five days and under fire each day.

Because Lieutenant General Ewell was sick,[25] the corps was under the command of Major General Early during these operations. Major General Stephen D. Ramseur was assigned to command Early's division. The Second Corps now consisted of the infantry divisions of Rodes, Gordon, and Ramseur, with the usual artillery. Since the battle of the Wilderness, May 5, our corps had lost heavily in men and officers. Brigadier Generals Stafford, Doles, Junius Daniel, and J. M. Jones had been killed. Brigadier Generals Pegram, J. A. Walker, R. D. Johnston, and Harry Hays had been wounded. Major General Edward Johnson and Brigadier General George H. Steuart were prisoners. Although we did not realize it at the time, Grant's "hammering" had commenced and was telling.

The Army of Northern Virginia had inflicted terrible losses on the enemy. It is said by their historians that Grant lost at this time about as many men as there were in General Lee's army, and that the loss he sustained before crossing the James River made the total about 10,000 more than Lee's whole force.[26]

One of the incidents of this campaign was the visit of an old up-country man, who came to see his son in our division. He wore a stovepipe hat, and the men had great fun over that hat. Yet he was a jolly old fellow and was not worried by them. He was very anxious to see a battle. While he was with us, we made one of our advances. He accompanied his son and returned unhurt with us. He was the most enthusiastic man I ever saw.

---

[25] Ewell suffered from "an acute intestinal malady," resulting in part at least, from a complete disregard for his health. He "recklessly slept on the ground and exerted himself ceaselessly;" consequently, throughout this campaign he was "in danger of collapse under his burdens." Ewell's wife wrote that on May 27 her husband "was attacked with something of the nature of scurvy, consequent on living on salt meat, and a terrible exertion . . ." On the following day, Ewell relinquished command to Early. Freeman, *Lee's Lieutenants*, III, 433, 498-99; Percy G. Hamlin (ed.), *The Making of a Soldier: Letters of General R. S. Ewell* (Richmond, 1935), p. 127.

[26] In the period May 5-June 24, 1864, Grant lost 54,926 men, including 7,621 killed. Lee's army at the outset of the campaign numbered about 64,000 effectives. *OR,* XXXVI, pt. 1, 188; Walter H. Taylor, *Four Years with General Lee,* ed. James I. Robertson, Jr. (Bloomington, Ind., 1962), p. 136.

While we were marching through Hanover County, an old lady came to the fence that ran along the road and wanted to know if we belonged to "Mr. Lee's Company." We told her we belonged to *General* Lee's *army*. She asked how her son was; when we informed her that we did not know him, she was perfectly astonished to think any man in "Mr. Lee's Company" did not know all the men in it.

Chapter IX

"HELL BROKE LOOSE NOW!"

On June 12, 1864, the Second Corps received orders to cook rations and be ready to move early the next morning. We were aroused about midnight and formed into line. Before day we marched out of the woods onto a road leading toward Mechanicsville. Arriving there we turned toward Richmond, thinking we were going to head Grant off on the south side of the Chickahominy. Soon after crossing that stream, we turned to the right (west), instead of the left as we had supposed. "What does this mean?" was the question among the men. We marched around Richmond to Three Chopt Road, then turned to the right again. We gave up guessing, except that possibly Jackson's old corps was going back to the Valley.

In marching around Richmond, our route was about a mile from the home of relatives of mine, and I went to see them. When I reached the house I found all the ladies of the family and two of Richmond's belles assembled on a large porch. I was welcomed most cordially and told I was just in time for luncheon. In a few minutes the dining-room servant appeared with a large waiter filled with ash cakes. Without formality I took one in each hand and, with one of the belles waiting on me, I was presented with a huge glass filled with buttermilk and ice. In this plain but whole-souled manner, we partook of our luncheon. That was a rich treat to me, and I know that it was enjoyed by the belles more than if set with fashion's formality. I can see those belles now, eating their ash cake and drinking their buttermilk—entering into the fun and mirth of the occasion in spite of the sound of distant cannon from Lee's and Grant's armies and the cheers from my own corps, marching we knew not whither.

Late in the afternoon, having marched over twenty-five miles, we went into camp near Ground Squirrel Bridge. On the following morning we marched again. About 10 o'clock General Gordon passed us and told us not to march so fast or the mules to the wagons would not be able to keep up with us, and in consequence we would not have supper. Gordon always had something pleasant to say to his men, and I will bear my testimony that he was the most gallant man I ever saw on a battlefield. He had a way of putting things to the men that was irresistible, and he showed them at all times that he shrank from nothing in battle. Many a time during this campaign I saw him ride along the skirmish line and say such things to the skirmishers as: "Let's drive those fellows away, and let our line of battle stay where they are! They are lazy fellows, anyway!" The skirmishers were devoted to him, and they would generally do as he wished.

On June 15 we came in sight of the Virginia Central Railroad, and we passed Trevilian's Depot, where Sheridan's cavalry and ours, under General Wade Hampton, had had a fight two or three days before.[1] We could see the dead horses, torn-down fences, etc., as if nothing had been touched. We saw the rail pens used by Hampton's men that Sheridan made such an ado about—saying he could not whip Hampton as his men were behind such strong fortifications!

On the evening of the 16th we went into camp about one mile beyond Keswich Depot. On the 17th my brigade got on railroad cars a little north of Keswich and rode to Lynchburg. Much to our surprise, we found the town in great excitement, because the enemy, under Major General David Hunter, had advanced to within two miles of the place. With only a small Confederate force in his front, the citizens expected immediately to see the enemy march into the town. Our presence brought an immediate change. We were cheered to the echo, and the ladies waved their hands and gave us lunches and cool water as we marched through the city.[2] All wished that Hunter would stay until Early could bring up all of his army.

We marched past the fairgrounds and formed a line of battle. We moved forward, halted near a schoolhouse, and remained there all night. We heard skirmishing in our front and cannonading on our left. We remained in line of battle until the afternoon of June 18, when we received orders to cook rations and be ready to move early the next morning. This meant that the remainder of our force was up, and that we were going to attack Hunter as soon as it was light enough to see. Our skirmish line advanced in the morning and found that Hunter had

[1] On June 11 Gen. P. H. Sheridan and 8,500 Federal troopers ran into 5,000 Confederate horsemen under Gen. Wade Hampton some twenty-eight miles east of Charlottesville. For two days ensued "as bewildering a fight as . . . cavalry ever had waged." Both sides won and lost advantages. In the end, nevertheless, "the operation could not be regarded otherwise than as a Southern victory." Freeman, *Lee's Lieutenants*, III, 518-22.

[2] J. Scott Moore of the 14th Va. Cavalry expressed the exhiliration of many of Lynchburg's meager defenders when he wrote: "Napoleon never looked upon his 'Old Guard,' or Cæsar his 'Tenth Legion,' with more pride than I did that evening upon the advance of Early's men through those fields of golden grain." SHSP, XXVII (1899), 190.

slipped out of the trap during the night and was in full retreat.[3] Immediate pursuit commenced, and we overtook him going into camp at Liberty in Bedford County. Our advance attacked him at once.[4] Hunter retreated further, and we camped in the place selected by him. During that day we marched twenty-five miles, and we did not let Hunter rest much. We followed him closely until we came to Salem in Roanoke County. Here General Early gave up the pursuit and turned toward the Valley. Before we reached Salem, he sent General John McCausland with his cavalry around to the rear of Hunter. McCausland succeeded in cutting off part of the enemy's wagon train, and he captured ten pieces of artillery.

One afternoon during this march, soon after passing Big Lick,[5] we approached one of the handsome residences in that part of the country. We noticed several ladies standing on the side of the road and, when we came nearer, we saw two beautiful young ladies and their maids. Near them were two huge wash tubs. The young ladies invited us to come forward and partake of some ice water and brandy julep. The men needed no second invitation. The head of the column marched up; the young ladies handed each man a drink, which was received eagerly with many grateful wishes for their future welfare. I was told that the tubs were repeatedly emptied and filled. This was the biggest julep treat of my experience.

We marched a short distance from Salem and encamped, remaining in camp the next day and taking a much-needed rest. Many men were barefooted—some for want of shoes, others having sore feet from new shoes and therefore unable to wear them. To the latter class I belonged. I started from Richmond wearing a new pair of heavy English shoes. When I took them off at the close of the first day's march, nearly all the skin on my feet came off with my socks. I therefore went through the campaign as far as Washington and back to Winchester barefooted, but I kept my place in the ranks. For several days I carried my shoes tied together and thrown over my shoulders. But I was troubled so much by questions and by requests to buy them that I finally gave them to a comrade who had none.

---

[3] A lieutenant in the 91st Ohio later wrote with disgust of Hunter: "Had the generalship that guided the movement been equal to the spirit and courage of the troops, Lynchburg would have fallen into our hands." *Sketches of War History, 1861-1865: Papers Prepared for the Ohio Commandery of the Military Order of the Loyal Legion of the United States,* II (1896), 146. Hereafter cited as *Sketches of War History.* See also Douglas, *Stonewall,* pp. 290, 292, 297-99.

[4] On June 19 Early attacked Hunter's rear guard, a cavalry division under Gen. W. W. Averell. It "stood the brunt of a severe attack for two hours," Averell reported, before falling back for want of ammunition. Federal losses numbered 122 men. *OR,* XXXVII, pt. 1, 101, 148.

[5] Now Roanoke, Va.

On June 23 we took up our march. The next day, at the request of the men, we marched over Natural Bridge and were allowed to rest there an hour or two and view the bridge. Resuming our march, we went into camp about sunset. The next morning, as we passed through Lexington, the whole corps marched through the burial ground and past Jackson's grave. What hallowed memories it brought up! Many a tear was seen trickling down the cheeks of his veterans. How many of them had crossed the river and were then resting "beneath the shade of the trees" with him!

We continued our march and on the 27th reached Staunton. Fourteen days had elapsed since we left Lee's line at Richmond. During that time we marched 235 miles in eleven days (marching only six miles the last day). On our march from Lynchburg, we passed many private places that had been pillaged or destroyed by Hunter's army. At Lexington we passed the ruins of the Virginia Military Institute, which Hunter burned while he was on his way to Lynchburg.

On June 28 we resumed our march down the Valley. We felt perfectly at home, since nearly all the Valley from Staunton to the Potomac River was familiar to us and many of its inhabitants old acquaintances. We stopped regularly at night and continued the march each day. On the afternoon of July 3 we reached Martinsburg and ran into the Yankees who were there so suddenly that they did not have time to move any of their stores. They were making big preparations to celebrate the Fourth, and many of the men had received boxes of good things from home and friends. The depot and express office were filled with articles of this kind. A guard was placed around these buildings and the enemy storehouses. The express office was put in charge of a quartermaster who was an old friend of mine. At night I went there and inquired of him, and the guard let me into the building. The quartermaster was very glad to see me, as he had only one man to help him get those articles in shape. I consented to help him if he would give me a barrel of cakes. He said all right. I found one, carried it out, and turned it over to my company. On returning, I went to work with a will. Yet with so many good things in sight, and with others that we knew were in the boxes, I was compelled to say to my friend that I must have something to eat before I could work any more. "I haven't had 'nary' mouthful for three days," I said.

Looking over some of the boxes, I chose one, opened it, and found it filled with cakes, oranges, bananas, lemons, and a bottle of wine. I got a chair—"a sure enough chair," as the soldiers said—and sat down to my box. I ate and ate until I could eat no more. Then I went to work again with renewed energy. The quartermaster just then wanted something from one of his associates who was at the depot. When I offered to go for him, he agreed and gave me directions. I reached the depot and found it filled with trunks, boxes, etc. After discharging my errand, I looked around the depot a few minutes and told the man in charge that he ought to send his friend, the quartermaster, one of the trunks for him to put some of the articles at the express office in to take with him. He said he would be much obliged if I would take one.

I shouldered one at once, carried it out, and got a comrade to help me carry it to the express office. I made my report and opened the trunk. In it was a magnificent saddle and a lot of clothing which I gave to the quartermaster, plus a fine pair of boots, a gold pen, a lot of writing paper, and a plum cake which I "confiscated." The boots fit me to a "T." When my feet healed enough for me to wear them, I wore them until I went home. I joined the members of my company, who were profuse in their thanks for the cakes, and soon fell asleep—dreaming of little cakes, big cakes, and a mountain made of cakes.

The next day was July 4, 1864. General Early did not move us at the usual early hour; rather, he issued to the men the good things captured the evening before. They were divided among the men as fairly as possible. F Company got a few oranges, lemons, cakes, candy, and a keg of lager beer. We certainly enjoyed the treat. We celebrated the day as well as we could for our hosts whom, we regretted, did not stay to preside for us. We drank to their health with the wish that they would do the like again. This was the biggest Fourth of July picnic celebration we enjoyed during the war.

We took up our march and crossed the Potomac at Shepherdstown. I took off my clothing, made a bundle, and secured it around my neck with my belt. I then walked into the water and commenced to ford. For about one-third of the way the river was covered with large round stones, after which was a smooth and level bed of granite that extended nearly to the opposite bank. I got along very well until I reached the level granite bottom, which was covered with minute shells so very sharp that they stuck into my feet at every step. I walked on them until I thought I could not take another step. Then I stopped, but I could not keep my feet still. I thought of sitting down, but the water was just deep enough to cover my mouth and nose if I did so. I thought of turning back, but I saw it was just as far to the other side. Tears actually came into my eyes. I was never in as much torture for the same length of time in my life. Finally I got over, with the resolve never to ford there again without shoes.

We went into camp that night on the banks of the Antietam and on ground occupied by a part of McClellan's army at the battle of Sharpsburg. The next day Gordon's division marched to Harper's Ferry, where we drove the enemy into their fortifications. We skirmished there the succeeding day, left during the night, and marched to Norristown, where we joined the remainder of our corps. The next morning we crossed South Mountain at Fox Gap and went into camp near Middletown.

During these operations Major General John C. Breckinridge's command, which we found at Lynchburg, joined General Early.[6] At this juncture Gordon's division was assigned to Breckinridge, thus making a corps or wing under his command.

Early on July 9 we left camp, or rather our bivouac, near Middletown. Taking the road to Frederick, Maryland, we marched around and in sight of the town. It was a beautiful day in this beautiful country. The sun was bright and hot, and a nice breeze was blowing that kept us from being too warm. The air was laden with the perfume of flowers; the birds were singing in bush and tree; all the fields were green with growing crops. The city, with its thriftiness, looked as if it had just been painted and whitened. A few floating clouds added effect to the landscape. It was a day and hour to impress all. We marched along quietly, talking about the scene and the day.

We left the city in our rear and neared the Monocacy, a river crossing the road on which we were marching. We soon heard the crack of muskets, and at almost the same moment the roar of cannon. We knew what that meant: the Yankees were going to dispute our crossing of the river. The two divisions in front of us were hurried forward. Our division halted after going a short distance, and we were told to stack arms and rest, as we would not go into the fight. The men took off blankets, oilcloths, etc., and stretched them in fence corners, on muskets, and on rails to make shelters from the sun. We were in the road and on a hill that overlooked the battle that was about to be fought in our front. We made ourselves comfortable and lay down under the shelter provided, to *look* at a battle. As Jackson's old "foot cavalry," this was something we had never done.

---

[6] Breckinridge's well-traveled force of 5,000 men consisted of two depleted brigades, four companies from VMI, a battery of artillery, and a skeleton cavalry brigade. On May 15 it had defeated Sigel at New Market, had rushed to Richmond in time to participate in the Cold Harbor campaign, and on June 7 had headed westward to Lynchburg.

We saw our men take position in line of battle. The skirmishers went forward and became engaged with the enemy on the opposite side of the river. A battery here and there on the other side shelled our men, while the continual *crack* of muskets told that the shelling made no impression on our skirmishers, who were now in the bushes along the river bank. Some of our guns went into position and opened fire; our line moved forward—all this in plain view of our division.

It was very exciting to us old Confederates, and a yell went up along our line every few minutes as we saw our men get into some better place and nearer the enemy. The men of our division were suggesting to each other a line on which our two divisions should cross the river. Suddenly our attention was called to a man riding up the road toward us and leaving a streak of dust behind him. He rode up to General Gordon, who was at the head of the division, and delivered a message. The general gave an order to the officers in front and then mounted his horse. We were called to attention, and the men took down thir blankets and oilcloths and rolled them up to take with them. "Take arms!" came the order. "No time now for blankets, but get into your places at once!"

All down the line came the command, "Right face! Forward march!" and away we went. "What is the matter?" was the question amongst the men. We thought we were to be spectators. We could not understand why, just as things had begun to get interesting in front, officers would break in upon us and actually make some of us leave our blankets and oilcloths—articles we had captured in some former battle. The men seemed more to dislike losing these articles than to miss seeing the battle.[7]

We hurried along the road for a short distance, then filed to the right and went through fields and over fences until we came to the river at a point we supposed was a mile or so from our line of battle. We found a small path on the river bank leading down to the water. On the opposite bank was a similar one, thus denoting a ford used by neighbors for crossing the river. The craking of muskets on the opposite side of the river told us that the front of our division, which had crossed, was engaged. My brigade was the rear one and, as the regiments crossed, they marched up the river along the low bank. We were formed in line and ordered forward to the attack.

---

[7] What Worsham and his compatriots did not know was that Ramseur's small division had assailed a Federal force of 6,000 men under Gen. Lew Wallace. When Early realized the situation, he ordered Gordon's division, with Gen. John McCausland's cavalry clearing the way, to cross the river and strike the Federal left flank.

As the Second Brigade mounted the hill, we saw in our front a field of corn about waist high and extending to a post and rail fence. Behind that fence was the Yankee line of battle. They began to shoot at us as soon as we were in sight. The men on our right were heavily engaged; we broke into a run with a yell and went toward the fence. In a moment or two we captured it, the Yankees running to another fence.[8]

An officer came along our line and said that we were not wanted there, that General Gordon was waiting for the Second Brigade, that we were wrong and must fall back through the corn, behind the hill, on the low bank, form at once and go to General Gordon. We had been fighting all this time, but as soon as the men could be made to understand, they ran to the rear. The brigade was soon formed and we marched by the flank further up the river. Then the head of the column turned to the right and we marched up on top of the hill. There was Gordon. I shall recollect him to my dying day. Not another man was in sight. He was sitting on his horse as quietly as if nothing was going on. He was wearing his old red shirt, with the sleeves pulled up a little—the only indication that he was ready for a fight.

Our division was heavily engaged on the right, and we could plainly hear that the troops on the other side of the river were keeping up their fire. We were to the left of the cornfield and marching obliquely from it. The ground had a gentle inclination, and the fields were enclosed with post and rail fences. As we approached General Gordon, he rode forward to meet us and said, "Hurry up, boys." He turned his horse and took the lead.

The head of the column was soon near a fence, and high enough up the hill to see some distance. Looking through this fence we could see another fence parallel to and about 200 yards from it. Just on the other side of the second fence was a line of Yankees marching toward the river. They were going at a double quick step and at right-shoulder-shift arms. Every man seemed to be in place, and the manner of their marching looked more like a drill than a movement in battle. Seeing this, the men at the head of our column gave a yell and sang out, "At them, boys!"

Now came General Gordon's part. He turned quietly in his saddle and said, "Keep quiet. We'll have our time presently."

As we neared the fence, General Gordon said, "Some of you pull down the fence so that we may get through."

---

[8] In reporting this assault Gordon stated that Terry's brigade "advanced with great spirit and in excellent order, driving the enemy from his position . . ." *OR*, XXXVII, pt. 1, 351. See also Gordon, *Reminiscences*, pp. 309-13.

In an instant several panels of the fence were down. The men quietly stepped aside to let the general go through and, as soon as this was done, they hurried through the fence. The first man to follow the general through the fence was a barefooted member of F Company.

General Gordon led in the direction in which we had been marching, and he tried to allay the excitement of the men. This he was able to do until about 100 men passed through the fence. Then a cry went up from them: "Charge them! Charge them!"

It was useless for General Gordon to try to stop it now—nothing but a shot through each man could have done it. With a yell we were at the fence. A volley from our guns, and that magnificent body of men who were taking their places in line were flying![9] The other men of our brigade came up as fast as they could run and delivered their fire at the fleeing enemy. Over the fence we went, the enemy running in all directions. Up went our old yell all along the line of our division, and it was answered by our comrades on the other side of the river.

A little way beyond the fence the hill fell abruptly to a small valley, and through this valley ran the road to Washington. Some of the enemy stopped at the road, turned and fired at us. It was just here that Porter Wren[10] of F Company received his fatal wound. He turned and managed to walk back to the fence; but when he tried to get over it, he fell back dead. Immediately on the brow of the hill I passed a Yankee colonel, lying dead on the ground.[11]

This was the most exciting time I witnessed during the war. The men, knowing as they did that the first line that fired would have the advantage of the other, were perfectly wild when they came in sight of the enemy's column. It was as much as General Gordon could do to keep the head of the column from making an attack.

Our division pursued the enemy a short distance. The pursuit was then taken up by Ramseur's division, which had crossed the river on the railroad bridge as soon as we cleared the way. It was about sunset now, and my brigade went into camp in an orchard near the road—on the same ground over which we had chased the enemy a few minutes

---

[9] "This movement," wrote Gordon, "promptly executed with a simultaneous attack from the front, resulted in the dislodging of [the Federal] line, and the complete rout of the enemy's forces." OR, XXXVII, pt. 1, 351-52.

[10] A clerk from Powhatan, Va., the thirty-three-year-old Wren was 6'1" tall, with blue eyes and dark hair. The death bullet at Monocacy struck him in the left breast and ripped through his right shoulder. He was buried on the field. Wren's personal service file, War Records Group 109, National Archives; Worsham to his mother, July 15, 1864, Worsham Papers.

[11] No Federal colonel was killed at Monocacy. The sixteen Union officers who lost their lives in the action included 7 captains and 9 lieutenants. OR, XXXVII, pt. 1, 202-03.

before. In this orchard were several wounded enemy. One of them asked me for some water; he stated that he had had a canteen but that one of our men had taken it from him. Poor fellow! I went to a spring, filled a canteen, and carried it to him. As I had two canteens, I gave him this one and told him that, in case some of our men wanted it, he must tell them what I had done for him, and I was sure none of our men would take it. I had a full haversack that I had taken from the body of a dead Yankee on the hill. I offered the wounded man something to eat, but he said he had his own haversack, and that it was full. He seemed to be very grateful for my little attention.

As a mill pond was near us, many of us took a bath, which refreshed us very much. I ate a good supper out of my Yankee haversack and soon went to bed for the night. In this battle F Company had J. Porter Wren killed and H. C. Fox wounded. Early's loss was not large and was confined principally to Gordon's division. Among the wounded was Brigadier General C. A. Evans. We captured five or six hundred prisoners; General Early sent us word to take no more, as he did not know what to do with them.[12] The tables were completely turned on Gordon's division. We thought we would *witness* the battle, but instead our little army saw our division of 2,300 men whip Wallace's force of 10,000.[13] General Breckinridge, who commanded his own and Gordon's division during this campaign, said to General Gordon about this battle: "If you had never made a fight before, this ought to immortalize you."

The road to Washington was now open, and on the morning of the next day, July 10, we hastened as fast as men could travel. We marched early, passing through Urbanna, Hyattstown and Clarksburg, and went into camp about sunset after marching twenty odd miles. The day was a terribly hot one and the men straggled a great deal, even though it was reported that the enemy cavalry we left at Harper's Ferry were following us and picking up all stragglers they could reach. We were up and moving early the next morning. We passed through Rockville, Maryland, and at 2 or 3 p.m. the head of Gordon's division passed the toll gate about four or five miles from Washington. We inquired what road we were on and were informed that it was the Seventh Street Pike. At this point the enemy were shelling the road

---

[12] Worsham erred about Early's directive; the Confederate commander did not order "no quarter given" in the battle's final stages.

[13] Wallace used but half of his 6,000 men in the engagement and suffered 1,649 casualties, including 700 prisoners. Although Wallace reported Early as having an "overwhelming force" of 20,000 troops, in reality only two Confederate divisions—numbering 3,500 men—took part in the battle. Their losses were less than 700. *OR*, XXXVII, pt. 1, 192; Douglas, *Stonewall*, p. 293.

with their big guns. We soon came in sight of the Soldiers' Home, where the enemy had a signal station. We could see the fortifications on each side of the road on which we were, and the men marching into them. Their dress induced us to think they were the town or city forces, for some of them looked as if they had on linen dusters, and none of them were in regular uniform. We were really at Washington.

Probably this day was hotter than the preceding one, and we had also been marching faster. Consequently, there was more straggling. Our division was stretched out almost like skirmishers, and all the men did not get up until night. Rodes' division was in front. He had formed a line of battle and sent forward his skirmishers, who had driven the enemy into their fortifications. Our division stacked arms on the side of the road; the men then broke ranks and looked around. A house between the two lines was burning.

I went to Silver Springs, the country home of Mr. Francis P. Blair,[14] one of Lincoln's cabinet members. I got water and examined the place. It was a splendid home. When I came back, I went to the front and looked out on the situation. As far as my eye could reach to the right and left were fortifications, and the most formidable looking I ever saw! The trees in their front had been cut down, and the sharpened limbs pointed toward us. About midway of the clearing was a creek that seemed to run near the fortifications and parallel to them. The enemy had a full sweep of the ground for at least a mile in their front. If their works were well manned, our force would not be able to take them—since, as I suppose, General Early's entire command did not number 10,000.

Night came on and found us occupying the same position. The next morning Gordon's division marched to the front and formed line of battle. We advanced to the edge of the wood and lay down, while our skirmish line was sent forward to the creek. We remained in our position all day. The enemy shelled us at intervals, and in the afternoon they sent skirmishers forward with a large force following them. They made an attack on Rodes' front. He repulsed them and drove them back into their works.[15] That night we left Washington and retraced our steps on the road as far as Rockville. There we took a road to the left, marched all night, and stopped about midway for several

---

[14] During his campaign against Washington, Early used Blair's Silver Springs home as his headquarters. A short distance away was the impressive residence of Postmaster General Montgomery Blair, which Confederates burned contrary to Early's orders against wanton destruction.

[15] Early reported that Rodes' men repulsed three Federal assaults. *OR,* XXXVII, pt. 1, 348-49. For the particulars of this engagement, see Frank E. Vandiver, *Jubal's Raid* (New York, 1960), pp. 167-71.

hours' rest near Darnestown. We then resumed the march and continued it all night. We passed Poolville, crossed the Potomac the next day at White's Ford, and went into camp near Leesburg.

Thirty-one days had passed since we left Lee's army at Richmond. During that time we had marched 469 miles, fought several combats and one battle, and threatened Washington, causing the biggest scare they ever had. It was believed by the men that we could have gone into the city on the evening of July 11 if our men had been up; but straggling prevented it.[16] I cannot say that they straggled without excuse because, as I said before, many of them were barefooted and footsore, and we had made a terrible campaign since we left our winter quarters on May 2. I was still barefooted; my feet were too sore to wear my boots. The scars made on that march are on my feet to this day. Many men, like myself, marched right along without shoes, but many of them were physically unable to keep up.

It is said that the enemy concentrated over 60,000 soldiers at Washington while we were threatening the city.[17] This force pursued us to the Potomac, but did us little damage.

The next day, July 15, the 21st Virginia was detailed to take charge of a lot of horses that had broken down on the way, others having been captured and put into their places. We immediately converted ourselves into a regiment of mounted infantry—the most motley ever seen. Some of the men secured saddles, some got bags and filled them with straw, and some merely used their blankets to ride on. Some horses had bridles, some had ropes, some had grape vines for bridles, and some were ridden without any form of bridles. As soon as we were mounted, we took up the march, driving the loose horses as we went. We passed through Union and Upperville, then stopped about sunset to let our horses graze. This was the only food they had had.

After several hours of rest we again mounted and continued the march. Riding all night, we passed through the Blue Ridge at Paris and moved into the Valley. We stopped the next morning near Millwood in Clarke County, and turned our horses loose to graze. We had marched about thirty-three miles, and we were the most completely used up men you ever saw. As we found out to our cost, foot cavalry could not be converted at once into mounted men. When the order to mount was given about midday, we were so sore and disabled that

---

[16] Worsham meant other men in the Confederate ranks. Ramseur voiced basically the same sentiments. See Freeman, *Lee's Lieutenants*, III, 567. See also the commentary of Lt. E. S. Dudley, 2nd U. S. Artillery, in *Sketches of War History*, I (1888), 122.

[17] This was a gross exaggeration. At no time during the siege did more than 20,000 men confront Early—and at least half of them were merchants, convalescing troops, youths, and other unorganized defenders. Vandiver, *Jubal's Raid*, pp. 142, 159.

nearly all the men needed assistance in mounting. We left this place and marched to Middletown on the Valley pike, stopping several times to graze our horses. On the morning of the 19th we turned our horses over to a quartermaster and marched to Winchester, where we joined our division.

The next day the army marched up the Valley. Reaching Middletown, Gordon's division was sent out in the direction of Berryville, for it had been reported that the enemy was advancing in that direction. After some brisk skirmishing, we drove them back. That night we marched to Hupp's Hill. The next day the army formed a line of battle and awaited an attack from the enemy. They came in sight of us, fired a few cannon, and sent out some skirmishers. Their army was now under the command of Major General George Crook, and the officer in command of their cavalry was Brigadier General William W. Averell.

The enemy soon left our front at Hupp's Hill and, on the morning of July 24, we marched down the Valley to Barton's Mill, where we learned that the enemy had made a stand at Kernstown. General Early immediately made plans to attack them. The Second Brigade was deployed as skirmishers, and it was posted on the left of the Valley pike, with its right resting on the pike. The rest of Gordon's division formed on the right of the pike with the remainder of Breckinridge's command. The Second Brigade was ordered forward in skirmish line. In our front was an open field almost level to the enemy's line of battle. There the country became gently rolling, and the enemy had stationed their artillery on the hills. Stone fences separated the fields, and several of them, occupied by the enemy, ran across our front. Soon after we began our advance, we came in sight of the hill occupied by a battery that fired at our regiment in March, 1862, when we crossed this same field.

They now sent shell after shell at us; and as soon as we were within range, the Yankees behind the first stone wall commenced to fire with their muskets. We were ordered to lie down. From this point we could see a long line of the enemy on the right of the pike, and on their extreme left was a body of cavalry. We also saw Breckinridge advancing against their left. The Yankees in front of our brigade were shooting rapidly at us.[18] Our men, lying down in the field, were becoming uneasy, since we had no opportunity to reply. Stooping down behind

---

[18] The Federals confronting Terry's brigade on the extreme left of Early's line were the 18th Conn., 2nd Md., and the 1st, 4th, and 12th (West) Va., under Col. William G. Ely. *OR*, XXXVII, pt. 1, 301-02.

the wall, the Yankees would load, rise, fire, and then lie down before we could locate them.

Our men sent a message along the line: "Let's take the wall!"

Back came the answer: "All right!"

We were up in a second, at the wall in a few more seconds, and the enemy retreated to the next wall. This wall was not very far from us; our men were mounting the wall already taken, some were over, and all were going to take the next wall!

Just then an officer came from General Early with an order for us to halt, retrace our steps, and lie down in the field again. Our brigade commander, Colonel R. H. Dungan[19] of the 48th Virginia, told him that he did not give the order to advance, but that he saw no reason to stop it after the men had started.

"Well, you must stop them now," said the officer.

Colonel Dungan gave the order to halt. It was obeyed very reluctantly—the men standing where they were with the Yankees shooting at them all the time. The officer from General Early, Major Mann Page[20] (an old F Company man), could not stand this. He was very impetuous and called to the men to return, but he could not induce them to do so. They cried out, "Let's drive them away from the wall!" and away we went, leaving the major stamping with rage.

We took the second wall in about the same time it takes to tell it, and we drove a line of battle from it. By this time Breckinridge had struck their left, and their whole line was in rapid retreat. As those on their left made for the Valley pike, nearly all of them passed us. We loaded and fired into their ranks as fast as we could. In their excitement some of our men sat on the stone wall, loading and firing from it. Yet the retreating column of the enemy seemed to be so intent on getting away that they gave no attention to our small line on the wall. As soon as all of them passed us, over the wall we went in close pursuit.

They went through the village of Kernstown, keeping on the pike until they reached an old stone church and burial yard. They turned to the left between them and went directly to the hills around Winchester.

---

[19] Robert Dungan enlisted as a lieutenant in the 48th Va., May 18, 1861, at the age of twenty-six. At Chancellorsville he narrowly escaped death when a spent cannon ball struck him in the chest but broke no bones. During this battle he commanded the 21st, 25th, 42nd, 44th, and 48th Va. Regts. in Terry's amalgamated brigade. Dungan's personal service file, War Records Group 109, National Archives; *OR*, XXV, pt. 1, 1029; XLIII, pt. 2, 928.

[20] Page, then twenty-nine years old, was normally an "inexhaustible fund of amusement and interest." Cited for gallantry at Kernstown, he was captured twice at Cedar Run but escaped both times. He served on Early's staff for the remainder of the war. *Ham Chamberlayne*, pp. 91, 135; Page's personal service file, War Records Group 109, National Archives; *OR*, XII, pt. 1, 403.

The first fire we received from them in their retreat was from a fence just beyond the old church. As we reached the church and turned around it toward the fence through which they went, a few of their skirmishers along the fence fired on us. Sergeant Addison W. Greever[21] of the 48th Virginia, who was carrying the flag, was shot dead at my side, and one or two more were wounded. The enemy had no time for a second fire, as we were upon them. From this fence to another about a quarter of a mile off, the field was filled with fleeing Yankees; and beyond the second fence, I could see them making their way over the hill. In order to help their men in the field, some of them were firing at us from the second fence. An officer on a white horse seemed to be directing them.[22] Some of us paid our respects to him, while the balance shot into the mass of the enemy in the field. Before we were halfway across the field, their fire ceased and they and the officer on the white horse disappeared over the hill.

When we reached the hill we were so tired that we could run no longer. Yet we continued the pursuit, followed their trail, and only came in sight of the enemy as they went up the hill just behind Winchester. On that hill they had one piece of artillery, which fired once at us, then limbered up and joined in the retreat. We continued the pursuit until sunset, when we halted, stacked arms, and soon lay down to rest for the night. Rodes' division kept up the pursuit into the night.

This was the most easily won battle of the war. We had very few casualties.[23] We could trace the line of the enemy's retreat to the hills by their dead and wounded—a loss inflicted on them mostly by the skirmishers of the Second Brigade. We were in the advance until we were stopped and ordered to stack arms, and we were within 100 yards of the enemy until they reached the hill.

The next day we followed the retreating enemy. Gordon's division went into camp at Bunker Hill. On July 26 we marched to Martinsburg, where we remained until the 31st, tearing up the Baltimore & Ohio Railroad for miles. This was the fourth time I took part in the ruin of this railroad. We left Martinsburg, marched to Darkesville, and remained there until August 4.

On August 2, while in camp at Darkesville, I made my last morning report of the company as orderly sergeant. It was made on a piece

---

[21] Greever enlisted May 18, 1861, at the age of twenty-two in Co. D, 48th Va. Greever's personal service file, War Records Group 109, National Archives.

[22] This was probably Adj. George B. Caldwell of the 12th (West) Va. See OR, XXXVII, pt. 1, 301.

[23] Crook's losses numbered 1,185, including 479 captured. Early reported his own casualties as "light." Ibid., 288-90; Early, War Memoirs, p. 400.

of paper torn out of an old account book. The ruling and heading I did with pokeberries, according to the form provided by the adjutant of the regiment. Here is a copy of it:

PRESENT

1864	CAPTAINS	1st LIEUTS.	SERGEANTS	CORPORALS	MUSIC	PRIVATES	EXTRA DUTY O.	N.C.O.	P.	SICK O.	N.C.O.	P.	IN ARREST O.	N.C.O.	P.	OFFICERS	ENLISTED MEN
Aug. 2		1	1	1		8		2	1					1		1	14
" 30		1		1		8		2	1					1		1	14

ABSENT

1864	DETACHED SERVICE O.	N.C.O.	P.	WITH LEAVE O.	N.C.O.	P.	WITHOUT LEAVE O.	N.C.O.	P.	SICK O.	N.C.O.	P.	MISSING O.	N.C.O.	P.	OFFICERS	ENLISTED MEN
Aug. 2		1	11		1	1			10	1	1	11		1	7	1	44
" 30		1	11		1	1			10	1	1	11		1	7	1	44

1864	PRESENT & ABSENT OFFICERS	ENLISTED MEN	AGGREGATE	AGGREGATE YESTERDAY	IN HANDS OF THE ENEMY	ALTERATIONS COOKS	DISCHARGED	TRANSFERRED	DIED	RECRUITS	NANCE, DISCHARGED	PEASTER, TRANSFERRED	CUMBIA, DIED	SMITH, RECRUIT
Aug. 2	2	58	60	60	1	1								
" 30	2	58	60	60	1	M. L. HUDGINS, 1st Lt.								

We moved to Shepherdstown and crossed the Potomac the following day. After marching through Sharpsburg and a few miles beyond, we went into camp for the night.

How soon the scars of war are removed when they are made in a country that is kept in a state of cultivation and improvement! We could see very little of the great battle of Sharpsburg. When we passed the Dunkard church, everything looked so nice and clean that one would not know that two years before it was the scene of the most severe fighting of the war! The battle of Jackson's Corps and McClellan's right was at its fiercest around this church. Lines were driven back and forward, around and around the old church; hundreds of musket balls struck it, and several cannon shots went through it. Dead and dying men by thousands were lying in sight.

The next day, August 6, we marched through Tillmantown, crossed the Potomac at Williamsport, and camped at Falling Waters. Thence we marched to Darkesville, Bunker Hill, and the Woolen Mill (not far from Winchester), camping for the night at each place. We arrived at the Woolen Mill in the afternoon. My brigade had stacked arms, broken ranks, and taken off accouterments, when the long roll was heard. We were ordered to fall in, and were marched some distance to repel an advance of the enemy's cavalry.[24] At Newtown on August 11 Gordon's division skirmished on the White Post Road with the enemy. There W. H. Divers of F Company received a terrible wound through the leg and died two days afterward.[25]

From Newtown we marched to Strasburg, where our army formed a line of battle and awaited an attack from the enemy. Thence we moved to Fisher's Hill and stayed there until August 17, when we marched to Winchester. There we found the enemy in line awaiting us. We made preparations for an immediate attack. Gordon's division formed a line of battle on the right of the Valley pike. We were divided into three sections. Our skirmishers were ordered forward, and the right section soon followed. As soon as they advanced their length ahead of the middle section, the middle section advanced. The third followed in line, and so our line advanced in echelon.

The Second Brigade was on the left of the line, and was the third or last section. We continued to advance in this way for a mile. Our skirmishers encountered the enemy in our front, who gave way at once. A battery posted on a hill to our left shelled our brigade heavily. We came to a cornfield and, as we passed through it, I took a well-filled haversack from a dead Yankee, swung it around by neck, and continued my march. Looking in it, I found it filled with roasting ears

---

[24] For reports of this skirmish, see OR, XLIII, pt. 1, 422, 438-39, 486, 568.
[25] Divers died Aug. 12, the day after the engagement. Divers's personal service file, War Records Group 109, National Archives.

that had been boiled and were still hot. I commenced to eat at once, and gave some ears to my comrades. Passing through the cornfield, we right-faced and joined the division, which was not marching by the flank. The skirmishers were so far off we decided that the enemy preferred a retreat to a fight. Night came on, so we stacked arms and bivouacked.

The next day, August 18, Lieutenant General Richard H. Anderson joined us with a division of infantry, his artillery, and some cavalry.[26] On the 19th we marched to Bunker Hill; the next day we moved toward Charlestown, encountered the enemy's cavalry in force, and finally came up with their army well fortified near Charlestown. Skirmishers were thrown forward and were heavily engaged all day. The enemy left during the night. When morning came and we ascertained that they had left, we were off at once in pursuit. Gordon's division passed through their fortifications, which were the best hurriedly thrown up works I saw during the war. About 100 yards in their front, rails from adjacent fences had been placed in the ground about six inches apart and leaning to the front. They were about waist high, and their ends were sharpened. When we reached them, we found it a heavy task to remove them for the division to pass through.

At Halltown we found the enemy again in position and fortified. It was reported to General Early that a fine lot of hogs was in the field on their right, inside their skirmish line. Gordon's division was immediately sent for the hogs, which we soon took, and that night all had fresh pork for supper.

We remained in the enemy's front until the morning of August 25, when Gordon's division, with some of the other divisions, marched toward Leetown. General Early accompanied us and left General Anderson in command of the force in front of the enemy. Soon after passing Leetown our division, which was in front, came in contact with the enemy's cavalry. A long line of skirmishers was thrown forward on each side of the road, our division formed in line of battle, and all were ordered forward. Soon the skirmishers became engaged and, as they advanced, fighting became heavy. Yet we drove the enemy at all points. Enemy cavalry made a charge on the left of the road in a large field and succeeded in capturing a few of our men, but they were

---

[26] The division was actually under Gen. Joseph B. Kershaw. Lee dispatched it to the Valley, along with Fitz Lee's cavalry division, as a counter to Federal reinforcements in the area. Gen. R. H. Anderson, then commanding the wounded Longstreet's corps, went to the Valley as leader of the Kershaw-Lee force.

hurriedly driven back. Occasionally we halted the line of battle to allow the skirmishers to clear the way.

During one of these halts, we stacked arms and lay down near our guns. A Yankee battery on our right occasionally sent a shot at us. One of these, a round shot, struck the ground near my front, ricocheted, and came directly toward us. Everyone in the locality was watching it, and it became evident that, in its second descent, it would strike a stack of muskets just to my right. The guns were loaded and, fearing that some of our line might be injured by the firing of the guns should they be struck, the men who owned them jumped to take arms and get away before the shot struck. In the hurry and confusion they became mixed, the shot fell in their midst, and men, guns, shot, and all went down together. In a few seconds the men were on their feet, hurrahing and laughing, and one man held up the shot. Neither men nor guns had been injured—but it was a close shave.

These men laughed and jested at death, as all soldiers do. Constant exposure to danger hardened the best of them.

We resumed the advance for a short distance. The enemy seemed to have had enough and to have withdrawn. Our skirmishers were recalled, and my division resumed its march by the flank in the road. We went along quietly, General Early and some other officers riding at the head of the column. Someone now approached General Early; he soon left the pike by a country road on our right and rode to the top of a hill. Then he turned and beckoned to the officers who was riding in our front, and he turned into this road. We followed a short distance and halted, and it was rumored that the enemy were just over the hill in our front. I ran to the top of the hill and found that it fell on the opposite side about as suddenly as it rose on our side. It was a ridge, at the foot of which on the other side was a cornfield extending to another pike. This pike ran at nearly right angles to the one on which we had been marching and joined it about a mile away. In this pike was a Yankee column of cavalry, marching along quietly and seemingly ignorant of the proximity of a Confederate. They were about 400 yards from us. I do not know how it affected General Early, but it was the most thrilling scene I ever saw, and it gave me the "shakes" at once.

I was ordered to run down the pike as fast as I could until I met some of the skirmishers. I was to give the officer in command an order to come to the front as fast as possible. I hastened away and soon met Captain O. J. Hays' command.[27] I delivered the order and described the situation to him. Poor fellow! He and his men were so completely exhausted from skirmishing with the enemy's cavalry for two or three hours that they could not double quick, but started off at a quick step. When they came to the front, they deployed in the cornfield and advanced at once.

Our line of battle was formed by regiments as fast as they could enter the cornfield, and each regiment was ordered forward. The skirmishers were near the road before they were observed by the enemy, and they poured a withering fire into them. The enemy attempted to reply; but when some of our regiments came into view, they broke and ran in every direction![28] We cut their column in two, some going toward Shepherdstown and the others returning toward Harper's Ferry whence they had come. Those returning to Harper's Ferry ran out a battery that shelled us for a few minutes. Then it limbered up and followed the crowd. Part of our division pursued them, and part pursued those going toward Shepherdstown.

When I came out of those two fights, I surely was the best equipped man in our army. I captured a horse with splendid equipment —even the poncho and blanket were rolled up behind the saddle. Before the fight was over, I got a Colt five-shooter, a sixteen-shot Winchester rifle,[29] a saber, nose bag for my horse and a bag of oats, plus a canteen, six extra saddles, and a Yankee haversack filled with rations.

About midnight, the division having come together, we went into camp and heard that Major General Fitzhugh Lee had captured the party that went toward Shepherdstown. All of us slept well on that news and after a heavy day's work. In the morning we learned that the enemy had escaped from Fitz Lee, although he at one time had them in a tight place.

August 27 found Gordon's division at Bunker Hill. On the 29th our division was ordered to the front. We found the enemy's cavalry

---

[27] Orlando Hays was a twenty-two-year-old Christiansville farmer in 1861 when he enlisted in Co. C, 21st Va. Elected lieutenant in April, 1862, he was promoted to captain on Feb. 5, 1863. A bullet wound in the right ankle at Fort Stedman in Mar., 1865, ended his military career. Hays' personal service file, War Records Group 109, National Archives.

[28] The routed Federal cavalry belonged to Gen. George A. Custer's brigade, consisting of the 1st, 5th, 6th, and 7th Michigan, and the 25th N. Y. One Federal officer stated that the Confederates attacked with "astonishing vigor." OR, XLIII, pt. 1, 425, 440, 464, 488, 517.

[29] Worsham erred about this weapon. No Winchester carbines were manufactured during the Civil War. He probably was referring to the 16-shot Henry rim-fire rifle, some 10,000 of which eventually got into service.

at Opequan Creek and attacked them at once, driving them about five miles.[30] We then returned to our camp. By September 3, Early's army was in camp around Winchester. On the 7th the enemy drove in the pickets of our brigade. Gordon's division moved out in support of the pickets and drove the enemy back across the Opequan, which was the dividing line between the two armies.

At this time I received the following communication:

Hd. Qrs. 21st Va. Infantry
Sept. 12th, 1864

Special Order.
   No. ....
      Sergt. J. H. Worsham Co. "F" is announced as Act. Adjt. of this Regt. from this date.

By order of Col. Moseley
E. E. England, Lt. & Act. Adjt.

This made three adjutants the company had furnished the regiment. It also furnished three sergeant-majors.

September 13 found Gordon's division near Brucetown. Here our pickets were again driven in by the enemy. The Second Brigade was ordered to their support and drove the enemy back across the Opequan. The 21st Virginia remained on picket. On September 14, General Anderson left us, taking his artillery and Kershaw's division of infantry with him, and leaving Fitz Lee's cavalry with us. The 17th found Gordon's and Rodes' divisions at Bunker Hill. The next day Gordon's division marched to Martinsburg. There we encountered some of the enemy's cavalry, who skirmished with us before retiring and then firing at long distance. We remained at Martinsburg a short time, then marched back to Bunker Hill and camped for the night.

For a week or two it had been rumored in our camp that Major General Philip H. Sheridan from Grant's army was in command of the enemy, and that he had been heavily reinforced.[31] Their force in the Valley had all along been three or four times as large as Early's; now, since Sheridan was receiving more men, it must be five or six times as large. It was believed by us that Sheridan had more men in his cavalry alone than the number of Early's entire army.

---

[30] Gordon struck the Federals' left flank while Ramseur simultaneously assailed their front. The Confederates drove the Federals for three miles in what one bluecoat termed "a right smart fight." Losses in Gordon's division were 10 killed, 75 wounded. *OR*, XLIII, pt. 1, 440-41, 469-70, 571, 956-57.
[31] Sheridan assumed command of the Federal army in the Valley on Aug. 6, 1864. Under him were about 40,000 infantry and 6,400 cavalry. To counter this force, Early had no more than 12,200 ragged and ill-equipped troops. *Ibid.*, 60-61, 709; Early, *War Memoirs*, pp. 415-16.

On the 19th we marched from Bunker Hill in the direction of Winchester, and in a short time we heard the boom of a cannon in our front. For the last month, some of the army had been engaged daily with the enemy. Considering this shot in our front to be a part of the daily attack, we paid little attention to it. We kept quietly on our way until we passed Stevenson's Depot. Then we saw a horseman approaching us hurriedly. When he rode up to General Gordon in our front, we recognized him as Colonel A. S. Pendleton, General Early's Adjutant General. Pendleton had a moment's talk with General Gordon, wheeled his horse, and rode off. We closed ranks and hurried up. Soon we turned left from the pike and marched across the fields. The firing in our front had become heavy, and we heard the musketry. We decided that it was a general attack by Sheridan; but our men were not disturbed by it, because we knew we could whip Sheridan easily, notwithstanding the large odds we believed he had against us.

We marched in the same direction for a mile or more. Coming in sight of a small body of cavalry, we learned it was part of Fitz Lee's force, and toward our right we saw some of our artillery firing. We marched toward and in front of this artillery. The fight was raging in our front, and in a wood on our left there was heavy skirmishing. We continued to march by the flank past this wood, the head of the column being nearly in front of our artillery. When we came to an open space between the woods just passed and another a little farther on, we saw our artillery firing through this opening at an enemy line of battle that was advancing through a field beyond the woods. Our column continued its march until it reached a line opposite the second woods, when we halted, were ordered to front face and load.

Our skirmishers, formed along the whole front of the division, were ordered forward. We followed them, our artillery firing over us at the advancing enemy. Terry's brigade was on the right, the Louisianians next, and Evans's[32] on the left. We saw our skirmishers in front engage the enemy, and from the increased firing in the woods on the left, we knew that they were in it too. We continued to advance and soon met the enemy with a volley. They turned and ran, we pursuing. We kept up the pursuit for three-quarters of a mile, when we were halted and ordered back.

We had made a clean sweep—not a Yankee could be seen in our front. Falling back about half a mile, Terry's brigade formed a line

---

[32] Commanding C. A. Evans's Georgia brigade of 7 regts. and 1 bttn. was Col. Edmund N. Atkinson.

with Rodes' division, which had arrived a little later than we and had advanced on the enemy in their front and had repulsed them as easily as we did. After we had made the connection with his line, we lay down to rest. We had been in action only about an hour, and we thought we had gained an easy victory. General Early said it was a grand sight to see those two divisions, numbering a little over 5,000 muskets, hurl back in utter disorder the immense body of the attacking force, which consisted of the Sixth and Nineteenth Corps![33]

We heard that General Rodes had been killed and was lying near Gordon's right.[34] Our men were much grieved, because Rodes had been associated with us so long, and Gordon's men had become very much attached to him. He was a gallant soldier and splendid fighter, and we lost a great man in his fall. The loss in Gordon's division at this time was very small. Brigadier General Zebulon York of the Louisiana Brigade was wounded, and General Terry had his horse killed under him.

Through an opening in the woods on our right, we saw Ramseur, on the extreme right of Early's line, still heavily engaged but gaining ground. Along the front of Gordon and Rodes, not a sound was heard and not an enemy was in sight. But the stillness was soon broken by the advance of a brigade of the enemy through a field on our left, toward the woods. Evans's brigade was in those woods, and these were the same woods occupied by the enemy in our attack on them—from which they had been driven by Evans. This enemy body advanced in splendid line. Our brigade on their flank could see down their entire line as they advanced on level ground. When they came within firing distance, Evans let them have his fire. They halted at once. We saw the dead and wounded on the ground, and many wounded going to the rear. They advanced again—many falling under Evans's fire as they advanced—and entered the woods, where we could hear heavy fighting. Soon we saw the enemy hurriedly driven out, and they disappeared behind the hills. This ended the fighting of Gordon's division at this part of the line.

Far around on our left, on the Valley pike, little fighting had taken place as only a few of the enemy had made their appearance. Now

---

[33] Gordon's fight was solely with Gen. William H. Emory's XIX Corps which, in the day's action, suffered 2,074 losses. *OR,* XLIII, pt. 1, 114-15.

[34] A professor and civil engineer before the war, Rodes (1829-1864) throughout the sectional struggle fluctuated between mediocrity and brilliance. He was bending from his saddle and giving orders to Col. S. D. Thruston when a bullet pierced his skull. Rodes slumped silently into Thruston's arms. *SHSP,* XIV (1886), 152. Cf. *ibid.,* II (1876), 26-27.

they came, nearly the whole of Sheridan's cavalry, and it must be recalled that they were as many as Early's entire army. A corps of infantry accompanied them. They advanced up the Valley pike and charged our weak force, consisting of a small cavalry force and a brigade of infantry from Brigadier General Gabriel C. Wharton's division. As stated by a Northern writer, "Hell broke loose now!"

Our cavalry and the small infantry force was soon driven back, but they fought so stubbornly that the Yankees made little progress. General Early sent reinforcements as soon as possible. Now the hardest fighting of the day took place. Our men were flanked; new lines were formed to be flanked again. But our men stood to their work, fighting every inch of the way. Orders now came for Gordon's division to go to the assistance of the left. We retired through some bushes, passed through a large open wood, and came out into an immense field that surrounded Winchester. We heard the heavy fighting on the left of our line as we went through the woods. Reaching the opening, we saw the whole field in the direction of the Valley pike filled with men fighting. We saw that our men were being driven, and that parts of the Yankee cavalry had possession of some of the hills that overlooked the surrounding country.

When we reached a large white house (the last outside Winchester), Generals Early, Breckinridge, and Gordon came riding together from our right toward the left. Reaching our division, they told the men they desired to make a stand there. As Major Moseley of the 21st Virginia was the only field officer at the time and was not in sight, I approached General Gordon and declared to him that our colorbearer would take his colors anywhere he might order them. I desired to know where he wished the line to be formed.

"Right here," was his answer.

I gave the command, "Men, form on the colors of the 21st!"

Our colorbearer, J. H. Cumbey,[35] halted and faced toward the enemy. He stepped out a few paces, stopped, and waved his flag. The 21st Virginia dressed on him, and the line grew each minute from other commands.

---

[35] A twenty-one-year-old farmer from Drapersville, Cumbey enlisted June, 1861, in Co. C, 21st Va. Following his capture and exchange at Kernstown, he became regimental colorbearer. At Cedar Creek, a month after the action described above, he lost two fingers when struck by a shell fragment. Yet he returned to duty late in 1864 and continued as colorbearer for the remainder of the war. He is probably the same bearer Worsham praised in his account of the Sept., 1863, review. Cumbey's personal service file, War Records Group 109, National Archives.

The sharpshooters of the enemy then made their appearance. A body of them took possession of the brick house and outbuildings about 300 or 400 yards in our front and opened fire on us at once. We then saw an enemy line of battle approaching that appeared to be a brigade. They advanced in splendid order; and when they were within about 400 yards of us, a colonel who was standing a short distance from me on my right, gave the order to fire. I ordered the 21st Virginia to hold its fire and, turning to the colonel, asked that the enemy be allowed to come nearer.

At this moment a shot wounded me in the knee but did not hurt much. I had been struck a few moments before on the shoulder by a spent ball which hit hard enough to raise a knot but did not break the skin. I had stooped down, picked up that ball, and put it in my pocket, thinking no more of it until I received this second shot which I thought was of the same character. Yet in a few minutes I became so sick that I was compelled to lie down. One of my comrades ran to me and asked if I was shot.

"I don't think I am," I replied. "It was a spent ball."

By this time I was so sick that I thought my time to die had come. As I looked at my knee, I saw the blood running freely down my pants. The enemy on the hill now had a battery on our flank, enfilading our line. Two of my comrades took me by my arms and carried me off the field. After going a short distance I begged to be allowed to lie down, thinking that I would otherwise die. They would not listen to me while the cannons were plowing great gaps in the earth all around us, but they promised that, as soon as we reached a large rock which we were approaching, they would let me lie down under its protection.

We soon reached it, and I lay at full length in hopes of getting some relief. But a cannon shot struck the rock, glanced off, and went up out of sight. In an instant I was taken up by my comrades and carried on until we reached the first house in Winchester, a small, one-story brick building at the corner of an alley. I was allowed to lie down behind this; almost instantly a cannon shot went crashing through it, throwing pieces of brick and mortar on us. They had me going again at once.

I met T. Richie Green, an old F Company man, who was sorry he could not do anything for me. Soon afterward we met Ira Blunt, our hospital steward and also an old member of F Company. Running to me, he put a canteen to my lips and told me to take a good pull. I drank some new apple brandy. Its effect was instantaneous; I felt perfectly well. Thanking him, I went on in search of our surgeon. As I turned the corner of the next street, I saw our surgeon, Dr. Malcolm N. Fleming, mounting his horse. I called him, and he rode to meet me. He said that he had sent all his stores to the rear and had just mounted his horse to follow, but that he would get me away if possible. Insofar as he knew, all the ambulances had gone. Just at this moment an ambulance turned the corner into our street and came toward us with the mules in a run. The surgeon ordered the driver to stop. For an answer, the driver whipped his team into a faster gait. Our surgeon mounted his horse and put him into a run. Overtaking the ambulance and catching one of the mules, he stopped the team by main force. I went forward to the ambulance, and my two comrades pitched me into the rear. The surgeon let the mules go, and we were off!

The ambulance was filled with medical chests, and I tried to arrange them so as to make a comfortable seat. But I could not. In the hinder part of the ambulance was a chest. At its end was a bucket, and the handle of the chest came over the bucket in such a manner that the bucket could not move. The other part of the ambulance was filled with chests piled one on top of the other, leaving only the chest in the rear on which to sit. I managed to put the foot of my wounded leg in the bucket, letting my good leg hang out.

By this time the ambulance had caught up with the wagon train, moving two abreast up the Valley pike. The enemy on the right of our line now opened on our wagon train with one piece of artillery. The first shot they fired went over the train a little in front of my ambulance. The next shot went through the top of the wagon just in front of us. Amidst the cracking of whips, yells, and oaths, the wagon train went in a hurry down the pike! In a few minutes they got behind the woods, and the firing from the Yankee gun ceased. Yet my ambulance driver had become demoralized. He wheeled his team to the right, and over a stone wall he went! How it was done, I shall never know, but he did it, and through the field his flying mules went! It was an old cornfield, and the reader may know how comfortable I was!

We went over several cross walls and finally, along in the night, we reached the pike again and continued our ride until about 8 o'clock the next morning, when a surgeon on the road side halted the ambulance. He told the driver to take out his mules, and to water and feed them. I was so sore that I could hardly move; I asked the driver to help me down, but he positively refused. However, I got out, made my way to a branch nearby, got a drink of water, and washed my face. I returned to the ambulance and breakfasted on articles in a Yankee haversack which I took the day before from one of their dead. I will state here that, from Winchester until I arrived at Staunton, the only rations I had were out of that haversack. Since it was such a good friend, I carried it home!

While I was eating my breakfast, a surgeon came and asked the driver whom he had in his ambulance. I gave him my name and command, and I asked him to look at my wound and say if it needed anything.

His inhuman reply was: "As you do not belong to my command, you must get your own surgeon."

After an hour or two of rest the driver hitched up the team. Fearing I might be left behind, I took my old place in the ambulance while the hitching was being done. Just before we started, I prevailed on the driver to pull off my boot. It was full of blood and running over the top! Soon after it was pulled off, my wound seemed to stop bleeding, and I proceeded more comfortably.

We rode until four o'clock in the afternoon, when we halted at a church in Woodstock. Here the ladies brought fruit, flowers, eatables, water and bandages, and made themselves very useful to two or three hundred wounded. A surgeon cut open my pants and drawers, examined my wound, and dressed it. This was the first time I had seen it myself. It had hurt me none to speak of. About sunset the wounded were put into wagons on a little straw and started up the pike. We rode all night, stopped a short time the next morning, and then continued until nightfall, when we rested. We traveled thusly for two days after leaving Woodstock until we reached Staunton. Here my wound was dressed the second time. The next morning we were carried from Staunton to Charlottesville, where the ball was taken out.

I write this lengthy narrative of myself because it was the experience of hundreds in this battle.

Returning to the account of the battle of Winchester: our left being driven back, the new line occupied some slight breastworks. Here the enemy were checked; as night approached, General Early's force retired up the Valley. On reaching Fisher's Hill he took position, when he was driven on September 22 with considerable loss. Among the killed in that engagement was our old comrade, Colonel A. S. Pendleton,

Adjutant General of the Second Corps. He was one of the first officers appointed to Jackson's staff and he had been with us since the commencement of the war. He was a gallant and splendid officer, and beloved by all the old command.

The battle of Winchester was as hotly contested as any of the war. It was a regular stand-up fight, but we were so outnumbered that we could not prevent being flanked by the enemy. I do not agree with the Northern writer who said: "Early was beaten before the battle commenced from the great disparity in numbers." This writer also said: "When Early was driven, he left a track of blue killed and wounded in his rear." Our loss in the evening was heavy. Among the wounded was Major General Fitzhugh Lee.[36] In F Company, Nathaniel Dowdy, J. C. English, and G. W. Houston were wounded.

Here is an interesting incident about the battle of Winchester taken from General Phil Sheridan's autobiography:[37]

"In a few days two of my scouts put me in the way of getting news conveyed from Winchester. They had learned that just outside of my lines, near Millwood, there was living an old colored man, who had a permit from the Confederate commander to go into Winchester and return three times a week, for the purpose of selling vegetables to the inhabitants. The scouts had sounded this man, and finding him both loyal and shrewd, suggested that he might be made useful to us within the enemy's lines; and the proposal struck me as feasible, provided there could be found in Winchester some reliable person who would be willing to co-operate and correspond with me. I asked General Crook, who was acquainted with many of the Union people of Winchester, if he knew of such a person, and he recommended a Miss Rebecca Wright,[38] a young lady whom he had met there before the battle of Kernstown, who, he said, was a member of the Society of Friends and the teacher of a small private school. He knew she was faithful and loyal to the Government, and thought she might be willing to render us assistance . . . I hesitated at first, but finally deciding

---

[36] A minie ball struck Lee in the thigh. The wound was not as serious as first thought, but it kept Lee out of action until Jan., 1865.

[37] *Personal Memoirs of P. H. Sheridan* (New York, 1888), II, 2-5.

[38] Miss Wright was an extremely attractive young Quaker who lived in a white frame house at the foot of Fort Hill. Prior to this time, she had lost a teaching position because of her unconcealed Unionist sentiments. With some misgivings "Becky" aided Sheridan throughout the campaign. She ran a boarding house in Winchester until 1868 when, with Sheridan's help, she received a clerkship in the U. S. Treasury Dept. This position she held for the remainder of her life. Sylvia G. L. Dannett, "Traitor or Patriot—Rebecca Wright," manuscript kindly loaned to the editor by Mrs. Dannett.

to try it, despatched the two scouts to the old negro's cabin, and they brought him to my headquarters late that night. I was soon convinced of the negro's fidelity, and asking him if he was acquainted with Miss Rebecca Wright of Winchester, he replied that he knew her well. Thereupon I told him what I wished to do, and after a little persuasion he agreed to carry a letter to her on his next marketing trip. My message was prepared by writing it on tissue paper, which was then compressed into a small pellet, and protected by wrapping it in tin-foil so that it could be safely carried in the man's mouth. The probability of his being searched when he came to the Confederate picket-line was not remote, and in such event he was to swallow the pellet. . . . Early the next morning it was delivered to Miss Wright, with an intimation that a letter of importance was enclosed in the tin-foil, the negro telling her at the same time that she might expect him to call for a message in reply before his return home. . . .

"The evening before a convalescent Confederate officer had visited her mother's house, and in conversation about the war had disclosed the fact that Kershaw's division of infantry and Cutshaw's battalion of artillery had started to rejoin General Lee. At the time Miss Wright heard this she attached little if any importance to it, but now she perceived the value of the intelligence, and, at her first venture, determined to send it to me at once, which she did with a promise that in the future she would with great pleasure continue to transmit information by the negro messenger."[39]

I thought while writing this that I would see if I could identify the Negro. So I wrote to Major Samuel J. C. Moore of Berryville, Virginia, an officer on General Early's staff, and asked him if he could give me the name of the Negro who carried the letter. Here is his answer:

"In 1869 I employed a negro man as gardener, whose name was Tom Laws. I had heard something about his being the man who was the bearer of the letter, and I broached the subject to him. At first he was not inclined to talk about it, but upon my assuring him that I would not harm him, I got him to talk freely about it. On the 17th of September, 1864, he went to Winchester to see some relations he had there. Miss Rebecca Wright, having heard he was in town, sought him and told him to come to her house before he left. He went there, when she asked him when he was going home, he told her he was ready to

---

[39] Following this passage in Worsham's original narrative was an exchange of letters between Miss Wright and Sheridan. They are printed in Sheridan's *Memoirs*, II, 5-6. Since they merely substantiate Sheridan's account of the episode, they have been omitted from this edition.

start at once. She then said she wanted him to carry a letter to Gen. Sheridan, and taking a small piece of thin tissue paper, she wrote upon it, and then enveloped it in a small piece of tin foil, which she gave him, and charged him that he must not let the rebels get it, and if they caught him he must swallow it, that if they found it on his person they would kill him, and it might cost her her life. She directed him to give it to no one but Gen. Sheridan in person. He found the general and gave the note to him, who read it, and promised him he should be paid fifty dollars in money for bringing it, but he never got the money."

General Sheridan said this information caused him to decide to attack Early the next morning. But having received a telegram from General Grant, who said he was coming to see him that day, he determined to defer it. After his conference with General Grant he decided to attack the next morning, and that letter brought on the battle of Winchester.[40]

---

[40] In his memoirs Worsham here added an organizational table of Early's army, which he compiled from OR, XLIII, pt. 1, 564-567, 1002-03, 1011-13. It has been omitted from this edition because it adds little to the narrative.

Chapter X

F COMPANY'S LAST BATTLES

The reader will want to know something of the old command after I left it. I can give some facts gathered from members of my company. After the battle of Fisher's Hill, Early retired up the Valley to Mt. Jackson. Sheridan followed him slowly. On September 24 Early's army marched about five miles beyond Tenth Legion on the Port Republic road. The next day the men moved to Brown's Gap in the Blue Ridge Mountains, and were there joined by Kershaw's division. On the 27th they marched from Brown's Gap toward Harrisonburg, then returned to Port Republic. There General Early learned that Sheridan's cavalry had gone in the direction of Staunton. Our army marched to Waynesboro and Rockfish Tunnel to intercept the enemy in case they marched to those places. Finding that the enemy had occupied Waynesboro a short time before, Early attacked at once and drove them back with some loss. Early camped in the neighborhood until October 1, when he marched on the Valley pike to Mt. Sidney. On October 5 Brigadier General Thomas L. Rosser's cavalry brigade joined him there. Early then marched down the Valley to Fisher's Hill, where he arrived on the 13th.

There he stayed until the night of the 18th, when he put his troops in motion to attack Sheridan, who was in a strongly fortified position along Cedar Creek. To Gordon was assigned the duty of attacking the enemy in their rear on the left of their line. Gordon moved down the Shenandoah River, fording it twice, and was in line at the designated place as the streaks of day appeared. With a yell his men dashed upon the enemy! This was the signal for Early's line in front to move forward, which they did. They swept everything before them, capturing the fortifications, guns, and camp of the enemy.[1] Sheridan's army was utterly routed with the exception of the Sixth Corps, which was encamped some distance in the rear. They formed a line and marched back with the fugitives until they reached Middletown. Here they formed a line of battle and required such of the fugi-

---

[1] Gordon's assault surprised and routed Gen. George Crook's Army of West Va. In addition to his camp and equipment, Crook lost 847 men in the brief conflict. *OR*, XLIII, pt. 1, 365-66.

tives as they could control to join them. Our line pursuing the enemy was so thin that it was not much more than a line of skirmishers.

The world will never know the extreme poverty of the Confederate soldier at this time! Hundreds of men who were in the charge and who captured the enemy's works were barefooted. Every one of them was ragged. Many had on everything they had, and *none* had eaten a square meal for weeks. As they passed through Sheridan's camp, a great temptation was thrown in their way. Many of the tents were open, and in plain sight were rations, shoes, overcoats, and blankets. The fighting continued farther and farther, yet some of the men stopped. They secured well-filled haversacks and, as they investigated the contents, the temptation to stop and eat was too great. Since most of them had had nothing to eat since the evening before, they yielded. While some tried on shoes, others put on warm pants in place of the tattered ones. Still others got overcoats and blankets—articles so much needed for the coming cold. They had already experienced several biting frosts to remind them of the winter near at hand.

In this way half of Early's men were straggling, and this accounts for his thin line in front. This was an awful hour! General Early noticed the thinness of his line. Being informed of its cause, he sent officers back to hurry up his men. By this time his advance line had come up to the enemy in their position at Middletown. The Confederates attacked at once, but so feebly that they were easily repulsed. Then the enemy felt emboldened, made an advance, and drove our men off the field of battle.[2] The stragglers who arrived were not in sufficient numbers to check the enemy's advance. The fighting continued until night put a stop to it. During the night General Early withdrew to Fisher's Hill; but, owing to the breaking down of a bridge, most of the captured guns and between fifteen and twenty of our own were taken by the enemy. We lost about 1,000 men taken prisoners, but we captured and brought off 1,900 of the enemy. Our loss was heavy, and among the killed was that splendid soldier, Major General Stephen D. Ramseur.[3]

---

[2] "The stampede of Early," one Confederate wrote cynically, "was uncalled for, unnecessary and disgraceful and I willingly assume my share of the blame and shame. My only title to fame rests upon my leading the Regiment in the grandest Stampede of the Southern Army . . . and I hope to be forgiven for saying with pardonable pride that I led them remarkably well to the rear for a boy of eighteen. A General could not have done better." C. Irvine Walker, *The Life of Lieutenant General Richard Heron Anderson of the Confederate States Army* (Charleston, S. C., 1917), pp. 189-90.

[3] Sheridan had 5,665 casualties. Early's losses, including an unusually high number of field commanders, were a little over 3,000 men plus 23 guns. *OR,* XLIII, pt. 1, 137, 564. For an article on Ramseur, who still awaits a good biographer, see *SHSP,* XVIII (1890), 217-60.

F Company lost Sergeant Robert M. Tabb,[4] killed; Corporal Henry C. Tyree and Private L. M. Couch, wounded. That gallant young officer, Lieutenant Malcolm L. Hudgins, had command of a line of skirmishers and was shot through both legs. Yet he succeeded in bringing off his command, and then took to the mountains! He was captured a few days later and taken to Winchester. From there he was sent to a Northern prison to stay until March 30, 1865. I was told that old man Joseph M. Mason of our company was quietly walking to the rear when a Yankee cavalryman rode up to him and, with uplifted saber, ordered the old man to halt. Mason looked over his shoulder; seeing who it was, he threw up his gun and shot the Yankee off his horse! However, the old fellow was captured not long after this.

General Early fell back to New Market, but Sheridan did not follow him. General Early stayed there until November 10. Learning that Sheridan had fallen back to Winchester, he advanced to Newtown. From there he fell back again to New Market, where, in December, Gordon's, Ramseur's, and Rodes' divisions left him and went to Petersburg to join General Lee.

On our march down the Valley we witnessed the vandalism of the Yankee general, Sheridan. All the barns and mills were in ruins, and it soon became evident that Sheridan intended to carry out his boast that when he was done with the Valley, a crow would have to carry his rations with him in order to get something to eat in going across it.[5]

From Woodstock, on October 7, 1864, General Sheridan reported to the authorities: "I commenced moving back from Port Republic, Mount Crawford, Bridgewater, and Harrisonburg yesterday morning. . . . In moving back to this point the whole country from the Blue Ridge to the North Mountains has been made untenable for a rebel army. I have destroyed over 2,000 barns filled with wheat, hay, and farming implements; over seventy mills filled with flour and wheat; have driven in front of the army over 4[000] head of stock, and have killed and issued to the troops not less than 3,000 sheep. . . . Lieut. John R. Meigs, my engineer officer, was murdered beyond Harrisonburg, near Dayton. For this atrocious act all the houses within an area of five miles were burned."

---

[4] A former clerk for Gen. W. B. Taliaferro, Tabb was thirty-three at the time of his death.

[5] Attributing this statement to Sheridan has long been a popular error. In reality, Grant made the remark in a dispatch of July 14, 1864, to Gen. David Hunter. Grant urged Hunter to push after Early's men with "veterans, militiamen, men on horseback, and everything that can be got to follow to eat up Virginia clear and clean as far as they can go, so that crows flying over it for the balance of this season will have to carry their provender with them." *OR*, XXXVII, pt. 2, 301.

As a matter of fact, Lieutenant Meigs was killed in a fight by a man named Martin of the Black Horse Cavalry.

From Newtown, on November 10, Sheridan reported: "I have had a small division of cavalry operating on the east side of the mountains in the vicinity of Upperville, Paris, Bloomfield, and surrounding country. . . . A lot of stock, horses, sheep, and cattle were brought in by this force, and the grain, barns, subsistence, &c., so far as practicable, were destroyed." The following day, from Kernstown, he stated that "a small division of my cavalry has just returned from the east side of the Blue Ridge. . . . They (sic.) brought back 300 head of cattle, a lot of sheep and horses, burned all the granaries and destroyed all the provisions they could on the road."[6]

This wanton destruction of the property of the citizens of the Valley—just because they were Southern sympathizers, was uncalled for, and no excuse can ever justify it.[7] This was a favored country, and to burn everything in the way of hay, grain, barns and mills, not excepting agricultural implements; to kill and drive off all the horses, stock, etc., belonging to those people because it would compel the Confederate army in the Valley to haul those articles, was a crime without reason or excuse, especially when those citizens were not paid a cent for their loss by the United States.

I think General Early did everything a commander could do in the Valley with the number of men he had in his command; and as a humble member of that army, I would like to ask those who have criticized General Early if they ever thought of the great disparity in numbers in the two armies? It is said that Sheridan's cavalry alone numbered as many as, if not more than, Early's entire force, and I never heard Sheridan's infantry placed at less than 30,000 men. General Early did not have more than 12,000 men in his entire army at the battle of Winchester—the first of his disasters.

Let me recall the fact that Early was detached from Lee's army at Richmond and sent to Lynchburg to intercept Hunter, who was marching on that place with a large force. He disposed of Hunter in quick time, driving him beyond the Allegheny Mountains. He was then ordered to threaten Washington, which he promptly did. On his arrival before that place the Yankees concentrated a force of over 60,000 men to repel him. A large part of this force was taken from Grant's army at a time that greatly helped Lee at Petersburg. By his activity Early kept

---

[6] *Ibid.*, XLIII, pt. 1, 30, 35; pt. 2, 602.
[7] Grant ordered the devastation and stated to Sheridan: "If the war is to last another year, we want the Shenandoah Valley to remain a barren waste." *Ibid.*, pt. 1, 916-17. The property that Sheridan captured or destroyed is listed in *Ibid.*, 37-38.

nearly all this force in his front until late in 1864. General Early certainly accomplished all that he was sent to the Valley to do, and he may have done more. It is needless for me to say anything about General Early's gallantry and fighting in the field. That is too well known.

Since the opening of the campaign on May 2, 1864, the Second Corps had marched over 1,600 miles and fought 75 battles and skirmishes. F Company participated in a majority of the engagements. The loss was heavy in officers and men as well as in guns, but we inflicted a loss on the enemy in men and officers twice as large as the Second Corps numbered—as well as a great loss in stores, etc.

On the arrival in Petersburg of the troops who left Early, Major General Gordon was made commander of the Second Corps. It was ordered to the front and, on February 5, 1865, it had a hard battle with Grant at Hatcher's Run. It was in this battle that the gallant Captain Reuben Jordan of F Company distinguished himself. While the brigade was marching by the flank through a dense pine wood, it was suddenly assailed by enemy sharpshooters. This threw our men into confusion, and they fell back out of fire to reform the line. Jordan at once turned toward the enemy and succeeded in getting seven men to join him. Two were from the 42nd Virginia, two from the 25th Virginia, and three from the 21st Virginia. Among the last-named was William R. Richeson of F Company. Jordan hurriedly placed those men along the road to stop the advance of the enemy at that point. The Yankees rapidly approached and commanded Jordan and his little band to surrender. For an answer the Yankees received bullets; and when the smoke cleared, one Yankee lay on the ground and the remainder were seeking safety!

At this moment General Gordon rode up and learned that the advance of the enemy had been stopped by Jordan and his few men. He complimented them on the spot in that peculiar way of his that bound those men to him forever. He then rode off to the brigade, made a speech, and closed by telling the men that "Captain Jordan, by his bravery and coolness, has with only seven men stopped the advance of the enemy." He hurried the troops forward, and the fight became general.

After the battle, when the troops had returned to camp, General Gordon sent a message to Captain Jordan, asking that the names of the seven men be forwarded through regular channels to his headquarters. He wished to publish their names as well as that of Captain Jordan for gallant and heroic conduct on the field of battle. This

Jordan did, but the end came before the account of this battle was published. Hence this incident is not known to the public.

I would like to say a word about W. R. Richeson, a humble man from Caroline County, who joined us in 1863 so infirm that he ought not to have been in the army. Yet in several battles he showed the mettle he was made of, and he well deserved this recognition from General Gordon. In this battle also, W. Bates and A. D. Brown[8] were wounded.

On March 25 Gordon made an attack on and briefly captured Fort Stedman. Of the members of F Company in this battle, George Hutchie Rennie, J. A. Kidd, and H. C. Fox were killed; Captain Jordan was wounded; and N. A. Dowdy was captured. Here is what one of the old company wrote of this engagement:

"On the night before the battle we were in camp, and quietly sleeping, when about midnight we were awakened and told to 'fall in' as soon as possible. As soon as the line was formed we were marched off hurriedly through the woods and fields, over ditches and fences, and finally formed a line of battle facing east. The streaks of day were just beginning to show themselves when we were turned loose, and we ran over two lines of the enemy's breastworks almost before I can tell about it, the troops on our right capturing at the same time the fort. We halted a short time after passing the second line of breastworks, reformed lines and then were ordered forward again. Soon I was captured, and that is all I know of the battle."

On the retreat from Petersburg, Gordon's command was the rear guard. After leaving Amelia Court House they were engaged every hour of the day and half of the night in repelling attacks by some body of the enemy. The hardships our men underwent in the retreat to Appomattox were such that it seems impossible for men to go through them and live! They left Petersburg without rations, on roads full of mud from the recent rains, and marched all night and nearly all the next day before stopping to rest. General Lee had ordered a train of cars, loaded with rations, to be at Amelia Court House depot on the Richmond & Danville Railroad, and he led his army there to get them. When they arrived, they learned that, by the mismanagement of some officials,[9] the train with rations had gone to Richmond and there fell into the hands of the enemy.

---

[8] "A splendid soldier," Worsham noted in the margin of his copy of his personal memoirs.

[9] Why these supplies did not reach Amelia has never been fully ascertained. For information on the subject, see *SHSP*, XXV (1897), 268-69; Freeman, *R. E. Lee*, IV, 509-13.

The men of Lee's army had been eating parched corn and anything else they could get their hands on, with the hope of getting something better on their arrival at Amelia Court House. When they learned that disappointment awaited them, they almost gave up. But the old spirit soon came back to the Army of Northern Virginia, and the men dragged themselves along the road to Lynchburg, where they knew rations could be gotten. Combats occurred nearly every hour with some portion of Grant's force, which by this time was in advance of our army as well as following close on our rear. The Confederates marched along this way until they neared Appomattox Court House, where they found awaiting them a train of provisions on the Norfolk & Western Railroad.[10] These were the first rations the men had had since they left Petersburg.

On April 5, the day before the Confederates reached Sailor's [Sayler's] Creek, Gordon was ordered to take the front. When he reached Appomattox Court House, General Lee ordered him to advance the next morning. If the enemy were encountered in numbers, Gordon was to cut his way through them. When morning came and Gordon found the enemy in large numbers in his front, he formed his line and ordered his men forward. They made the attack with so much spirit that they succeeded in driving the Yankees and in capturing two pieces of artillery. When Gordon sent General Lee word that he "had fought his troops to a frazzle," those old fellows could be seen, and heard from too, in that frazzle![11] My brother, who was one of them, told me that at the time General Lee raised the white flag, this same "frazzle" was driving the enemy in its front.[12]

You might like to know what became of the colors of the 21st Virginia. After it was known positively that General Lee was going to surrender, the gallant John H. Cumbey, who had carried the colors for such a long time, tore them from the staff—which was a short one, as it had been shot off by a cannon ball some months before. He broke the staff and threw it away. Then he tore the flag into small pieces, which he gave to each man. That was a great flag! Inscribed upon it were the names of all the battles, from Kernstown on, in which Jack-

---

10 Then known as the Southside Railroad, the line connected with the Virginia & Tennessee at Lynchburg.
11 Yet the battle was a Confederate defeat. Lee reported that Gordon's men "bravely resisted and twice repulsed" Federal assaults, but that they were soon flanked and "driven from the field in much confusion." On the other hand, the Federals paid for the victory with 1,200 losses. *OR*, XLVI, pt. 1, 682, 909, 917, 1266; Gordon, *Reminiscences,* pp. 437-38.
12 Worsham's reference was to a final attack by Gordon's 1600-man "corps" at dawn, Apr. 9, 1865. Massed Federals astride the Confederate line of retreat repulsed it handily. See Freeman, *Lee's Lieutenants,* III, 726-33.

son's old division had been engaged. Three cannon balls had been shot through it; and when I left the regiment in September, 1864, over 100 musket shots through it could be counted.

As for myself, I was in Richmond confined to my bed by my wound when the city was evacuated. I cannot say that I saw or heard much of what went on outside of our house, as there was not a man on the place at the time except myself, and the women were too much alarmed to go out. We heard many rumors on Sunday afternoon, April 2. The first definite news was about midnight, when a soldier friend came to bid us goodbye. He was going away with the soldiers who were then marching through the city. He stated that the President, his cabinet, other officials of the government, the archives, etc., had left the city by the Richmond & Danville Railroad, and that as soon as the troops crossed the James River, the bridges would be burned. Soon afterward, a member of the legislature called and told us goodbye. He said that the legislators were going to Lynchburg on the packet boat that ran up the James River and Kanawha Canal.

This created a feeling of great uneasiness in our household. We well knew that the ever long wish of the enemy to get to Richmond would soon be gratified, but what would be the result? I dreaded the coming day, and I listened to every noise I heard outside. Occasionally I would hear a report as if something had been blown up—an arsenal, steamer, or something of that kind. Not long before daybreak, a flash of light came into my room, brighter than the brightest lightning. It was accompanied immediately by a loud report that rumbled and shook the house, and by a crash that sounded as if the front had fallen! The ladies were in my room in an instant; and as soon as the outer door could be opened, the servants came in too! As best I could, I explained to them that it was the explosion of a large quantity of powder—probably one of the magazines.[13] After they were quieted, one of them went into the front room to see if anything had been broken. She soon returned and stated that the sash of one of the windows had been blown into the middle of the room, and that all the glass was broken.

About sunrise on Monday, April 3, 1865, the ladies left me and went to their rooms to dress for the day. The servants went about their accustomed duties. When the ladies returned, they reported that a great fire was raging in town, and that it looked as if the whole city would be burned! A friend now called and stated that the rear guard of our army had set fire to the Shockoe, the Public, the Myers & Anderson

---

[13] This particular explosion was the powder magazine situated 100 yards from Shockoe Hill Cemetery in almost the heart of the city. Rembert W. Patrick, *The Fall of Richmond* (Baton Rouge, 1960), pp. 44-46.

tobacco warehouses, as well as the arsenals, magazines, etc. Those fires had spread to adjacent buildings, the greater part of the business portion of the city was in flames, and there was no prospect of checking the fires. He also said that the city council and some of the prominent citizens had held a meeting and decided to destroy all liquor in the government buildings and large warehouses. It was taken into the streets and emptied into the nearest culverts. Yet hundreds of citizens were pillaging the burning stores, breaking into others, and taking everything. He concluded that the town was in the hands of a mob!

About 7:30 a.m. a little Negro boy about eight to ten years old brought my breakfast. He was devoted to me and, as he was very quick and smart, he was a great favorite of mine.

He said to me, "Marse John, let me run down to the corner and see if I can see any of the Yankees."

At that time he had a great horror of them. After some begging on his part, I let him go, and he promised to return before his mistress could miss him. He returned before I finished my breakfast. On entering the room he said, "Marse John, they is here." He had seen a squad coming up toward the Capitol, and he had run home.

During the boy's absence, one of the Negro girls ran down to Capitol Square; on her return she came into my room and stated that she saw fifteen Yankees on horseback ride up Ninth Street to the Capitol gate, enter, and ride up to the building. Some of them dismounted, went inside, and soon came out on the roof, where they hoisted a United States flag on the flagstaff. That was the first flag hoisted by the enemy in Richmond.[14]

This party of Yankees made a deep impression on the girl, for they were the first body of armed Yankees she had seen. She seemed particularly struck by their uniforms and long buck gauntlets. She went out again soon afterward and stayed two or three hours. She came back with a large blanket filled with articles as numerous and as varied as are in a peddler's sack. She had gotten them, she said, out of stores on Main Street. All were open, everybody was helping himself, and she thought she would do the same.

From the great clouds of smoke hovering over the city, it seemed that all downtown must be burning up! Large chunks of fire were falling on our house and in the yard. Although the house had been on fire several times, one of the Negro servants had come home from fear

---

[14] The first Federal banners raised over the Capitol were two guidons of Maj. Atherton H. Stevens's 4th Mass. Cavalry. Later in the day, with the arrival of the occupational army, Gen. George F. Shepley ordered a flag he had carried throughout the war for just such an occasion, run up the Capitol flagpole. *Ibid.*, p. 67.

and we had stationed him on top of the house to watch for fires. He stayed there all day. A man or boy was on nearly every house, although in some places the women were doing this duty. We were about half a mile from the nearest fire, and the smoke at our house was so dense all day that the sun could not be seen. The appearance outdoors was like that of a heavy fog in the morning.

About midday we heard the music, cheers, and some firing by a body of the enemy marching on the next street. In our yard near my window was a small peach tree. I was sitting up in bed and looking at the tree when the firing took place. I saw a small twig on the tree fall; almost at the same moment, I heard the quick thud of a ball striking the fence. This I call the last shot of Richmond. We were sure now that the enemy were in the city. A friend called and told us that nearly all the business portion of the city had been burned, that the Yankees had quelled the mob, and that they were then engaged in stopping the fires. This they succeeded in doing after severe exertion and by blowing up several buildings ahead of the fire. One of our old Negro women prayed nearly all day. She was in the yard and terribly frightened by the thought that the fire would reach us and burn her up.

Hundreds of residents of the burned district were bivouacking in Capitol Square, and they had brought with them everything they could. The place presented the appearance of a vast camp, filled with household goods, women, and children. Many had built fires and were cooking to feed their hungry children. All the people remained there until the next day, and some stayed several days.

In the evening we heard that quiet had been restored. Yankee soldiers were patrolling the streets. Guards had been placed throughout the city to preserve order among citizens as well as soldiers. They had marched outside the city and would allow no soldier except the guard to go about the streets. This had a very soothing effect, for the citizens had not known what would be done for the city. We saw none of the Yankees except for a few who now and then passed the house—although we heard that all the houses would be searched for contraband goods and Confederate soldiers. The next morning one of my good neighbors sent me a piece of cornbread and herring for breakfast, with the message that it was the last of the Confederacy.

On Wednesday or Thursday, April 5 or 6, our doorbell rang; the servant answering it met three Yankee officers at the door! Invited to enter, they introduced themselves by name and stated that they were members of the staff of General Canby, who was in command of the city.[15] One of the household came and informed me. Thinking the best thing to do was to be candid with them, I sent them information of my presence and condition in the house, and I asked them to come to my room and see me. This they did at once, and they were very polite and courteous to me. Hidden about the house in various places were articles of value and other possessions we desired to keep. In my room was a large lounge whose springs were out of order. I had placed two sabers in this lounge because I thought that, on account of the bad springs, they would not be detected. When I invited the officers to take seats, all sat down on this lounge.

I noticed that some of them occasionally moved about on the lounge, but I could not tell whether their suspicions were aroused. After talking a little while, I told them of the hiding-place. They laughed; and when they left, they told me to let them remain there for the present—as well as anything else that was hidden. If anyone molested us or any articles in the house, they said, we were to let them know at headquarters. The next day a guard was placed on the square in front of our house, and guards remained at this post for several weeks.

On Sunday, April 9, it was rumored in Richmond that General Lee had surrendered his army. None of the Confederate people believed this. It was confirmed the next day. What a blow! The Army of Northern Virginia, the greatest army the world ever saw, and commanded by that great soldier, General Lee, had surrendered.[16] It seemed impossible! However few, they would die fighting. Yet the officers thought it best to save those few men and determined to surrender. General Grant, Commander-in-Chief of the United States Army and who commanded the Army of the Potomac in person, paid the Army of Northern Virginia its greatest tribute when he stated the previous year that *that* army could not be beaten—it could only be destroyed. This he intended to do by mere attrition, knowing full well that when he destroyed one man, we had no other to put in his place. If necessary, he was willing to sacrifice ten of his men to one of ours. How well he carried this out, his campaign will tell, for the Army of Northern Virginia destroyed for him several times its own number before it was finally destroyed.

---

[15] Worsham's memory lapsed at this point. Gen. E. R. S. Canby was then leading an expedition against Mobile, Ala. Gen. Shepley was military governor of Richmond, with Col. Frederick S. Manning acting provost marshal of the city.

[16] At Lee's surrender only 57 men remained in the 21st Va. Worsham's F Company contained a corporal and two privates. *SHSP,* XV (1887), 4, 85, 228-29.

A few days after the confirmation of the surrender, the men of Lee's army began to arrive in Richmond. Shortly afterward, the old Chief himself came riding alone to the city.

About the middle of April, 1861, I had been standing in the door of our headquarters in Richmond when my attention was attracted to a man approaching me. He wore a uniform; yet it was not the uniform that attracted my attention but the man himself. He was tall and straight, and I thought him the handsomest specimen of manhood, both in face and figure, that I had ever seen. He made such an impression that, as he came opposite me, I could not keep from looking at him. When he had passed my eyes still followed him, and I actually stepped outside the door to keep him in sight. About an hour later, he returned up the street and went into the Spottswood Hotel. I followed and asked a friend if he could identify that splendid looking man. He informed me that it was Colonel Robert E. Lee.

The next time I saw him was on Valley Mountain in Pocahontas County, Virginia (now West Virginia). He was a general in the Confederate army and in command of our department. I saw him daily until he was ordered to another command. In our advance to attack McClellan near Cold Harbor in 1862, after passing through some woods and reaching a field, the first man we saw was our beloved old general on his gray horse. Although he was at some distance, we recognized him at once. He was then in command of the Army of Northern Virginia, and we joined him to remain until the end came at Appomattox. I saw him several times after this around Richmond. The next time I saw him he was sitting on a stump on the battlefield of Second Manassas and observing Longstreet's men taking position in line of battle as they came on the field to join Jackson. I saw him often from that time until Grant's campaign of 1864. When last I saw him, he was at Spotsylvania Court House. It was the day our corps left to head off Grant at Hanover Junction. He appeared to me then the same ideal man, except that his hair had become almost white and the dark mustache of my first acquaintance had been exchanged for a full beard of gray. As our column approached him, an old private stepped out of ranks and advanced to General Lee. They shook hands like acquaintances and entered into a lively conversation. As I moved on I looked back, and the old man, still talking, had his gun in one hand and the other hand on Traveler's neck.

It was such scenes as this that made General Lee so popular. He believed in his men and thought they could do anything that mortals could do. His men worshipped him, and I think the greatest man the world ever saw was Robert E. Lee.

Now, as Lee came riding alone into Richmond, his old followers immediately recognized him. They formed in line and followed him to his home where, with uncovered heads, they saw him enter his door. Then they silently dispersed.[17]

This was the last of the Confederacy! All realized that the last hope was gone, and that the great struggle for secession was at an end. Thus ended the war, and at that time the inhabitants of the South were a ruined people.

> Furl that Banner! true, 'tis gory,
> Yet 'tis wreathed around with glory,
> And 'twill live in song and story,
>   Though its folds are in the dust:
> For its fame on brightest pages,
> Penned by poets and by sages,
> Shall go sounding down the ages—
>   Furl its folds though now we must.
>
> Furl that Banner, softly, slowly;
> Treat it gently—it is holy—
>   For it droops above the dead.
> Touch it not—unfold it never,
> Let it droop there, furled forever,
>   For its people's hopes are dead![18]

---

[17] A more vivid description of this scene is in Freeman, *R. E. Lee,* IV, 163-64.

[18] From "The Conquered Banner," by Abram J. Ryan. The full text of the seven-stanza poem is in A. J. Ryan, *Father Ryan's Poems* (Mobile, 1879), pp. 150-51.

Appendix A

RETURNING HOME

When the Confederate soldiers returned from the army after the war, a majority of them literally had nothing but the ragged clothing on their backs! They did not even have a change of clothing. Yet what a sight met them on their arrival home! Desolation was everywhere. Many found their families scattered all over the state, different members having taken up their abode with relatives or friends in such sections as had not been overrun by the enemy. Many found dwellings, barns, stables, outbuildings, fences, and literally everything except the land gone. Some found a few outbuildings remaining but no fences, while others found the fences remaining but everything else gone. One could travel for miles along the roads in certain sections of the country and see no fence, no house, not a single living thing—unless a fox or other wild animal should cross his path.

While some of the soldiers had their land, that was all they had. If one had stock, farming utensils, or provisions, he was an exception. The world will never know the poverty to which these men were reduced, and their conduct at this time shines out with more brilliancy, if such could be the case, than did their services in the army. They literally turned the sword into the plowshare, and they went to work with a determination to make a living and, if possible, to recuperate their fortunes. Poverty is a great leveler, and all were on the same footing now. The men accepted any honorable work. In the burnt districts of Richmond, men who a short time ago were worth thousands were actually seen cleaning brick!

It was not uncommon to see a private and a colonel in their old uniforms working side by side. The men in the country went to work with the same determination. A family that had been raised in affluence and luxury lived in a log cabin; the lady of the house did the cooking, and the landed proprietor followed a plow drawn by the only horse on the place.

For several months all the money made by the men was spent in meeting actual needs, and generally it took all they made to feed the family. In consequence, the old soldiers still wore their old uniforms.

This became a great annoyance to the Yankee armies stationed in the South. The sight of the old Confederate soldier going about daily in his old uniform reminded them to forcibly of the hard times they had undergone during the last four years. In order to remove the sight of these uniforms as much as possible, the military authorities issued an order that the brass buttons on the coats and jackets of late Confederate soldiers must come off by a certain day. They allowed them the choice of either covering the buttons with some material that would hide the shining brass, or else cutting them off.

In any event, the brass buttons had to be hidden from sight by that date. If any were found on clothing after that date, the United States soldiers had orders to cut the buttons off and arrest the offender. If a man submitted to the button-cutting and made no resistance, he was allowed to go free; if he was caught a second time, he was imprisoned. Some of our men thought this such a foolish order for the great United States government to issue that they paid no attention to it. Many were then stopped in the streets of Richmond and had their buttons cut off! This accounts for the many old uniforms that are seen at this day with buttons covered or without brass or military buttons.

Appendix B

THE WOMEN OF THE SOUTH

What had the women of the South been doing all this time? Would that I had a gifted pen to tell of the noble deeds done by them! They had not been idle. Wherever woman could work or administer comfort, there she was found.

As soon as Virginia seceded, women organized work societies throughout the state. In Richmond they met daily at certain houses and in the basement of nearly every church. There, using all the old cotton and linen clothing they had, they made bandages by the mile and lint by the hundred pounds—as well as haversacks and all kinds of clothing. To show the energy with which they could work when it was necessary, I will narrate a circumstance told me soon after it occurred.

During the retreat of General Joseph E. Johnston from Yorktown, Richmond was thought to be deficient in fortifications. It was suggested that, if the government had bags that could be filled with sand and earth and placed in position, thus forming a wall, earth could then be thrown against this on the outside and earthworks of great strength could be made very quickly. But how to get enough bags was the trouble. Hearing of this, the ladies sent a committee to see the Secretary of War, George W. Randolph. They offered to make the bags if he would supply the material. Mr. Randolph gladly accepted this offer, and in an hour he had delivered to the ladies, at various places which they had designated, many huge rolls of cotton. The ladies were ready; cutting and making commenced and went on all night. The next morning thousands of finished bags were delivered to the authorities, and in a few hours the work of erecting the fortifications was begun.[1]

The hospital committee was ever present, administering to the sick and wounded. I have heard numerous soldiers say they were glad they were wounded, as the careful attention received from those women

---

[1] Judith McGuire related this incident of Apr. 21, 1862, in her *Diary of a Southern Refugee during the War* (Richmond, 1889), pp. 108-09.

more than repaid them for the suffering they endured.[2] Here is a little incident told me after the war by one of the fashionable young ladies who lived on one of the fashionable streets of wartime Richmond. She was a member of one of the hospital committees. In one of the hospitals which she attended was a soldier from one of the Southern states. Although desperately wounded, he had been saved by devoted nursing. He appreciated it and showed his obligation as well as a man could. When he was well and was ordered to his command in the field, he asked this young lady if he might call on her at her home. She told him she would be glad to see him at any time, and she gave him the number of her residence.

He called a day or two afterward. After conversing a short while, he told her he knew that the care given him by the ladies had saved his life, and he had asked to call in order that he might thank her and at the same time present her with a little gift. This had given him a great deal of thought, as his means were very limited, but he had bought what he considered the best thing in the world. He presented her with a small package of "goobers" (peanuts), saying that he wished he were able to give her a bushel! The young lady said to me that she considered that the most valuable present she ever received, and she prized it as such because it came from the man's heart. She thinks it took every cent of money he had to purchase it.

There were also committees to look after the poor. They had a hard time, as everyone was poor. Yet they did their duty as nobly and as faithfully as the others.

Many households were without any males. This entailed much work and anxiety on the women left at the head of them. Especially was this true in the country, where it was necessary to attend to the business of the farm as well as that of the house. Many farms, including some large ones, were operated very successfully by women.

After the war they cheerfully shared every hardship. With an abiding faith in the men, they upheld them in all honorable work. They welcomed the mens' old army acquaintances to their homes with great cordiality, regardless of the rough hands and ragged clothing of the visitors.

God bless the Southern women of those days! Would that I were able to build a monument to them. I would have it as high as the steeple of St. Paul's Church. At its base would be a room, the walls of

---

[2] For an excellent narrative by one of Richmond's nurses, see Phoebe Yates Pember, *A Southern Woman's Story*, edited by Bell I. Wiley (Jackson, Tenn., 1959).

which I would adorn with paintings to tell the story of women's lives during those trying times. In the center of this room would be a statue of a Southern mother, dressed in plain Confederate clothes, and hand‹ing to her boy, who is not old enough to wear a coat, a pocket Bible. Her other hand would be pointing to the open door; and with tears streaming down her cheeks she would be telling him that his country's needs are more than hers, and for him to go and join the army.

Among the paintings would be one of the wife and daughters of General Robert E. Lee knitting socks for the private soldiers of his army. Another would show Mrs. John B. Gordon administering to a sick or wounded soldier on the roadside in the field. (She accompanied the general in the field during the war.) I would fill the room with such scenes as these.

Appendix C

ROSTER OF F COMPANY, 21st VIRGINIA INFANTRY

This roster was compiled for the most part from personal service records in the National Archives. Additional information was gleaned from muster rolls—also on deposit in the National Archives—and from Worsham's own, fragmentary listing. Ages given for some individuals were their ages at the time of enlistment. In instances where men transferred from the company, no service record subsequent to transfer has been given unless the individual performed exceptional service. To facilitate reference, officers and enlisted men are arranged in alphabetical order.

ANDERSON, Archer: enlisted Apr. 21, 1861, Richmond; aged 23; promoted to captain and transferred to Gen. Trimble's staff, 1861; became lieutenant colonel and served on the staffs of Gens. Holmes, D. H. Hill, and J. E. Johnston.

ANDERSON, Henry V.: enlisted Apr. 21, 1861, Richmond; aged 21; killed at Cedar Run, Aug. 9, 1862.

ANDERSON, James H.: enlisted Apr. 11, 1863, Culpeper County; promoted to corporal, 1864.

ANDERSON, Junius H.: enlisted Apr. 21, 1861, Richmond; aged 26; promoted to corporal, July 6, 1863; deserted, Feb., 1865.

ARCHER, William S., Jr.: enlisted Apr. 21, 1861, Richmond; aged 17; promoted to ordnance sergeant, Apr. 22, 1862; promoted to lieutenant in 48th Va., Dec. 24, 1863; wounded at Cold Harbor, June 3, 1864; captured at Winchester, Sept. 19, 1864.[1]

AYERS, Edward S.: enlisted Apr. 21, 1861, Richmond; transferred, 1861.[2]

BARBER, Nathaniel: enlisted Feb. 4, 1863; Franklin County; captured at Winchester, Sept. 19, 1864, and sent to Point Lookout; exchanged, Feb. 24, 1865.

[1] See OR, XLVI, pt. 1, 1275; SHSP, XXI (1893), 242-44.
[2] For criticism of Ayers, see Ham Chamberlayne, p. 255.

BARKER, William C.: enlisted Apr. 21, 1861, Richmond; aged 28; transferred to Richmond Howitzers, Apr. 10, 1862.

BATES, Edward: enlisted Feb. 4, 1863, Pittsylvania County; died from chronic diarrhea, Mar. 10, 1864.[3]

BATES, W.: enlisted Mar. 30, 1863, Pittsylvania County; discharged for chronic diarrhea, Dec. 24, 1864.

BAUGHMAN, Charles C.: enlisted Apr. 21, 1861, Richmond; aged 19; discharged, Feb. 1, 1862.

BAUGHMAN, George C.: enlisted Apr. 21, 1861, Richmond; aged 32; promoted to lieutenant in Caskie's Battery, June, 1861.

BAUGHMAN, Greer H.: enlisted Apr. 21, 1861, Richmond; aged 21; promoted to sergeant in Caskie's Battery, July, 1861; wounded at Cold Harbor, June 3, 1864.

BEERS, Henry H.: enlisted Apr. 21, 1861, Richmond; aged 20; transferred to Caskie's Battery, 1862.

BINFORD, James M.: enlisted Apr. 21, 1861, Richmond; discharged for chronic rheumatism, 1862.

BINFORD, Robert E.: enlisted Apr. 21, 1861, Richmond; promoted to lieutenant in artillery, 1862.

BLUNT, Ira W.: enlisted Apr. 21, 1861, Richmond; aged 29; assigned as hospital steward, Jan. 24, 1862.

BOWE, H. C.: enlisted 1863; discharged June, 1864.

BOYD, James N.: enlisted Apr., 1865, Namozine Creek; aged 15; captured Sayler's Creek, Apr. 6, 1865.

BRIDGERS, David B., Jr.: enlisted Apr. 21, 1861, Richmond; aged 19; transferred to Richmond Howitzers, May 1, 1862.

BRIDGERS, Richard M.: enlisted Apr. 21, 1861, Richmond; aged 17; promoted to captain, Mar. 18, 1862; resigned from service, Nov., 1862.

BROCK, Robert Alonzo: enlisted Apr. 21, 1861, Richmond; aged 22; promoted to corporal, Apr. 22, 1862; assigned as hospital steward, June 12, 1862.

BROWN, A. D.: enlisted Feb. 18, 1863, Culpeper; wounded at Hatcher's Run, Feb. 6, 1865.

BROWN, A. H.: enlisted Feb. 24, 1863, Culpeper; hospitalized, Sept., 1863, until end of war because of hernia.

BROWN, George W.: enlisted Feb. 21, 1863, Culpeper; lost a leg at the Wilderness, May 5, 1864.

---

[3] In his roster Worsham stated that Bates died "from effects of campaign."

BROWN, Henry: enlisted Feb. 24, 1863, Campbell County; captured at Cedar Creek, Oct. 19, 1864.

BROWN, James R.: enlisted Feb. 18, 1863, Culpeper; reported missing after May 5, 1864.

BULLINGTON, Henry N.: enlisted Apr. 21, 1861, Richmond; aged 20; assigned as clerk to Col. A. P. Hill, 1861.

CABELL, J. Caskie: enlisted Apr. 21, 1861, Richmond; promoted to lieutenant in 60th Va., 1861.

CALLIS, G.: enlisted Feb. 3, 1863, Richmond; on sick list after Aug., 1863.

CARY, R. Milton: enlisted Apr. 21, 1861, Richmond; captain of F Company at its muster; promoted to colonel of 30th Va., June 15, 1861; assigned to Belona Arsenal in 1862 to supervise manufacture of cannon; surrendered with J. E. Johnston's army, Apr. 26, 1865.

CHAMBERLAYNE, J. Hampden: enlisted Apr. 21, 1861, Richmond; aged 22; promoted to lieutenant and assigned as adjutant of an artillery battalion, Mar. 4, 1862; captured at Chambersburg, Pa., June 29, 1863; exchanged; subsequently became major.[4]

CHAPMAN, Isaac W.: enlisted Apr. 21, 1861, Richmond; aged 21; discharged for disability, 1862.

CHILD, Jesse: enlisted Apr. 21, 1861, Richmond; aged 30; promoted to corporal, June 6, 1861; promoted to sergeant, Apr. 22, 1862; assigned as hospital steward of 42nd Va., Dec. 24, 1863.

CLARKE, Maxwell T.: enlisted Apr. 21, 1861, Richmond; aged 31; transferred to C. S. Navy, June 1861; subsequently commanded gunboat on James River.

CLOPTON, John: enlisted Apr. 21, 1861, Richmond; transferred June 6, 1861.

COCKE, Lorenzo G.: enlisted Apr. 21, 1861, Richmond; aged 25; died in camp, Dec. 1, 1861.

COLE, Addison C.: enlisted Apr. 21, 1861, Richmond; aged 30; discharged from service, Jan. 25, 1862.

COLEMAN, N.: enlisted Feb. 18, 1863, Liberty.

COUCH, L. M.: enlisted Feb. 9, 1863, Richmond; wounded at Mine Run, Nov. 27, 1863, at the Wilderness, May 5, 1864 and at Cedar Creek, Oct. 19, 1864.

---

[4] Chamberlayne's memoirs, *Ham Chamberlayne—Virginian,* have been quoted extensively in the footnotes for this edition.

COWARDIN, John L.: enlisted Apr. 21, 1861, Richmond; promoted to adjutant of 50th Va., 1861.[5]

CRAIG, John A.: enlisted Apr. 21, 1861, Richmond; aged 21; assigned as hospital steward, Nov., 1862.

CRENSHAW, James R.: enlisted Apr. 21, 1861, Richmond; promoted to lieutenant colonel and transferred to 26th Va., 1862.

CUMBIE, W. S.: enlisted Nov. 9, 1862, Appomattox.

CUMBIE, William E.: enlisted Jan. 20, 1862, Mecklenberg County, in 22nd Va. Battalion; transferred to 21st Va., Sept. 4, 1863; wounded at the Wilderness, May 5, 1864; died May 24, 1864.

CUNNINGHAM, Frank: enlisted Apr. 21, 1861, Richmond, as company surgeon; promoted to division surgeon, 1862.

CUNNINGHAM, Richard H., Jr.: enlisted Apr. 21, 1861, Richmond; aged 27; 2nd lieutenant at muster; promoted to captain, May 16, 1861, elected lieutenant colonel of 21st Va., Apr. 22, 1862; killed at Cedar Run, Aug. 9, 1862.

DANFORTH, Henry D.: enlisted Apr. 21, 1861, Richmond; aged 20; slightly wounded at Kernstown, Mar. 23, 1862; promoted to lieutenant of ordnance, May 19, 1862.

DILL, Adolph, Jr.: enlisted Apr. 21, 1861, Richmond; aged 20; detailed to commissary department, June, 1862.

DILLARD, R. H.: enlisted Mar. 6, 1863, Franklin County; slightly wounded at the Wilderness, May 5, 1864; wounded and captured at Spotsylvania, May 12, 1864; exchanged from Elmira, Mar. 14, 1865.

DIVERS, W. H.: enlisted Feb. 9, 1863, Franklin County; died from wounds at Newtown, Aug. 12, 1864.

DOGGETT, Francis W.: enlisted Apr. 21, 1861, Richmond; aged 27; discharged for disability, Nov. 22, 1861.

DOWDY, Nathaniel A.: enlisted Jan. 26, 1863, Cumberland County; promoted to corporal, Jan. 1, 1864; shot twice in arm at the Wilderness, May 5, 1864; wounded at Winchester, Sept. 19, 1864; captured at Fort Stedman, Mar. 25, 1865; paroled, June 12, 1865.

EDMUNDS, William B.: enlisted May 1, 1863, Lynchburg; wounded and captured at Chancellorsville, May 3, 1863.

ELLERSON, John H.: enlisted Apr. 21, 1861, Richmond; transferred, June, 1861.

---

[5] On Apr. 1, 1865, Lt. Cowardin was ordered to proceed to Halifax, Va., to recruit Negro troops for the Confederate armies. *OR*, Ser. IV, III, 1194. See also *ibid.*, Ser. I, LI, pt. 1, 41-42.

ELLET, Robert: enlisted Apr. 21, 1861, Richmond; aged 18; promoted to lieutenant in Letcher's Battery, Sept. 23, 1861; killed at Petersburg, Apr. 2, 1865.

ELLET, Thomas: enlisted Apr. 21, 1861, Richmond; aged 28; sergeant at company's muster; promoted to lieutenant in Crenshaw's Battery, May, 1862.

ENGLISH, James C.: enlisted Apr. 15, 1863, Bedford County; aged 28; shot in right thigh at Winchester, Sept. 19, 1864; captured at Fort Stedman, Mar. 25, 1865; paroled from Elmira, July, 1865.

ETTING, Samuel: enlisted Apr. 21, 1861, Richmond; transferred to Caskie's Battery, June 27, 1861.[6]

EXALL, Charles H.: enlisted Apr. 21, 1861, Richmond; aged 20; promoted to sergeant and transferred to Letcher's Battery, Oct., 1862.

EXALL, William: enlisted Apr. 21, 1861, Richmond; aged 20; killed at Bath, Jan. 3, 1862.

FIELD, William G.: enlisted Apr. 21, 1861, Richmond; transferred to cavalry, 1861; killed at Malvern Hill, July 1, 1862.

FLOYD, George J.: enlisted Feb. 19, 1863, Richmond; absent without leave after June 5, 1864.

FONTAINE, R. Morris: enlisted Apr. 21, 1861, Richmond; aged 17; discharged from service, Nov. 26, 1861, as a result of typhoid fever.

FOX, Henry C.: enlisted June 18, 1863, Augusta County; wounded and captured, July, 1864; exchanged from Elmira, Oct. 29, 1864; killed at Fort Stedman, Mar. 25, 1865.

GENTRY, John W.: enlisted Apr. 21, 1861, Richmond; aged 22; promoted to corporal, Apr. 22, 1862; discharged for coronary ailment, Aug. 31, 1862.

GENTRY, M. C.: enlisted Feb. 4, 1863, Richmond; declared unfit for field service, Mar., 1864; detailed to Richmond as prison guard, Sept. 2, 1864.

GIBSON, William T.: enlisted Apr. 21, 1861, Richmond; slightly wounded at Kernstown, Mar. 23, 1862; promoted to sergeant, Apr. 22, 1862; discharged from service, Oct. 23, 1862.

GILLIAN, Robert H.: enlisted Apr. 21, 1861, Richmond; aged 22; wounded at Cedar Run, Aug. 9, 1862; promoted to lieutenant in 25th Va. Battalion, Feb., 1864; captured at Sayler's Creek, Apr. 6, 1865.

---

[6] Etting won promotion to lieutenant and in at least one battle distinguished himself for valor. *Ibid.,* XII, pt. 1, 771.

GILMORE, J. Harvie: joined regiment in 1861 as chaplain; remained behind at Gettysburg to minister to sick and wounded; taken prisoner and confined in Fort McHenry; exchanged, Aug., 1863.

GOULDMAN, E.: enlisted Feb. 10, 1863, Caroline County; promoted to corporal, May, 1863; promoted to sergeant, July 6, 1864; hospitalized for diarrhea after July, 1864.

GRAY, Somerville: enlisted Apr. 21, 1861, Richmond; aged 20; wounded at Kernstown, Mar. 23, 1862; transferred to Richmond Howitzers, Jan. 8, 1863.

GRAY, William Granville, Jr.: enlisted Apr. 21, 1861, Richmond; aged 35; promoted to lieutenant, Dec. 6, 1861; resigned from service, Mar. 25, 1864, because of "frequent attacks of rheumatism."[7]

GREEN, John W.: enlisted Apr. 21, 1861, Richmond; aged 23; transferred to artillery, Mar. 2, 1862; killed at Liberty Mills, Sept. 22, 1863.

GREEN, T. Richie: enlisted Apr. 21, 1861, Richmond; aged 24; transferred to artillery, 1861.

HARRISON, Thomas R.: enlisted Apr. 21, 1861, Richmond; transferred to Richmond Howitzers, May 27, 1861; wounded and captured at Gettysburg, July, 1863.

HARVIE, William O.: enlisted Apr. 21, 1861, Richmond; promoted to major and transferred to quartermaster department, 1861.

HAWKINS, Laban A.: enlisted Feb. 5, 1863, Richmond; discharged for œdena of both legs, Apr. 9, 1864.

HAYNES, George A.: enlisted Apr. 21, 1861, Richmond; aged 22; promoted to corporal, Apr. 22, 1862; promoted to orderly sergeant, Aug., 1862.[8]

HENRY, Patrick: enlisted May 16, 1861, Richmond; aged 24; promoted to regimental assistant surgeon, 1861.

HOBSON, Deane: enlisted Apr. 21, 1861, Richmond; transferred to artillery, May 20, 1861.

HOUSTON, George W.: enlisted Feb. 19, 1863, Richmond; shot in left leg and captured at Winchester, Sept. 19, 1864; sent to Elmira.

HUDGINS, Malcolm L.: enlisted May 16, 1861, Game Point; aged 17; promoted to sergeant, Apr. 22, 1862; promoted to lieutenant, May, 1863; wounded and captured at Cedar Creek, Oct. 19, 1864.

---

[7] Gray to Sec. of War, Mar. 25, 1864, Gray's personal service file, War Records Group 109, National Archives.
[8] For more on Haynes, see DeLeon, *Four Years in Rebel Capitals,* p. 105.

HULL, Irving: enlisted May 16, 1861, Game Point; transferred, 1861.

JENKINS, William S.: enlisted Apr. 21, 1861, Richmond; aged 27; discharged from service, Oct. 24, 1862.

JOHNSTON, J. W.: enlisted Jan. 1, 1863, Henry County; captured at the Wilderness, May 5, 1864; sent to Elmira.

JONES, David B.: enlisted Apr. 21, 1861, Richmond; aged 25; promoted to sergeant, June 15, 1862; acting quartermaster of 21st Va., 1864.

JONES, Philip B., Jr.: enlisted Apr. 21, 1861, Richmond; promoted to captain in quartermaster's department, Oct. 26, 1861.[9]

JORDAN, Reuben J.: enlisted Apr. 21, 1861, Richmond; aged 18; promoted to orderly sergeant, 1862; promoted to lieutenant, May 20, 1863; promoted to captain, May, 1864; wounded at Cold Harbor, June 3, 1864; shot in right side at Fort Stedman, Mar. 25, 1865.

KAYTON, Patrick W.: enlisted June 16, 1863, Richmond; captured at Spotsylvania, May 12, 1864; sent to Fort Delaware.

KELLOGG, Timothy H.: enlisted Apr. 21, 1861, Richmond; aged 30; promoted to lieutenant in H Company, Apr. 21, 1862; promoted to major, Nov., 1862.

KIDD, J. A.: enlisted Apr. 9, 1863, Bedford County; wounded in arm at Mine Run, Nov. 27, 1863; killed at Fort Stedman, Mar. 25, 1865.

KING, Shirley: enlisted Apr. 21, 1861, Richmond; aged 19; corporal at company's muster; reduced to private in Apr., 1862, elections; transferred to quartermaster's department, Sept., 1863, because of coronary condition.

LEGG, A. C.: enlisted Nov. 10, 1863, Orange County; wounded at the Wilderness, May 5, 1864; died of gangrene, June 26, 1864.

LINDSAY, Roswell S.: enlisted Apr. 21, 1861, Richmond; aged 20; promoted to corporal, Apr. 22, 1862; killed at Cedar Run, Aug. 9, 1862.

LORENTZ, A.: enlisted Apr. 21, 1861, Richmond; transferred, 1861.

LYONS, Peter: enlisted Apr. 21, 1861, Richmond, as assistant company surgeon; promoted to regimental surgeon, 1862.

McEVOY, Charles A.: enlisted Apr. 21, 1861, Richmond; resigned from service, June 27, 1861.

---

[9] An incident of Jones' valor is mentioned in *OR*, XIX, pt. 1, 887.

MACMURDO, Richard C.: enlisted May 18, 1861, Richmond; aged 26; promoted to captain and transferred, May 29, 1862.

MADDOX, R. G.: enlisted May 16, 1861, Game Point; transferred, 1861.

MASON, Joseph M.: enlisted Feb. 10, 1863; aged 41; captured at Cedar Creek, Oct. 19, 1864.

MAYO, Edward: enlisted May 10, 1861, Richmond; aged 30; resigned from the company, Oct., 1861.

MAYO, Joseph E.: enlisted May 10, 1861, Richmond; aged 21; transferred to Signal Corps, Apr. 24, 1863.

MEADE, Everard B.: enlisted Apr. 21, 1861, Richmond; aged 22; promoted to lieutenant in engineer corps, Nov. 2, 1861.[10]

MEBANE, James A.: enlisted Apr. 21, 1861, Richmond; aged 19; assigned as hospital steward, Nov. 25, 1861.

MEREDITH, J. French: enlisted Apr. 21, 1861, Richmond; transferred June 6, 1861.

MERRYMAN, John T.: enlisted Mar. 2, 1863, New Kent; captured at Spotsylvania, May 12, 1864; exchanged from Fort Delaware, Oct. 30, 1864.

MILLER, Henry T.: enlisted Apr. 21, 1861, Richmond; aged 26; sergeant at company's muster; promoted to lieutenant, June 6, 1861; transferred to 26th Va., Nov., 1861.

MITCHELL, Samuel D.: enlisted Apr. 21, 1861, Richmond; aged 19; promoted to lieutenant and aide-de-camp to Gen. C. S. Winder, May 9, 1862; killed at Gaines's Mill, June 27, 1862.[11]

MITTLEDORFER, Charles: enlisted Apr. 21, 1861, Richmond; aged 22; transferred, 1861.

MORGAN, William H.: enlisted June, 1861, Richmond, as adjutant of 21st Va.; elected captain of F Company, Apr. 21, 1862; killed at Cedar Run, Aug. 9, 1862.

MORRIS, Walter H. P.: enlisted Apr. 21, 1861, Richmond; aged 21; transferred to artillery, 1861.

MOUNTCASTLE, John R.: enlisted Apr. 21, 1861, Richmond; aged 20; promoted to lieutenant of cavalry, Mar. 21, 1862.

MUNT, Henry F.: enlisted Feb. 14, 1863, Prince George County; promoted to corporal, May, 1863; captured at the Wilderness, May 5, 1864; sent to Elmira.

---

[10] Gen. J. H. Lane commended his behavior in *ibid.*, XLVI, pt. 1, 1286.
[11] For praise of Mitchell by Gen. Winder, see *ibid.*, XI, pt. 2, 571. Details of his death are in Howard, *Recollections*, p. 141; SHSP, XXX (1902), 148.

NANCE, J. L.: enlisted Feb. 8, 1863, Pittsylvania County; discharged from service, Nov. 29, 1863, because of epilepsia.

NORWOOD, William, Jr.: enlisted Apr. 21, 1861, Richmond; promoted to lieutenant and transferred, Sept. 11, 1861.

NUNNALLY, Joseph N.: enlisted Apr. 21, 1861, Richmond; aged 20; wounded in head at Kernstown, Mar. 23, 1862; killed at Cedar Run, Aug. 9, 1862.

PACE, George R.: enlisted Apr. 21, 1861, Richmond; aged 25; promoted to corporal, June 5, 1861; discharged from service, Feb. 1, 1862.

PACE, Theodore A.: enlisted May 6, 1861, Fredericksburg; aged 16; discharged from service, June, 1862.

PAGE, Mann: enlisted Apr. 21, 1861, Richmond; aged 26; promoted to sergeant major, June, 1861; promoted to lieutenant, 1862; on Gen. J. A. Early's staff at end of war.

PARDIGON, C. F.: enlisted Apr. 21, 1861, Richmond; transferred, 1861.

PAYNE, James B., Jr.: enlisted Apr. 21, 1861, Richmond; aged 24; promoted to lieutenant, Dec. 28, 1861; wounded at Bath, Jan. 3, 1862; resigned from service, Apr. 21, 1862.

PEASTER, Henry: enlisted Apr. 21, 1861, Richmond; aged 25; wounded in abdomen at Mine Run, Nov. 27, 1863; transferred to Maryland Line, Mar. 3, 1864.

PEGRAM, William A.: enlisted Apr. 21, 1861, Richmond; aged 23; promoted to sergeant, 1862; promoted to captain, May 20, 1863; killed at Williamsport, Md., July 6, 1863.

PEGRAM, William R. J.: enlisted Apr. 21, 1861, Richmond; aged 20; promoted to lieutenant of artillery, May, 1861; was colonel of artillery when killed at Five Forks, Apr. 1, 1865.

PETERKIN, George W.: enlisted Apr. 21, 1861, Richmond; aged 20; promoted to sergeant, 1861; elected lieutenant, Apr. 19, 1862; assigned to staff of W. N. Pendleton, June, 1862.[12]

PICOT, Henry V.: enlisted Apr. 21, 1861, Richmond; aged 24; mortally wounded at Kernstown, Mar. 23, 1862.

PIET, William A.: enlisted Apr. 21, 1861, Richmond; aged 23; promoted to corporal, Apr. 22, 1862; transferred to Richmond Howitzers, May 2, 1862.

---

[12] Peterkin, like Pendleton, was an ardent Episcopalian. As mentioned in footnote 8 for Chap. II, he subsequently became a rector and then Bishop of West Va.

PILCHER, Samuel F.: enlisted Apr. 21, 1861, Richmond; promoted to sergeant, 1861; died of ill health, 1863.

PIZZINI, John A.: enlisted Apr. 21, 1861, Richmond; aged 27; sergeant at company's muster; wounded on Romney campaign, Jan., 1862; promoted to lieutenant and transferred, Apr., 1862.

POLLARD, William G.: enlisted Apr. 21, 1861, Richmond; aged 24; promoted to sergeant, Apr. 19, 1862; killed at Cedar Run, Aug. 9, 1862.

POWELL, John G.: enlisted Apr. 21, 1861, Richmond; aged 26; killed at Cedar Run, Aug. 9, 1862.

POWELL, John W.: enlisted Apr. 21, 1861, Richmond; aged 26; transferred, 1861.

PRICE, R. Channing: enlisted May 16, 1861, Fredericksburg; transferred to cavalry, 1861; became major and assistant adjutant general to J. E. B. Stuart; killed at Chancellorsville, May 3, 1863.[13]

RANDOLPH, J. Tucker: enlisted Apr. 21, 1861, Richmond; aged 17; promoted to corporal, June 5, 1861; promoted to sergeant, Nov., 1861; wounded in foot and stomach at Kernstown, Mar. 23, 1862; promoted to lieutenant and assigned to Gen. John Pegram's staff, June, 1862; killed at Bethesda Church, May 30, 1864.[14]

RANDOLPH, Merewether Lewis: enlisted Apr. 21, 1861, Richmond; promoted to corporal, May, 1861; promoted to lieutenant of 1st Va. Battalion, June 4, 1861; later became captain in the Signal Corps.[15]

RAWLINGS, Edward G., Jr.: enlisted Apr. 21, 1861, Richmond; aged 36; sergeant at company's muster; elected lieutenant, Apr. 21, 1862; killed at Second Manassas, Aug. 30, 1862.

REDD, Clarence M.: enlisted Apr. 21, 1861, Richmond; aged 21; shot in left wrist at Cedar Run, Aug. 9, 1862; transferred to Hanover Artillery, Oct., 1862.

REEVE, John J.: enlisted May 10, 1861, Fredericksburg; aged 20; promoted to captain and A.A.G. on Gen. Loring's staff, Apr. 7, 1862; promoted to major and A.A.G. on Gen. C. L. Stevenson's staff, 1862.

---

[13] For Gen. J. E. B. Stuart's laudatory mention of Price see *OR*, XII, pt. 2, 738.

[14] Worsham wrote that Randolph had "a determination of countenance that made him look much older than he was." Worsham manuscript, Randolph Papers. After a March, 1863, nocturnal expedition, Gen. Pegram stated of him: "By his personal actions during the whole night he rendered such service as commanded the admiration of all who saw him." *OR*, XXIII, pt. 1, 173.

[15] Gen. Rodes praised Randolph's conduct at Gettysburg. See *ibid.*, XXVII, pt. 2, 560.

RENNIE, George Hutchie: enlisted May 18, 1861, Game Point; aged 20; wounded in neck at Kernstown, Mar. 23, 1862; promoted to sergeant, Oct. 20, 1864; killed at Fort Stedman, Mar. 25, 1865.

RICHESON, P. S.: enlisted Feb. 10, 1863, Caroline County; wounded and captured at Spotsylvania, May 12, 1864; exchanged; shot in left foot at Cedar Creek, Oct. 19, 1864.

RICHESON, William R.: enlisted Feb. 10, 1863, Caroline County.

RISON, John W.: enlisted Apr. 21, 1861, Richmond; transferred, 1861.

ROBERTSON, William S.: enlisted May 18, 1861, Game Point; aged 18; promoted to corporal, Sept., 1863; promoted to sergeant, Jan. 1, 1864; captured at Waynesboro, Mar. 2, 1865; sent to Fort Delaware.

ROBINSON, Christopher A.: enlisted Apr. 21, 1861, Richmond; transferred to engineer corps, 1862.

ROBINSON, Richard F.: enlisted Apr. 21, 1861, Richmond; aged 22; discharged from service, Apr. 21, 1862.

RUTLEDGE, William: enlisted Feb. 25, 1863, Richmond.

SEARLES, Samuel: enlisted Feb. 28, 1863, Richmond; hospitalized, Aug. 16, 1864, until end of the war.

SEAY, Morton: enlisted Feb. 20, 1863, Richmond; hospitalized for rheumatism from May 2, 1864, until end of the war.

SEAY, W. C.: enlisted Sept. 26, 1863, Richmond; died May 14, 1864, of wounds received at Spotsylvania.

SIMPSON, Frederick J.: enlisted Feb. 17, 1863, Richmond; captured at Spotsylvania, May 19, 1864; sent to Fort Delaware.

SINGLETON, Andrew Jackson: enlisted Apr. 21, 1861, Richmond; aged 22; discharged from service, Feb. 28, 1862.

SIZER, Milton D.: enlisted Apr. 21, 1861, Richmond; aged 19; discharged from service for disability, Feb. 16, 1862.

SKINKER, Charles R.: enlisted Apr. 21, 1861, Richmond; aged 21; wounded in heel at Kernstown, Mar. 23, 1862; transferred to Richmond Howitzers, Apr. 10, 1862.

SMITH, Edward H.: enlisted Apr. 21, 1861, Richmond; aged 22; transferred to Richmond Howitzers, Nov. 25, 1861.

SMITH, Horace: enlisted Aug. 6, 1864, Richmond; aged 39; shot in both thighs and captured at Cedar Creek, Oct. 19, 1864; exchanged Mar., 1865.

SMITH, Joseph T.: enlisted Feb. 14, 1863, Culpeper.

SMITH, Thomas: enlisted Feb. 14, 1863, Culpeper; captured Sept. 29, 1863; sent to Point Lookout.

SOLES, Peter D.: enlisted Feb. 25, 1863, Richmond; hospitalized, Nov., 1863, until end of the war.

SUBLETT, Peter A.: enlisted Apr. 21, 1861, Richmond; aged 29; transferred to Richmond Howitzers, Aug., 1862.

TABB, Robert M.: enlisted Apr. 21, 1861, Richmond; aged 30; promoted to corporal, Apr. 30, 1863; promoted to sergeant, May, 1863; killed at Cedar Creek, Oct. 19, 1864.

TALLEY, Daniel D.: enlisted Apr. 21, 1861, Richmond; aged 20; appointed to Gov. Letcher's staff, Apr., 1862.

TATUM, A. Randolph: enlisted Apr. 21, 1861, Richmond; aged 20; assigned to duty with Gen. J. H. Winder, Feb., 1862.

TATUM, Vivian H.; enlisted Apr. 21, 1861, Richmond; aged 23; transferred to commissary department, Feb., 1862.

TAYLOR, Charles E.: enlisted Apr. 21, 1861, Richmond; aged 18; wounded at Kernstown, Mar. 23, 1862; transferred to 10th Va. Cavalry, Sept. 2, 1862.

TAYLOR, Clarence E.: enlisted Apr. 21, 1861, Richmond; aged 27; slightly wounded at Kernstown, Mar. 23, 1862; wounded at Cedar Run, Aug. 9, 1862; detailed to quartermaster's department in Richmond, 1862.

TAYLOR, Edward B.: enlisted Apr. 21, 1861, Richmond; aged 29; shot in back at Kernstown, Mar. 23, 1862; transferred to ordnance department, Apr., 1863.

TAYLOR, Robert T.: enlisted Apr. 21, 1861, Richmond; aged 24; promoted to major and transferred to quartermaster department, Apr. 15, 1862.[16]

TINEY, W. C.: enlisted Feb. 16, 1863, Prince George County; promoted to corporal, May, 1863; killed at Williamsport, Md., July 6, 1863.

TOMPKINS, Edward G.: enlisted Apr. 21, 1861, Richmond; aged 25; permanently disabled by wounds at Cedar Run, Aug. 9, 1862.

TRAINUM, Charles: enlisted Feb. 3, 1863; discharged from service for idiocy, Apr. 11, 1864.

TYLER, James E.: enlisted Apr. 21, 1861, Richmond; aged 20; promoted to sergeant and transferred to Letcher's Battery, Mar. 27, 1862.

---

[16] That Taylor was a skilled quartermaster is borne out in *OR*, XI, pt. 2, 880.

TYLER, John: enlisted Apr. 21, 1861, Richmond; aged 25; promoted to sergeant, Feb., 1862; transferred to Crenshaw's Battery, Mar., 1862.

TYLER, Robert Emmet: enlisted Apr. 21, 1861, Richmond; aged 24; promoted to corporal, Apr. 22, 1862; transferred to ordnance department, 1862.

TYREE, Henry C.: enlisted Feb. 9, 1863, Franklin County; aged 37; promoted corporal, July 6, 1864; shot in right thigh and captured at Cedar Creek, Oct. 19, 1864; exchanged Oct. 29, 1864.

VAN BUREN, Benjamin B.: enlisted Apr. 21, 1861, Richmond; aged 24; discharged from service, Mar., 1862, for disability.

WALDROP, Richard W.: enlisted Apr. 21, 1861, Richmond; promoted to commissary sergeant of 21st Va., Apr., 1863.

WALKER, Thomas B.: enlisted Feb. 4, 1863, Franklin County; promoted to sergeant, May, 1863; killed at Williamsport, Md., July 6, 1863.

WALLACE, Richard H.: enlisted May 15, 1863, Lynchburg; aged 32; transferred to 24th Va. Battalion, Sept. 4, 1863.

WATKINS, Aurelius Salle: enlisted Apr. 21, 1861, Richmond; promoted to lieutenant in 3rd Va. Battalion, May 17, 1864.

WATKINS, Henry Harrison: enlisted Apr. 21, 1861, Richmond; aged 20; wounded and permanently disabled at Cedar Run, Aug. 9, 1862.

WELLFORD, Philip A.: enlisted Apr. 21, 1861, Richmond; aged 27; promoted to lieutenant, May 1, 1861; promoted to captain and Assistant Commissary of Subsistence, 1863.

WHITE, Robert C.: enlisted Apr. 21, 1861, Richmond; aged 21; transferred to Crenshaw's Battery, Aug. 13, 1863.

WILKINS, J. M.: enlisted Feb. 12, 1863, Gloucester; hospitalized from June, 1863, until end of the war because of chronic rheumatism and diarrhea.

WILLIS, Joseph N.: enlisted Apr. 21, 1861, Richmond; aged 21; assigned as hospital steward, Apr., 1863.

WOOD, S. E., enlisted Feb. 9, 1863, Bedford County; wounded in head and captured at Winchester, Sept. 19, 1864; exchanged, Oct. 31, 1864.

WORSHAM, John H.; enlisted Apr. 21, 1861, Richmond; aged 21; promoted to sergeant, July, 1863; appointed adjutant of 21st Va., Sept. 12, 1864; wounded and permanently disabled at Winchester, Sept. 19, 1864.

WORSHAM, Thomas R.: enlisted Apr. 21, 1861, Richmond; transferred to Letcher's Battery, Mar. 21, 1862; subsequently became
lieutenant; wounded at Spotsylvania, May 12, 1864.

WREN, Joseph Porter: enlisted Apr. 21, 1861, Richmond; aged 30;
wounded at Cedar Run, Aug. 9, 1862; promoted to sergeant, Apr.,
1863; wounded at Mine Run, Nov. 27, 1863; killed at Monocacy,
Md., July 9, 1864.

WRIGHT, Philip A.: enlisted Apr. 21, 1861, Richmond; transferred,
1861.

ZIMMER, Louis: enlisted Apr. 21, 1861, Richmond; promoted to
captain in ordnance department, 1861.

INDEX

NOTE: Unless otherwise specified, all places listed in the index are in Virginia.

Ambulances, 34, 171
Amelia, 181-82
Amissville, 69
Anderson, Archer, 194
Anderson, David W., 140
Anderson, Henry V., 66, 194
Anderson, James H., 143, 194
Anderson, Junius H., 194
Anderson, Richard H., 56-57, 101, 163, 166
Antietam Creek, Md., battle of, xx, 86-90, 112, 151, 162
Appomattox, 24n., 142, 182, 187
Aquia Creek, xvi, 3, 5-8
Archer, William S., Jr., 100, 105, 194
Arkansas Infantry—1st: 7
Arms, 60-61, 123, 165
Ashby, Turner: death of, 49; praised, 49-50; ment., 26, 35, 42, 53
Ashland, 54-55
Atkinson, Edmund T., 167n.
Averell, William W., 148n., 158
Ayers, Edward S., 194

Baldwin, John B., 9
Baltimore, Md., 7n., 10, 11
Baltimore & Ohio R.R., xxiv, 31, 82, 84, 91, 110, 160
Banks, Nathaniel P., xix, xxvii, 30, 38, 41, 47
Barber, Nathaniel, 116, 194
Barker, William C., 195
Barnett's Ford, 62
Bartley's Mill, 126
Barton's Mill, 31, 158
Baskerville, H. E. C., 11
Bates, Edward, 195
Bates, W., 109, 181, 195
Bath, W. Va., 25, 27n.
Bath Alum Springs, W. Va., 21-22
Battle, Cullen A., 128n.
Baughman, Charles C., 195
Baughman, George C., 195
Baughman, Greer H., 195
Bayard, George D., 62n.
Beaver Dam, 54, 61
Beers, Henry H., 195
Benjamin, Judah P., 29n.
Berkeley, William R., 11, 101
Bermuda Hundred, xiv
Berryville, 158, 174
Bethesda Church, 143
Big Lick, 148
Big Spring, 24, 36
Binford, James M., 195
Binford, Robert E., 195

Black Horse Cavalry, 179
Blair, Francis P., 156
Blair, Montgomery, 156n.
"Bloody Angle," 132-37
Bloomfield, 179
Blunt, Ira W., 99, 170, 195
Booker, John A., 89
Boonsboro, Md., 83-84
Boteler's Ford, 86
Bowe, H. C., 195
Boyd, James N., 195
Breckinridge, John C., 151, 155, 158-59, 169
Bridgers, David B., Jr., 195
Bridgers, Richard M., 195
Bridgewater, 50, 178
Bristoe Station, 114
Brock, Robert A., 195
Brown, A. D., 116, 181, 195
Brown, A. H., 195
Brown, George W., 116, 130, 195
Brown, Henry, 196
Brown, James R., 116, 196
Brown, John, 8
Brown's Gap, 51, 176
Brucetown, 166
Buffalo Gap, 13, 39
Buford, John, 105n., 108
Bull Run—see Manassas
Bullington, Henry N., 196
Bunker Hill, 160, 162, 163, 165-67
Burnside, Ambrose E., 92, 94n., 121n.
Butterfield, Daniel, 4n., 70n.

Cabell, J. Caskie, 196
Cabler, Nicholas, 77
Caldwell, George B., 160n.
Callis, G., 106, 196
Camp Lee, 7, 9-11, 99-100
Camp Mercer, 4
Campbell, John A., 45
Canby, Edward R. S., 186 and n.
Carrick's Ford, W. Va., 14
Cary, R. Milton, 8, 196
Caskie's Battery, 195, 198
Casler, John O., xiv, xxvii
Catlett's Station, 62 and n.
Cedar Creek: battle of, 169n., 176; ment., 43, 48
Cedar Run: battle of, xix-xx, xxvi, 63-66, 77, 79, 101n., 112, 159n.
Cedarville, 43
Centreville, 115
Chamberlayne, J. Hampden, 196
Chambersburg, Pa., 196

Chancellorsville: battle of, xxi, 87n., 92, 102, 108, 112, 159n.; ment., 121, 122
Chantilly, battle of, 81
Chapman, Isaac W., 196
Charlestown, W. Va., 163
Charlottesville, xix, 53, 54, 147n., 172
Child, Jesse, 8, 196
Clark's Mountain, 123
Clarke, J. Lyle, 7, 11
Clarke, Maxwell T., 196
Clarksburg, Md., 155
Clary, William H. H., 140
Clopton, John, 196
Cocke, Lorenzo G., 196
Cold Harbor, battle of, xxiii, 101n., 143, 151n.
Cole, Addison C., 196
Coleman, N., 196
Coleman, Robert T., 11, 15n., 88n., 99
Colorbearers, 65, 112, 113, 169, 182
Connecticut Infantry— *5th:* 64n.; *18th:* 158n.
Conrad's Store, W. Va., xvii, 17
Cooke, John Esten, 2n.
Couch, L. M., 116, 118, 130, 178, 196
Couch, Nicholas, 2n
Cowardin, John L., 197
Cox, William R., 142n.
Craig, John A., 197
Crawford, Samuel W., 64n.
Crenshaw, James R., 8, 197
Crenshaw's Battery, 97n, 198, 206
Crook, George, 158, 160n., 173, 176n.
Cross Keys, battle of, xix, 49-50, 52
Crow, Sgt., 93
Culpeper, 62, 115
Cumbey, John H., 169, 182
Cumbie, W. E., 101, 116, 127-28, 131, 197
Cumbie, W. S., 116, 197
Cunningham, Frank, 197
Cunningham, Richard H., Jr.: death of, 65, 66; praised, 67; ment., 8, 11, 29n., 37, 40, 52, 197
Custer, George A., 165n.
Cutshaw, Wilfred E., 174

Dabney, Robert L., 67, 103n.
Dabney, Virginius, 11, 72
Danforth, Henry D., 197
Daniel, Junius, 127n., 144
Darkesville, 160, 162
Darnestown, Md., 157
Davis, Jefferson: described, 56; ment., xxvii, 10, 20, 30n., 41, 54n., 183
Davis, Joseph R., 135
Dayton, 178
Dead, the: robbing of, xxvii, 129-30, 155; ment., xix, 17, 58 and n., 59, 68, 77, 80, 90
Desertions, 120n., 194, 198
Dill, Adolph, Jr., 197
Dillard, R. H., 197

Divers, W. H., 162, 197
Doggett, Francis W., 197
Doles, George, 133, 144
Doswell, 61
Dowdy, Nathaniel A., 116, 130, 173, 181, 197
Dungan, Robert H., 159

Early, Jubal A.: praised, xxiv, 179-80; ment., xxiii, xxiv, 67-68, 88, 89, 112, 142, 143n., 144, 147, 150-51, 152n., 155-56, 158-59, 163, 164, 166, 167, 168-69, 172-74, 176-78
Early, Robert D., 130n.
Edinburg, 35
Edmunds, William B., 116, 140, 197
Edray, W. Va., 19
Elk Mountain, W. Va., 18-19
Ellerson, John H., 197
Ellet, Robert, 198
Ellet, Thomas, 8, 97, 198
Elmira, N. Y., 118n., 197, 198, 199, 200, 201
Ely, William G., 158n.
Emory, William H., 168n.
England, Edmund E., 79n., 166
English, James C., 173, 198
Equipment, 1-2, 8, 12, 60-61, 83, 91, 92, 138-39, 165
Etting, Samuel, 198
Evans, Clement A., 142, 155, 167-68
Evans, Randall, 29
Ewell, Richard S.: illness of, 144; ment., 41-44, 48, 63, 66, 70, 75, 84, 86, 108-10, 113, 126, 130n., 131n., 135, 138n.
Exall, Charles H., 198
Exall, William, 25, 198
Execution, 120

F Company: described, xv-xvi, 1-2; ment., *passim*
Fair Oaks, battle of, 58n.
Falling Waters, W. Va., 109, 162
Field, William G., 198
Fisher's Gap, 92
Fisher's Hill, 31, 162, 172, 176-77
Five Forks, 202
Fleming, Malcolm N., 171
Floyd, George J., 100, 198
Floyd, John B., 17
Fontaine, R. Morris, 198
Food—see Rations
Foraging, 36
Fort Delaware, Del., 200, 201, 204
Fort McHenry, Md., 199
Fort Stedman, 165n., 181, 197, 198
Fort Sumter, S. C., xv
Fox, Henry C., 116, 155, 181, 198
Franklin, W. Va., 41
Fraternization, xxi, xxii, 68, 94, 96, 128-29, 155
Frayser's Farm, 59
Frederick, Md., 71, 72n., 82-83, 151

Fredericksburg: battle of, xx-xxi, 93-95, 112, 121n.; ment., xvi, 3-5, 8, 30n., 54, 69n., 121, 126
Fremont, John C., 42n., 47-51
Front Royal, xviii-xix, xxvi, 42-44, 48, 131

Gaines's Mill, battle of, xix, xxvii, 55-57, 58n., 112, 187
Gainesville, 69
Gaither, George R., 74n.
Game Point, 5
Garnett, Robert S., 14
Garnett, Thomas S., 67
Gatling gun, 57n.
Geary, John W., 64n., 65n.
Gentry, John W., 198
Gentry, M. C., 198
Georgia Infantry—3rd: 105n.; 10th: 88n.;
Germanna Ford, 121
Gettysburg, Pa., battle of, xxi, 95n., 104, 108, 109, 110n., 112, 130n., 135n., 199
Gibbons, Simeon B., 39n.
Gibson, William T., 198
Gilham, William, 11, 17, 24, 27
Gillian, Robert H., 66, 198
Gilmore, J. Harvie, 199
Goddin, John, 140
Gordon, John B.: described, 153; praised, 137 and n., 146-47; ment., xxiii, 127n., 136, 142, 144, 151, 152-56, 158, 160, 162, 165-69, 176, 178, 180-82
Gordon, Mrs. John B., 193
Gordonsville, 54, 61, 68
Gouldman, E., 100, 116, 199
Grant, Ulysses S., xxiii, 126, 130 and n., 140, 141, 142-44, 146, 166, 175, 178n., 179n., 180, 182, 186, 187
Gray, Somerville, 199
Gray, W. Granville, Jr., 17, 22, 24, 37, 199
Green, John W., 199
Green, T. Richie, 24, 170, 199
Greenbrier River, W. Va., 19-20
Greever, Addison W., 160
Gregg, Maxcy, 95
Griffin, J., 100, 116
Griffin, Tom, 29
Grigsby, Andrew J., 45, 86, 89, 90
Ground Squirrel Bridge, 146
Grover, Cuvier, 77n.
Groveton, battle of, xx, 72-74
Guiney's Station, 92-93

Hagerstown, Md., 83, 86, 108-09
Halltown, W. Va., 163
Hampton, Wade, 147
Hampton, 8n., 87n.
Hancock, Winfield S., 134, 136-38
Hancock, Md., 26
Hanover, 142, 187
Hanover Artillery, 203

Harpers Ferry, W. Va., xx, xxi, 8, 31n., 48, 84-85, 88, 89, 109, 112, 151, 165
Harrison, T. Randolph, 199
Harrisonburg, 36, 38, 41, 52, 87n., 176, 178
Harrison's Landing, 59
Harvie, William O., 199
Hatcher's Run, 180, 195
Hawkins, Laban A., 199
Haymarket, 69
Haynes, George A., 199
Hays, Harry, 144
Hays, Orlando J., 165
Hedley, William, xxv
Henry, Patrick, 199
Higginbotham, John C., 110n.
Hill, A. Powell, 55, 58, 62, 63, 70, 75, 77n., 78, 81n., 84, 86, 89, 90, 114, 119, 135, 143n., 196
Hill, D. Harvey, 55, 94, 194
Hinson's Mill, 69
Hobson, Deane, 199
Hoffman, John S., 104n.
Homesickness, xx
Hooker, Joseph, 77n., 102
Hospitals, 58, 83, 191-92
Houston, George W., 173, 199
Hudgins, Malcolm L., 87, 100, 178, 199
Hull, Irving, 200
Hundley's Corner, 55
Hunter, David, xxiii, 147, 148 and n., 149, 178n., 179
Huntersville, W. Va., 14, 15n.
Hupp's Hill, 158
Hyattstown, Md., 155

Illinois Cavalry—8th: 107n.
Illinois Infantry—39th: 25n.
Indiana Infantry—7th: 127; 14th: 33n.
Irish Battalion, 17, 24, 63-64, 72, 79n., 95
Irving, Francis D., 11

Jackson, Alfred H., 68n.
Jackson, Thomas J.: bravery of, xviii, 41, 45; criticized, 30n., 43n.; death of, xxi, 102; described, 23, 102; discipline of, 38; grave of, 149; incidents of, xix, 26, 29n., 33, 38, 40, 42, 44-46, 52, 70n., 81, 83-84, 93, 102-03; loved by troops, 103, 149; strategy of, xviii, xix, 30, 31, 34-35, 37-38, 48-49, 69n., 91, 102; ment., xvii, xx, xxi, 14n., 22, 25, 27, 32, 37, 39, 41, 47, 50-51, 62-95 passim, 98, 107, 113, 134-35, 141, 143, 146, 162, 173, 187
Jeffersonton, 69
Jenkins, William S., 200
Johnson, Bradley T.: incident of, 76; praised, 80; ment., 72-74, 77n., 79, 83, 117
Johnson, Mrs. Bradley T., 117 and n.

Johnson, Edward, 39-40, 42, 72n., 108, 112, 113, 115, 117-19, 120n., 121, 126, 132, 133, 135, 140, 141, 144
Johnson, John C., 118
Johnson's Island, O., 87n.
Johnston, J. W., 116, 200
Johnston, Joseph E., 30, 191, 194, 196
Johnston, Robert D., 144
Jones, David B., 200
Jones, John M., 108, 130-31, 144
Jones, John R., 87, 95
Jones, Philip B., Jr., 200
Jordan, Reuben J., 87-89, 100, 116, 143, 180-81, 200

Kayton, Patrick W., 116, 200
Kearny, Philip, 81
Kelley, Alfred D., 101
Kelley, John H., 38
Kellogg, Timothy H., 11, 200
Kelly's Ford, 115
Kernstown: 1862 battle of, xviii, 31n., 32-35, 37, 47n., 112, 143, 169n., 182; 1864 battle of, xxiv, 158-60, 173
Kershaw, Joseph B., 163n., 166, 174, 176
Keswich Depot, 147
Kidd, J. A., 116, 118, 181, 200
Kimball, Nathan, 33n.
King, Shirley, 8, 200

Laburnam, 140
Lacy's Spring, 24
Laws, Tom, 173-74
Leach, James P., 11
Lebanon Springs, 41
Lee, Fitzhugh, 62n., 163n., 165-67, 173
Lee, Robert E.: compassion of, 15-16; described, 56, 187; incidents of, 113, 136; loved by troops, 15, 102, 187; praised, 187-88; ment., xxvii, 7n., 17, 54 and n., 55, 58, 60, 69 and n., 71, 87n., 88-90, 92, 95, 103-04, 108, 110, 112, 118, 119, 120n., 121n., 130 and n., 138, 140-42, 144, 146, 149, 157, 163n., 174, 178, 179, 181-82, 186, 193
Leesburg, 157
Leetown, W. Va., 163
Legg, A. C., 116, 130, 200
Letcher, John, 205
Letcher's Battery, 198, 205, 207
Lewis, R., 11
Lexington, 31n., 149
Liberty, 148
Liberty Mills, 61-62, 110
Lindsay, Roswell S., 65, 66, 200
Linton, Samuel S., 25n.
Litchfield, Connally T., 55n.
Locust Grove, 126
Longstreet, James, 55, 56, 58, 59, 69, 78, 94, 101, 163n., 187
Lorentz, A., 200
Loring, William W.: criticized, 14; incidents of, 15, 28n.-29n.; ment., 18, 28, 30n., 203

Louisa, 54, 61
Louisiana Infantry—6th: 46n.; 7th: 46n.; 8th: 46n.; 9th: 46n.
Lowe, T. S. C., 58n.
Luray, 42
Lynchburg, 53, 147, 149, 151, 179, 182, 183
Lyons, Peter, 200

McCausland, John, 148, 152n.
McClellan, George B., 31n., 52n., 54, 55, 58, 60, 86, 143, 151, 162, 187
McDowell, Irvin, 47, 54, 74n.
McDowell: battle of, xviii, 40-41, 112; ment., 14, 39n.
McEvoy, Charles A., 200
McLaws, Lafayette, 84, 88, 89

Macmurdo, Richard C., 201
Maddox, R. G., 201
Madison, 62, 92, 110
Magruder, John B., 58
Mail, 97-98
Maine Infantry—10th: 64n.
Malvern Hill, battle of, xix, 58-59, 112
Manassas: capture of supply depot at, 70-71; first battle of, 13-14, 49n., 81; second battle of, xx, xxvi, 75-81, 95n., 112, 187; ment., xx, 30, 32, 34, 62
Manassas Gap R.R., 31
Marching, 96-97, 103, 110, 149, 157
Martinsburg, W. Va., 30, 31, 84, 91, 149, 160, 166
Maryland Infantry (CSA)—1st: 72n.
Maryland Infantry (USA)—2nd: 158n.
Mason, Joseph M., 116, 178, 201
Masonic Order, 76
Massachusetts Cavalry—4th: 184n.
Massachusetts Infantry—1st: 77n.; 11th: 77n.; 16th: 77n.
Mayo, Edward, 8, 18, 22, 201
Mayo, Joseph E., 22, 201
Meachum's Depot, 38
Meade, Everard B., 201
Meade, George G., 94n., 109, 115, 118, 119, 121n.
Mebane, James A., 201
Mechanicsville, xxvii, 56n., 60, 146
Medical treatment, xxiv and n., 98-99, 170-72
Medill, William H., 107n.
Meigs, John R., 178-79
Meredith, J. French, 201
Merryman, John T., 116, 201
Michigan Cavalry—1st: 165n.; 5th: 165n.; 6th: 165n.; 7th: 165n.
Middletown, Md., 151
Middletown, Va., 33, 43, 158, 176-77
Milboro, W. Va., 17, 22
Miller, Henry T., 8, 24, 201
Milroy, Robert H., 40
Milwood, 157, 173
Mine Run Campaign, xxii, 117-19

Mississippi Infantry—*2nd:* 135n.; *11th:* 135n.; *42nd:* 135n.
Mitchell, Samuel D., 201
Mittledorfer, Charles, 201
Monocacy River, Md., battle of, xxiii, 118n., 151-55
Monterey, 14
Montpelier, xxi, 110, 111, 113-14
Moore, Samuel J. C., 174
Morgan, William H., 11, 37, 58, 63, 66, 201
Morris, Walter H. P., 201
Morris farm, 60
Morton's Ford, 116, 120
Moseley, John B., 11, 37, 101
Moseley, William P., 101, 137, 166, 169
Moss Neck, 95
Mount Crawford, 178
Mount Jackson, 23, 30, 31, 35-36, 49, 176
Mount Pisgah Church, xxii, 116, 119, 122
Mount Sidney, 176
Mountcastle, John R., 201
"Mud Campaign," 120-21
Munt, Henry F., 100, 116, 201
Murchison, Kenneth M., 107n.
Music, 131
Mustain, Sherwood T., 11

Nance, J. L., 202
Natural Bridge, 149
Neff, John, 45n.
Negroes: freedmen, 29, 70, 173-75; servants, 4, 28, 124-25, 183-85; soldiers, 197n.
New Creek Station, 42n.
New Hampshire Infantry—*2nd:* 77n.
New Hope, 52
New Jersey Cavalry—*1st:* 52n., 62n.
New Market: battle of, 27n., 151n.; ment., 36, 42, 49, 92, 178
Newtown, 43, 162, 178, 179, 197
New York Infantry—*28th:* 64n.
Norristown, Md., 151
North Carolina Infantry—*1st:* 142n.; *3rd:* 142n.; *21st:* 70n.; *54th:* 107n.; *55th:* 135n.
North Garden, 53
Norwood, William, Jr., 202
Nunnally, Joseph N., 34, 66, 202

Ohio Infantry—*5th:* 64n.; *7th:* 64n.; *8th:* 33n.; *29th:* 64n.; *66th:* 64n.; *67th:* 33n.
Oliver, James, 11
Opequan Creek, 166
Orange, 62, 92, 112, 119
Orange & Alexandria R.R., 53, 115
Orleans, 69

Pace, George R., 8, 202
Pace, Theodore A., 202
Page, Archer C., 87-89
Page, Mann, 159, 202
Pardigon, C. F., 202

Paris, 157, 179
Patrick, Marsena R., 140
Patriotism, xvii, xviii, xxii
Patton, John M., Jr., 11, 32n, 37, 43n., 45, 101
Pawnee (USN), xvi, 2-3, 6
"Pawnee Sunday," xvi, 2-3
Payne, James B., Jr., 24, 25, 202
Payne's Farm, battle of, 117-18
Peaster, Henry, 116, 118, 202
Pegram, John, 143, 144, 203
Pegram, William A., 100, 105-08, 202
Pegram, William R. J., 4-5, 202
Pelham, John, 94
Pendleton, Alexander S., 167, 172-73
Pendleton, William N., 44n., 202
Penn, John E., 72, 89
Pennsylvania Infantry—*13th Reserve:* 55n.; *26th:* 77n.; *46th:* 64n.; *84th:* 33n.; *118th:* 90n.
Peterkin, George W., 6 and n., 15n., 17n., 37, 202
Petersburg, xxiv, 178-82, 198
Picket duty, 95-96
Picot, Henry V., 34, 202
Piet, William A., 202
Pilcher, Mary B., xxv
Pilcher, Samuel F., 203
Pizzini, John A., 8, 203
Point Lookout, Md., 194, 205
Pole Green Church, 54-55, 143
Poolville, Md., 157
Pollard, William G., 66, 203
Pope, John: criticized, 79; described, 61-62; ment., xx, xxvii, 62n., 63, 68, 69 and n., 70
Port Republic: battle of, xix, 50-51; ment., 38, 49, 52, 176, 178
Powell, John G., 66, 203
Powell, John W., 203
Powhatan, 154n.
Price, R. Channing, 203
Prince, Henry, 66n.
Prisoners of war, 43, 47-49, 51-53, 84-85, 87n., 127
Provost Marshal (CSA), 92-93, 103
Pughtown, 24
Punishments, 5, 19, 91-92, 123
Purcell's Battery, 4

"Quaker cannon," 62

Raccoon Ford, 115, 119
Ramseur, Stephen D., 144, 152n., 154, 157n., 166n., 168, 177, 178
Randolph, George W., 191
Randolph, J. Tucker, 8, 33-34, 143, 203
Randolph, Lewis, 79n.
Randolph, M. Louis, 8, 203
Rations, 5, 13, 61, 69-71, 82, 118, 122-23, 146, 149, 163, 177, 182
Rawlings, Edward G., 8, 23, 37, 79, 80, 203

Redd, Clarence M., 66, 203
Reeve, John J., 203
Religion, 5, 9, 41, 113-14, 119-20
Rennie, George H., 181, 204
Reviews, military, 112-13
Reynolds, John F., 74n.
Richeson, P. S., 116, 140, 204
Richeson, William R., 116, 180-81, 204
Richmond: occupied, xxv, 183-87; raid on, 140-41; ment., xiii-xv, xxiv-xxv, 1-5, 7-13, 54, 59-61, 92-93, 99-100, 130n., 146, 148, 149, 151n., 157, 179, 188-89, 191-92
Richmond & Danville R.R., 181, 183
Richmond, Fredericksburg & Potomac R.R., 3, 5, 8, 61, 92, 142
Richmond Howitzers, 2, 134, 194, 195, 199, 202, 204, 205
Richmond Light Infantry Blues, 3, 5, 6
Richmond Press, xxv
Rison, John W., 204
Robertson, William S., 116, 204
Robinson, Christopher A., 204
Robinson, Edward T., 8
Robinson, J. A., 110n.
Robinson, Richard F., 204
Robinson, Thomas B., 11
Rockbridge Artillery, 32-33, 44-46
Rocketts, 2-3
Rockville, Md., 155-56
Rodes, Robert E.: praised, 168; ment., 112, 138, 142n., 144, 156 and n., 160, 166, 178
Romney, W. Va., campaign of, xvii, 24-29
Rosser, Thomas L., 176
Rude's Hill, 30-31, 36
Ruggles, Daniel, 5, 6n., 7n.
Rumors, xxi-xxii
Rutledge, William, 204
Ryan, Abram J., 188
Ryan's, 13-14, 39

Salem, 148
Saunders, Jane C., 117n.
Savage Station, battle of, xix, xxviii, 58
Sayler's Creek, battle of, 182, 195, 198
Scottsville, xxv
Searles, Samuel, 116, 204
Seay, Morton, 204
Seay, W. C., 116, 140, 204
Seddon, John, 17n., 72
Semmes, Paul J., 88n.
Seven Days Campaign, xix, 55-59
Sewell's Mountain, W. Va., 17
Sharpsburg, Md., 86, 161
"Shebangs," 91
Sheetz, George F., 42
Shepherdstown, W. Va., 86, 150, 161, 165
Shepley, George H., 184n., 186n.
Sheppard, William L., 2n.
Sheridan, Philip H.: criticized, 178-79; ment., xxvii, 140, 147, 166-67, 169, 173-76

Shields, James, 31n., 42n., 47-49
Shipp, Scott, 11, 27
Sickness, xvii, 14, 15, 29, 30n.
Sigel, Franz, 74n., 151n.
Silver Spring, Md., 156
Simpson, Frederick J., 204
Singleton, Andrew J., 204
Sizer, Milton D., 204
Skinker, Charles R., 34, 204
Slaughter Mountain, battle of—see Cedar Run
Smith, Edward H., 204
Smith, Francis H., 39n.
Smith, Horace, 204
Smith, Joseph T., 116, 204
Smith, Thomas, 205
Soap, 111
Soles, Peter D., 205
Southside R.R., 182n.
Spotsylvania, battle of, xxii-xxiii, 132-37, 141, 187
Stafford, Leroy A., 62, 120n., 130, 144
Starke, William E., 68, 77n., 78, 80, 86
Staunton, 12-13, 18, 22, 23, 34, 37n., 39, 100, 103, 149, 172, 176
Stephens, Alexander H., 21
Steuart, George H., 128n., 133, 140, 144
Stevens, Atherton H., 184n.
Stevens, Isaac I., 81n.
Stevenson, Carter L., 203
Stonewall Brigade, 39, 44, 45, 48, 55, 65-66, 68, 86, 132, 134, 136, 139, 141-42
Stragglers, 103, 157, 177
Strasburg, 23, 31, 35, 43, 47-52, 162
Stuart, Carrie, 112n.
Stuart, James E. B., 55, 62, 68, 88, 105n., 203
Stuart, Margaret, 112n.
Sublett, Peter A., 20, 205
Summerville Ford, 69
Sutlers, 39
Swift Run Gap, 35, 41-42

Tabb, Robert M., 178, 205
Taliaferro, William B., 67, 75, 80, 178n.
Talley, Daniel D., 205
"Taps," 4
Tatum, A. Randolph, 205
Tatum, Vivian H., 205
Taylor, Charles E., 34, 205
Taylor, Clarence E., 66, 205
Taylor, Edward B., 34, 205
Taylor, George W., 70n.
Taylor, Richard, 41-43, 45-46
Taylor, Robert T., 205
"Telescope" rifles, 123
Tennessee Infantry—Walker's Legion: 7; 1st: 30n.; 7th: 30n.; 14th: 30n.
Tenth Legion, 176
Terry, William, 142, 153n., 158n., 167-68
Thruston, Stephen D., 168n.
Tillmantown, Md., 162
Tiney, W. C., 100, 107, 205

Tompkins, Edward G., 66, 205
Trainum, Charles, 205
Trevilian's Depot, 147
Trimble, Isaac R., 50-51, 70n., 95, 194
Tyler, James E., 205
Tyler, John, 8, 206
Tyler, Robert E., 206
Tyler, Robert O., 138n.
Tyree, Henry C., 116, 178, 206

Unger's Crossroads, 25-26
Union, 157
Upperville, 157, 179
Urbanna, Md., 155

Valley Mountain, W. Va., 17-18
Valley of Virginia: characterized, xxvi; described, 24; 1862 campaign in, xviii-xix, 30-50, 58; 1864 campaign in, 158-80
Van Buren, Benjamin B., 206
Virginia Artillery—see specifically named units: Rockbridge Artillery, etc.
Virginia Cavalry—1st: 55n., 74n.; 10th: 205. See also specifically named units: Black Horse Cavalry, etc.
Virginia Central R.R., 54, 61, 100, 147
Virginia Infantry: Battalions—1st: 203; 3rd: 206; 22nd: 128n., 197; 24th: 101, 206; 25th: 24n., 198; 30th: 7n., 8n. Regiments—2nd: 48; 4th: 142n.; 5th: 33; 10th: 38-39; 11th: 92n.; 15th: 88n.; 21st: passim; 25th: 110, 130, 159n., 180; 26th: 24n., 197, 201; 27th: 34n., 45n.; 31st: 58n., 68n., 104n.; 32nd: 88n.; 33rd: 45n.; 42nd: 24, 63-64, 77, 89n., 159n., 180, 196; 44th: 95, 140, 159n.; 46th: 3n.; 48th: 24, 63-64, 72, 159, 160, 194; 50th: 95, 118, 127, 197; 60th: 195. See also specifically named units: Stonewall Brigade, etc.
Virginia Military Institute, 11, 27, 39, 87n., 149, 151n.
Virginia State Insurance Co., xxv

Wadsworth, James S., 127n.
Walcott, Charles F., 81n.
Waldrop, Richard W., 206
Walker, James A., 139-40, 144
Walker, John G., 84
Walker, Lindsay, 4-6
Walker, Thomas B., 100, 107, 206
Wallace, Lew, 152n., 155
Wallace, Richard H., 101, 206
Walsh, Meret C., 127
Ward, Michael, 105
Warm Springs, W. Va., 21
Warren, Edward T. H., 39n.
Warrenton, 62n., 72, 74, 75, 81
Washington, D. C.: raid on, xxiii-xxiv, 155-57, 179; ment., 54, 61n., 69n., 70, 72, 79, 148, 154

Watkins, Aurelius S., 206
Watkins, Henry H., 66, 206
Waynesboro, 52-53, 176, 204
Wellford, Philip A., 8, 22, 206
West Virginia Infantry—1st: 158n.; 4th: 158n.; 12th: 158n., 160n.
Weyer's Gap, 51
Wharton, Gabriel C., 169
Wheat, C. Roberdeau, 46n.
White, Robert C., 206
White Oak Swamp, 58-59
White's Ford, 82, 157
Whiting, W. H. Chase, 54-55
Wilderness, battle of, xxii-xxiii, 89n., 121, 126-30, 137n., 144
Wilkins, J. M., 206
Williamsport, Md.: battle of, 105-08; ment., 84, 103-04, 109, 162
Willis, Joseph N., 206
Wilton, 2
Winchester: 1862 battle of, xix, xxvi, 44-47, 112; 1864 battle of, xiii, xxiv, xxv, 101n., 167-70, 172-75, 179; ment., 22-23, 28-31, 43, 48, 50n., 92, 110, 158-63, 166, 178
Winder, Charles S., 66-67, 201
Winder, John H., 205
Winslow, George B., 128n.
Winter quarters, 96, 119-21, 125
Wise, Henry A., 8
Wise, O. Jennings, 3n.
Witcher, William A., 11, 63n., 65n., 72, 101, 134-35, 137, 140
Women: incidents involving, 18-19, 23-24, 27-28, 43-44, 104-05, 109, 112-13, 116, 117, 131, 140-41, 145, 148; tribute to, 191-93
Wood, S. E., 116, 206
Woodstock, 35, 172, 178
Worsham, John H.: birth and prewar career of, xiv-xv; death of, xxv; described, xv, xxv, 206; memoirs of, xiii-xiv, xxvi-xxviii; postwar career of, xxiv-xxv; wounded, xxiv, 170
Worsham, Mrs. John H., xxv
Worsham, Richard, xiv-xv
Worsham, Thomas R., 207
Wounded, the, 57, 58
Wren, J. Porter, 66, 100, 118, 154, 155, 207
Wright, Horatio G., 134
Wright, Philip A., 207
Wright, Rebecca, 173-75
Wyndham, Percy, 52-53

York, Zebulon, 142, 168
York River R.R., 59
Yorktown, 191

Zimmer, Louis, 207